THE HAUNTING OF
ALMA FIELDING

ALSO BY KATE SUMMERSCALE

The Queen of Whale Cay
The Suspicions of Mr Whicher
Mrs Robinson's Disgrace
The Wicked Boy

THE HAUNTING OF ALMA FIELDING

A True Ghost Story

Kate Summerscale

BLOOMSBURY CIRCUS
LONDON · OXFORD · NEW YORK · NEW DELHI · SYDNEY

BLOOMSBURY CIRCUS
Bloomsbury Publishing Plc
50 Bedford Square, London, WC1B 3DP, UK

BLOOMSBURY, BLOOMSBURY CIRCUS and the Bloomsbury Circus logo
are trademarks of Bloomsbury Publishing Plc

First published in Great Britain 2020

A catalogue record for this book is available from the British Library

ISBN: HB: 978-1-4088-9545-0; TPB: 978-1-4088-9544-3;
EBOOK: 978-1-4088-9543-6; SIGNED SPECIAL EDITION: 978-1-5266-3105-3

2 4 6 8 10 9 7 5 3

Typeset by Newgen KnowledgeWorks Pvt., Ltd, Chennai, India
Printed and bound in Australia by Griffin Press, part of Ovato

To find out more about our authors and books visit www.bloomsbury.com
and sign up for our newsletters

For David Miller

O plunge your hands in water,
Plunge them in up to the wrist;
Stare, stare in the basin
And wonder what you've missed.

The glacier knocks in the cupboard,
The desert sighs in the bed,
And the crack in the tea-cup opens
A lane to the land of the dead.

W. H. Auden, 'As I Walked Out
One Evening' (1940)

Alma Fielding

CONTENTS

CONTENTS

PROLOGUE

In January 2017 I visited the Society for Psychical Research archive in Cambridge to look up some references to the ghost hunter Nandor Fodor, a Hungarian emigré who had been a pioneer of supernatural study in London between the wars. I wanted to know more about Fodor's investigation of a housewife called Alma Fielding, a poltergeist case from which he deduced, to the horror of his colleagues, that repressed traumatic experiences could generate terrifying physical events.

I had seen several references to Fodor in the catalogue to the SPR archive, but I didn't expect to find anything directly relevant in its files: he had investigated Alma for a rival organisation, the International Institute for Psychical Research, whose papers were said to have been destroyed by German bombs. But when the documents were delivered to the university library's manuscripts room, I discovered that they were Fodor's original International Institute papers. The SPR must have acquired the smaller organisation's archive when it was disbanded in the 1940s. To my delight, one of the files turned out to be Fodor's dossier on Alma, mistakenly catalogued as a holding on 'Mr' Fielding.

The manila folder contained the documents that the Institute had confiscated when it expelled Fodor in the autumn of 1938: transcripts of Alma's seances and of his interviews with her, lab reports, X-rays, copies of her contracts, scribbled notes, sketches, photographs of the damage wrought by her poltergeist in her house and on her body. The pages were dense with facts and figures: measurements, times, dates, weights. This fat folder of evidence seemed a wonderful object: a documentary account of fictional and magical events, a historical record of the imagination. I hoped it would explain the radical link that Fodor had made between suffering and the supernatural.

In the taxi from Cambridge railway station to the library the next day, my driver asked me what I was researching. I told him that I was studying psychical material from the 1930s. Was I an expert? he asked. No, I replied, I was new to it. He told me that, as it happened, psychical research was his speciality. He had read widely in the subject and had become pretty good at the clairvoyant skill of 'remote viewing'. Sometimes he annoyed his girlfriend by calling her at work and telling her what she was doing, or which sandwiches she had chosen for lunch. I asked the driver when this started. He said that his great-grandmother had been a medium. He said that I wouldn't believe the things that he had seen in the spirit world: dragons, monsters – everything that I had read about in stories. We drew up outside the library and he turned in his seat to face me.

'In fact I've got one with me right now,' he smiled, 'hanging round my neck.' It was an amphisbaena, he said, a two-headed snake. According to Greek myth, the amphisbaena is the spawn of blood dripped from the Medusa's head. It feeds on corpses and its two mouths spew poison.

Why's it there? I asked, looking at the cab driver's bare neck and laughing a little uneasily. Protection? 'Yes,' he said. 'Healing.'

Part One

THE GHOST HUNTER

'Nowadays, we find that nearly everything
comes from within – from our
subconscious self'

Agatha Christie, 'The Red Signal' (1933)

Nandor Fodor

ONE

The crack in the teacup

At his office in South Kensington on Monday 21 February 1938, Nandor Fodor opened a letter from an East End clergyman of his acquaintance. The Reverend Francis Nicolle wanted to alert him to a poltergeist attack in the suburb of Thornton Heath, just south of London, which had been the subject of a report in that weekend's *Sunday Pictorial*.

'I wonder whether you have seen it?' wrote Nicolle. 'Unfortunately the actual address is not given.' The minister thought that the haunting sounded even more remarkable than a similar case in east London that he had helped Fodor to investigate that month.

Fodor, a Jewish-Hungarian journalist, had for four years been chief ghost hunter at the International Institute for Psychical Research. He loved his job, which required him to investigate and verify weird events, but the spiritualist press had recently turned against him. The bestselling weekly *Psychic News* accused him of being cynical about the supernatural and unkind to mediums, charges that were so damaging to his reputation as a psychical researcher – and his future in England – that in January he had sued for libel. He was now desperate to prove his sincerity and his aptitude: he needed to find a ghost.

Fodor obtained a copy of the latest *Pictorial*. The paper had run the poltergeist story next to a giant cut-out photograph of Adolf Hitler, who was poised to invade Austria, so that the news of the haunting seemed to issue from the Führer's shouting mouth. '"GHOST" WRECKS HOME,' ran the headline, 'FAMILY TERRORISED.'

According to the *Pictorial*'s report, the disturbance emanated from Alma Fielding, a thirty-four-year-old housewife who lived in Thornton Heath, in the borough of Croydon, with her husband, their son and a lodger. A week earlier, on Sunday 13 February, Alma had been seized by a pain in her pelvis while she was visiting friends in the neighbourhood. She hurried home, trembling and burning, and took herself to bed. Having suffered from kidney complaints since she was a girl, she had a stock of antibacterial medicine to fight infection and sedatives to help her sleep. She dosed herself with both. As she shivered and sweated in her bedroom, a strong wind swept across south-east England, driving sheets of rain, sleet and snow through the streets of Croydon at eighty miles an hour.

Alma was laid up for days. In the middle of the week, she was joined in bed by her husband, Leslie, who usually worked as a builder and decorator. His gums were bleeding heavily, his teeth having been pulled so that he could be fitted with dentures. Through Wednesday, Thursday and Friday, reported the *Sunday Pictorial*, Les and Alma lay together, his mouth leaking blood, her abdomen pulsing with pain, a bright frost lining the trees and walls outside their twin windows. The storms died down, but the air remained wintry and sharp. Alma noticed a peculiar, six-digit handprint on the mirror above the bedroom fireplace. Perhaps her fever or the drugs were inducing hallucinations.

Towards midnight on Friday, Alma and Les were trying to sleep when they heard something shatter nearby. Alma turned on her bedside lamp. She and Les saw the shards of a broken tumbler on the floor and then, suddenly, another glass flew past and splintered against the wall. They waited, terrified. The room fell quiet. 'Put the light out,' said Les. 'Let's see what happens.' When Alma turned off her lamp a dank wind moved through the room, lifting the eiderdown so that it swam up at them and fell over their faces. 'Switch on the light,' said Les. 'Quickly.' Alma tried to turn on the lamp, but nothing happened. Nor did the light come on when Les reached over and pressed the switch himself. Alma shouted for help. Their sixteen-year-old son, Donald, crossed the landing from his bedroom, but as he opened the door he had to duck to dodge a flying pot of face cream. George, the lodger, edged in after him, and was hit by two coins – a shilling and a penny. The pair of them drew back, and Don hurried downstairs to fetch matches. When he returned he struck a match and made his way by its flame to the lamp at his mother's bedside. The bulb had vanished from the socket. It was found, unbroken and still hot to the touch, on a chair on the other side of the room.

Everyone was shaken, but after half an hour things seemed to have calmed down. At about twenty to one Don and George went to their beds. They all eventually fell asleep.

The next morning Alma was feeling well enough to go downstairs, but an egg smashed when she was in the kitchen; a saucer snapped. She didn't know what to do – a ghost hardly seemed a matter for the police – so she placed a call to the offices of the *Sunday Pictorial*. The newspaper was running a series on the supernatural and had invited readers to write in with their experiences.

'Come to my house,' Alma implored the *Pictorial*'s news desk. 'There are things going on here I cannot explain.'

The *Sunday Pic*, as it was known to its readers, despatched two reporters to Thornton Heath.

As Alma opened the front door to the *Pictorial* men that afternoon, they saw an egg fly down the corridor to land a yard from their feet. As she led them to the kitchen, a pink china dog rattled to the floor and a sharp-bladed tin opener cut through the air at head height. In the front parlour, a teacup and saucer lifted out of Alma's hands as she sat with her guests, the saucer spinning and splintering as if shot in mid-air. She screamed as a second saucer exploded in her fingers and sliced into her thumb. While the gash was being bandaged, the reporters heard smashing in the kitchen: a wine glass had apparently escaped a locked cabinet and shattered on the floor. They saw an egg whirl in through the living-room door to crack against the sideboard. A giant chunk of coal rose from the grate, sailed across the room, inches from the head of one of the reporters, and smacked into the wall. The house seemed to be under siege from itself.

Les, Don and George were at home but, as far as the *Pictorial* men could tell, none of them was responsible for the phenomena: the objects were propelled by an unseen force.

A crowd had gathered in the street outside. Among the bystanders, the reporters found a palm reader who went by the name of Professor Morisone (otherwise Mr Morrison), and invited him in to the house. The clairvoyant advised Alma that she was a very strong 'carrier' of ectoplasm, the floating filmy substance with which some mediums materialised spirits. He said that the tumult in her home was a message of warning, and that her son was in danger.

The *Pictorial* published its piece the next morning, under the slogan: 'This is the most curious front page story we have ever printed.' In an ordinary terrace in Thornton Heath, it declared, 'some malevolent, ghostly force is working miracles. Poltergeist... That's what the scientists call it. The Spiritualists? They say it's all caused by a mischievous earth-bound spirit.'

On an inside page, the paper ran a photograph of Alma, Don and George – 'the occupants of the house of fear' – gazing warily at a large lump of coal.

Fodor was gripped by the *Pictorial*'s story. He hoped that this poltergeist would provide him with the proof of the supernatural that he needed. It might also help him to develop his more daring ideas about the occult. The word 'poltergeist', from the German for 'noisy spirit', had been popularised in Britain in the 1920s, but no one knew what poltergeists really were: hoaxes by the living; hauntings by the dead; spontaneous discharges of electrical energy. Fodor, having read the work of Sigmund Freud, wondered if they might be kinetic forces unleashed by the unconscious mind. He noticed that the Thornton Heath poltergeist centred on one woman. It had sparked into life in the bedroom, and seemed at first to direct its violence at the men of the house.

Fodor knew that he must act quickly. The International Institute was one of several psychical research bodies in London, and other ghost hunters would be sure to take an interest in this haunting. Poltergeist attacks were in any case usually short-lived, sometimes lasting for only a few days. He composed a letter to the *Sunday Pictorial*'s new editor, the twenty-four-year-old wunderkind Hugh Cudlipp, asking if he could 'come in' on the case. Would Cudlipp be good enough to give him the haunted family's address in Thornton Heath? Reminding Cudlipp that he had already submitted several articles about uncanny events to the *Pictorial*, Fodor promised to report back on anything that he found.

Like everyone in Britain, Fodor was also following the political news with disquiet. The *Pictorial* reported that the prime minister, Neville Chamberlain, had called an emergency Cabinet meeting to address the threat posed by the Italian dictator Benito Mussolini; and that Adolf Hitler had massed 80,000 troops on the Austrian border, ready to invade. That Sunday, Hitler made a defiant three-hour speech in which he demanded the return of German land surrendered in the Treaty of Versailles.

Britain was braced for war. Twenty-five million gas masks had been manufactured by late February, schools were being commandeered for air-raid training, and trial blackouts were being staged throughout the land. The town of Jarrow in north-eastern England was seized with panic when an oxygen works went up in flames that month, reported the *Pictorial*. As exploding metal canisters shot across the River Tyne, the residents fled their homes in terror, convinced that enemy planes were bombing the munitions factories. 'It was an amazing scene,' said the paper. 'Cripples, frantic women pushing prams, aged people, all scantily dressed, massed in a terrified throng.' Several war veterans collapsed, apparently with symptoms of shell shock.

'Ordinary chaps that I meet everywhere,' says the narrator of George Orwell's *Coming Up For Air*, 'chaps that I run across in pubs, bus drivers, and travelling salesmen for hardware firms, have a feeling that the world's gone wrong. They can feel things cracking and collapsing under their feet.' They have a 'kind of prophetic feeling', he says, 'that war's just around the corner and that war's the end of all things'. For many, the dread was sharpened with flashbacks – 'mental pictures of the shellbursts and the mud'. If the first world war of the century had been devastating, the next was expected to be apocalyptic.

The ghosts of Britain, meanwhile, were livelier than ever. Almost a thousand people had written to the *Pictorial* in February to describe their encounters with wraiths and revenants, while other papers reported on a spirit vandalising a house in Stornoway, in the Outer Hebrides, and on a white-draped figure seen gliding through the Hawker aircraft factory in Kingston upon Thames. The nation's phantoms were distractions from anxiety, expressions of anxiety, symptoms of a nervous age. Fodor had been in Britain for less than a decade, but as a ghost hunter he had already become intimate with his new country's fantasies and fears.

While Fodor waited he gleaned a few further details about the Thornton Heath poltergeist. The *Daily Mirror*, the *Pictorial*'s weekday sister paper, disclosed that it had sent three men to the Fieldings' house on Sunday: they had seen a book slide from the bookcase when Alma was in the dining room, a glass leap from the table and a mirror drop from the wall. She was frail and hollow-eyed, the reporters observed, and no wonder.

The *Mirror* also reported that Anthony Eden had resigned as foreign secretary of Chamberlain's coalition government, having failed to persuade the prime minister to stand up to Mussolini. When Eden emerged from 10 Downing Street after their meeting, said the *Mirror,* he looked like a ghost.

On Wednesday, Hugh Cudlipp replied to Fodor with the Fieldings' address. Fodor couldn't make it to Croydon that afternoon, so he despatched his assistant, a young film technician called Laurence Evans, to check out the story. Laurie had been an investigator at the Institute for just three months, but he was keen, enterprising and personable. At only twenty-five, he had already squandered his inheritance in Hollywood and been married twice. He now had a day job as a sound recordist at Twickenham Studios, near London, and lived in Surrey with his girlfriend, a film actress. He was a 'brilliant young inventor', according to Fodor, as well as an enthusiastic ghost hunter. Fodor told Laurie to let him know at once if the Thornton Heath case seemed genuine, so that they could stake a claim before any of the other psychical research organisations in London.

Laurie stayed late at Beverstone Road and reported back to Fodor early the next morning. He had witnessed amazing things, he told him. In the living room, he saw a wine glass jump from Alma Fielding's hand, shattering in mid-air and falling to the wooden floor. A second glass did the same, this time landing on a rug. A third hit the electric light fixture on the ceiling. Alma was shaking violently and her heart was racing, said Laurie. He put his fingers to her wrist and felt her pulse leap. Upstairs, he was shown a wardrobe that the poltergeist had thrown on the sixteen-year-old Don Fielding's bed. Luckily, Don had been sleeping at a neighbour's house at the time, being already so alarmed by the weird events that he had decided to stay away from home. Laurie noticed a broken white china cat lying between two blue vases on the far side of the boy's room. He was downstairs in the hall a few minutes later when he heard a smash, and turned to see the pieces of a blue vase lying by the grandfather clock at the foot of the stairs. He ran up to Don's room and saw that one of the pair had vanished.

Laurie told Fodor that no one could have smuggled the vase out of the bedroom. Alma had been in the kitchen when it hit the hall floor. He had never known anything like it, he said. 'I unhesitatingly label it as supernormal.'

Fodor couldn't wait to meet Alma. He immediately set out for Thornton Heath himself.

TWO

Feel my heart

At 11.30 a.m. on Thursday 24 February Fodor reached the Fieldings' house in Beverstone Road, a red-brick end-of-terrace Victorian villa with a dark slate roof and bright white gables. He introduced himself to Les Fielding at the door, and handed him three eggs and three tumblers, explaining cheerfully that he had brought them along in case the ghost would like to break them. Les was tall, fair, broad-shouldered. Fodor, at forty-two, was four years older than his host and a little shorter, with a solid build, dark stubble and curly hair.

Les took Fodor into the living room, pushed the door shut, and showed him a tray of glass and china fragments, relics of the poltergeist's rampage. Les seemed straightforward and down-to-earth, thought Fodor, but badly shaken by the events of the past few days. 'He had an anxious and worried look in his eyes,' he noted. 'The removal of all his teeth and three days in bed with haemorrhage had already affected his nerves.' Les had been hit by a hand grenade while serving on the Western Front in the Great War, and still scratched the back of his right thigh where the shrapnel had lodged in his flesh.

Les said that he and Alma had barely slept all week. The previous day he had taken part in a seance in the dining room – his first such experience – in which a local medium tried to exorcise the ghost. The psychic warned the Fieldings that there might be murdered babies in a well in their back garden, and advised them to plant marigolds over the site. That night, Les told Fodor, he and Alma had drunk double whisky and sodas to help them get off to sleep.

Les said that he didn't like all the people peering in through the windows. The crowd had been building since Saturday, when Alma first called the *Pictorial*, and had grown so large that police had been sent to protect the house. On Tuesday, one of the constables claimed that the Fieldings' door mat had wrapped itself around his head.

Fodor tried to put Les at ease, telling him how excited he was at the prospect of meeting the poltergeist. He took the eggs that he had brought, placed them inside the tumblers and lined them up on the mantelpiece. Suddenly something whacked the other side of the living-room door. Les opened the door, and found a Bakelite clock on the hall floor, its case cracked. A dent had been made in one of the door's panels. The clock, Les said, came from his and Alma's bedroom.

Les introduced Fodor to Alma when she came down-stairs. She was tremulous and nervy, Fodor observed, and very attractive: about five feet three inches tall, deli-cately built, dark-eyed and dark-haired. Fodor also met the Fieldings' lodger, George Saunders, a short, balding man with thick black eyebrows. George mended boots and shoes for a living, and had been living with the Fieldings since the breakdown of his marriage in 1928; he had chosen to rent a room in a family home rather than a boarding house. George walked with crutches, having been badly injured playing football at the age of seven, but he had no 'inferiority complex', Fodor observed. He was affable and self-assured, and of all the household the least rattled by the poltergeist.

Alma and Les showed Fodor round, pointing out the astonishing array of items that had been smashed over the previous few days: thirty-six tumblers, twenty-four wine glasses, fifteen china egg cups, five teacups, four saucers, a salad bowl, three light bulbs, nine eggs, two plates, a pudding basin, two vases, a water jug, a milk jug and a jar of face cream. Fodor saw the dents that had been punched in an aluminium saucepan and an orna-mental brass kettle. He saw some of the objects that had been chucked at Alma: chairs, rugs, a fire screen. In Don's room, at the back of the building, he saw the capsized wardrobe, askew and splintered on the bed.

The Fieldings' house was more comfortable than most working-class homes that Fodor had visited. Unusually, it had its own telephone as well as being fitted with electricity, gas and water. The entrance hall gave on to the living room and dining room, both amply furnished, and a small kitchen. The sash windows in the front room were topped with squares of stained glass – purple, orange, pale green – and hung with thick lace curtains. Les kept his business ledger and invoices in a desk in this room. The three bedrooms upstairs were served by a bathroom with a flushing lavatory. George's shoe-mending workshop was in the garden, near the coal shed.

After his tour, Fodor interviewed Alma alone. She confirmed the accuracy of the piece in the *Pictorial*. He asked about the injuries that she and Les had sustained. As well as cutting her thumb, she said, she had bruised her head when she fell on the stairs and again when a tin of polish whirled out of the kitchen cupboard. A vase had hit Les on the head when he was on the landing outside the bathroom. 'I don't think these bruises were intentional,' Alma said. 'I think it just happened we were in the way.' She seemed to want to play down the poltergeist's aggression.

When Fodor asked if any of the incidents of the past few days had been comical, she recalled that on Tuesday the lid to the whistling kettle had gone missing, only to be found in Don's room, perched like a beret on the head of the white china cat. But most of the phenomena frightened her. Alma described what it was like to have a glass snatched from her hand: she felt a chill and a sudden pressure before the glass flew up and shattered in the air or fell unbroken to the ground. Objects could be taken in any room, she said, whether or not she was present.

'Do you think you are psychic?' asked Fodor.

'I don't know. I am told I am because sometimes I tell people things that come to pass. I dreamed once that Don had met with an accident. I warned him to look out. That morning he was knocked down by a bicycle.' She cited other premonitory dreams. One night she dreamt that the State cinema in Thornton Heath had crumbled and collapsed, so the next evening she insisted that the family go to the Empire instead. She afterwards heard that the film reel at the State had burnt out, though the building itself was not damaged.

Fodor asked whether the Fieldings' dog Judy – a black-and-tan Manchester terrier – ever showed signs of alarm. 'Sometimes we see Judy with his hair standing up and shivering,' Alma said. One of their three cats was behaving queerly, she added.

Alma said that she did not believe in ghosts and was not a churchgoer or a spiritualist, but she thought 'there are things which we are not meant to know'.

Fodor asked Alma about her sexual relations with Les: 'Do you mind telling me something about your marital life?' Alma replied that it was 'perfectly normal', though both she and Les were 'rather cold, untemperamental'. Fodor asked if Don was fond of the company of girls. Alma said not: 'He is very shy, reserved, and has almost no friends. He has reverent views about sex. He is innocent.'

Alma had undergone other odd experiences over the past few months, she told Fodor. Towards the end of 1937 she heard a voice in the dining room, whispering, 'Hurry up, hurry up.' Soon afterwards a powder puff and a tube of lipstick sprang out of her hand and disappeared.

Last Christmas Day, she said, while the men of the house were out at the pub, she was walking down the stairs with a tray when she felt a cold hand clutch her shoulder. She froze at the touch, faltered, fell. She came round to find herself lying in the hallway, her crockery broken about her.

With the arrival of the poltergeist, Alma's private experiences had become public, the whispers in her ear turning into bangs and crashes in her home. The chilly hand that she had felt on her shoulder on Christmas Day, the voice in the dining room, the disappearing powder puff had all been omens: flickers of this future.

Alma seemed frightened, but Fodor had so far not seen the poltergeist in action. This changed at lunchtime.

Don turned up at one o'clock, as he and Les had a decorating job booked that afternoon. At sixteen, Don had already been working as his father's apprentice for two years. He was a quiet, dutiful boy, as his mother had said, and at school had excelled at mathematics and practical work. He looked like Les: slim, tidily dressed, his light brown hair cut short at the back and sides.

Fodor was about to go out to buy something to eat, but Les and Alma encouraged him to stay. Something might happen while he was away, they said. He instead sent out for sandwiches, and sat on the dining-room sofa, reading the Fieldings' insurance policy, while Alma put lunch on the table for Les, Don and George. The sofa faced the back window. Along the wall to Fodor's left was a heavy oak sideboard, laden with ornaments; and to his right were a fireplace and mirror. The room was papered with a geometric print. Through the doorway on the left, Fodor could see the hall and part of the kitchen entrance.

At 1.50 p.m., as Alma was bringing in a plate, a tumbler flew off the kitchen table. Fodor went to the kitchen to see the glass, which was undamaged, and then returned to the sofa. Next Alma brought the pudding plates to the dining room. 'From sheer nervousness she is holding everything with both hands,' wrote Fodor in his log. 'She is in full view. Ping. Behind her in the kitchen the same glass flies off the table again, falling away from her and remaining unbroken.' The tumbler was put back on the table. Five minutes later she fetched a saucer and three cups for tea. 'She is hugging them close to her breast with both hands. She is in full view. Ping. The same tumbler flies off the kitchen table, again unbroken.'

Alma became more agitated and fearful with each crash. She let Fodor put his fingers to her pulse, which was racing. 'Feel my heart,' she said, and he placed his palm against her pounding chest.

At 2.15 p.m. Alma was sitting on the fender by the dining-room fireplace when her teacup sailed through the air at Les, missing his head by a fraction of an inch; her saucer simultaneously smashed on the hearthstone. When Les left for work with Don, Alma's cup jumped across the table at George, blasting his face with hot tea. Fodor was caught in the spray. Then two tumblers in succession leapt from Alma's hand at speed, one hitting the wall with a rap as sharp as a rifle shot.

There were comings and goings throughout the afternoon, a bustle of people to match the flurry of objects. Several of Fodor's psychical research colleagues turned up. The first was Dr Gerald Wills, a spare, rangy man of forty-seven who had taken early retirement from his job as an anaesthetist at St Thomas's Hospital in London. He was joined by Fodor's assistant Laurie Evans and by the Reverend Nicolle, who had alerted Fodor to the Thornton Heath poltergeist. A Croydon physician, Dr Frayworth, came to offer his help. It emerged that he was of Hungarian descent, and distantly related to Fodor.

Laurie, who had brought six tumblers with him for the poltergeist, went out at four to buy cakes for the Fieldings and their visitors. A reporter from the *Croydon Advertiser* arrived at teatime, and Alma's unmarried older sister, Doris Smith, called round with their mother, Alice, who lived nearby. Dorrie admitted that she had been impatient with Alma's supernatural stories in the past. 'We always used to think they were fairy tales Alma told us,' she said. 'We used to say, "Oh, Alma, you and your china again!" Now I've had the china break in my hands.' Alma's mother claimed to have had the sensation of being 'nearly strangled' on a previous visit to the house.

Rose Saunders, Alma's best friend and George's sister-in-law, was in and out all day. Don was staying with her family, who were neighbours of Alma's mother in Haslemere Road. Rose told Fodor that she had seen the spout fly off a teapot in the kitchen on Tuesday.

Fodor was alone in the living room, speaking on the telephone to the *Sunday Pictorial,* when a saucepan thudded against the door. He noticed that one of the eggs that he had placed on the mantelpiece had disappeared, and minutes later saw an egg zip down the hallway to smash on the carpet.

At 5.30 Dr Wills informed Fodor that he had just witnessed an unmistakably supernatural event in the kitchen. He had been facing Les, who had come in through the garden door and was taking off his shirt collar. Alma was standing with her back to them, using both hands to fill the kettle at the sink. Suddenly Dr Wills saw a saucer appear at eye level, about four feet away from him, and crack itself on the corner of the back door.

Gerald Wills had joined the International Institute three years earlier, but this was the first time that he had witnessed an event of this nature. He drew up a plan of the ground floor of the house, marking the kitchen's measurements and the positions of Les, Alma and himself at the time of the smash. The kitchen was a bare and narrow room with a linoleum floor, eight feet nine inches long and eight feet eight inches high. Along its left-hand side were a fitted corner cupboard, a gas cooker, a draining board and a sink. A small table was pushed against the right-hand wall. Gauze curtains covered the window above the sink and the glass panels in the back door. On his diagram, Dr Wills placed a small cross in the far right corner, where he had seen the saucer burst. Les and Alma identified the plate as the cat's saucer, which was usually on the concrete path outside. The investigators found scraps of fish on the door frame where it had hit the wood.

In his log of the day's action, Fodor listed the strange incidents witnessed by himself or another member of the Institute. He entered most as 'not evidential': that is, they could conceivably have been engineered by someone in the house. But a few, including the episode of the flying cat saucer, seemed impossible to explain.

Fodor interviewed Don, who said that he had not witnessed anything supernatural. According to his mother, he was 'picture-mad' – obsessed with the movies, like many of his generation – and thought spiritualism was 'just bunk'. Nonetheless, he had been unnerved by the chaos and by Professor Morisone's warnings about his safety. He was the only member of the household frightened enough to move out.

In the front room, Fodor took a call from a reporter at the *Croydon Times*, a rival of the *Advertiser*, who asked for news of Alma. 'She is fine,' said Fodor, 'but she does not want to see anyone. There are a lot of relatives here, and the occurrences are still going on. In the first place, when they started happening, she got in touch with the press because she thought they could help her. Now she is tired of all the publicity this is getting.'

Fodor wanted to limit access to Alma for his own reasons too. Some of his rivals had already shown an interest in his new find. This might prove a sensational case, and he hoped to keep it between the Institute and the three newspapers that had been first on the scene.

The reporter for the *Croydon Advertiser*, Jack, told Fodor that he had been calling at the house all week. Les had said to him: 'I would have laughed at the wife and said she had been "on the razzle" if it had been just her telling me of these things. But I know she doesn't drink, and I have seen the things for myself.' Jack had slept over on the Tuesday night that the wardrobe fell on Don's bed. He and the newspaper's photographer had still been playing darts with Les and George when Alma finally put out the cats and headed to bed at 2.30 a.m., telling the visitors that they could stay in Don's room. A few minutes later they heard a heavy thud overhead. Jack, Les and the photographer rushed upstairs. Alma was emerging from her bedroom, pulling on a dressing gown as she crossed the landing and opened the door to her son's room. Jack saw the wardrobe lying across the empty bed, its mirror cracked where it had hit the bedpost. Just then a cry came from the hallway: George had followed the others upstairs, and as he climbed the steps with the help of a crutch he had fallen backwards and tumbled to the ground. An invisible hand had pushed him in the chest, he said.

Jack told Fodor that he, the photographer, Alma, Les and George all slept downstairs that night. They went up in pairs to use the bathroom.

Alma mentioned to Fodor that she recognised his name from reports of the Bethnal Green poltergeist, which he had investigated with Laurie Evans and the Reverend Nicolle earlier in the month. The story had run in

the *Daily Express*, the *Daily Mail*, the *Daily Sketch*
and the *Evening Standard*. The BBC – which had just
finished airing *Things I Cannot Explain*, a radio series
about listeners' eerie experiences – had considered
broadcasting from the haunted house. Alma was curious
about what Fodor had discovered in east London. What
lay behind the phenomena? she asked. Had the ghost
been laid to rest?

Fodor and Laurie first visited the house in Teesdale
Street, Bethnal Green, on 5 February, having obtained
the address from the editor of the *Standard*. Almost
2,000 people were gathered outside the building.
A Mrs Davis had died in the house in September, and
her spectre had apparently returned to haunt her family
and a young couple with a baby who lodged in the
upstairs rooms. Pictures fell off walls, doors unbolted
themselves, chairs flipped onto their backs. The house
would shudder as Mrs Davis had shuddered when she
suffered an epileptic fit, and wails echoed down the
stairways, like the shrieks that she had once made as
she convulsed. Mrs Davis's twenty-year-old daughter,
Grace, said that on Armistice Day she had seen the
earth move at her mother's grave, as if her fits were
persisting in the spirit world.

The widowed George Davis, a print compositor of
sixty-one, lived on the first two floors of the house with
Grace and two of his sons. On the top floor were the
lodgers: Mr Harrison, a lorry driver, his wife, Minnie,
and their eighteen-month-old baby, Maureen. The ghost
was making mischief in their rooms, too: when Minnie

Harrison found that a jar of Bovril beef extract in the kitchen cupboard had been emptied, she remembered that Bovril had been Mrs Davis's favourite drink. The tiny Maureen, she said, could do an uncanny impression of the bloodcurdling cries that their landlady had made during an epileptic episode.

Fodor and Laurie tried to trace the ghost – or hoaxer – with detective techniques. They sprinkled powdered starch on the floor of Mr Davis's bedroom, where many of the phenomena had taken place, before locking the door and sealing it with tape, copper wires and staples. When they opened the door the next day, they found the starch untouched.

Fodor interviewed Grace and Minnie. Both women's nerves seemed shattered. Grace suggested that the spirit of her dead mother might have returned to take revenge on Mr Davis and Minnie Harrison, whom she had suspected were lovers. Minnie agreed that there had been tension between her landlady and herself. 'She has been very jealous of me,' she said.

Fodor noticed that either Grace or Minnie was always present when something strange took place. One or both of them seemed to be causing the phenomena. But why? Perhaps the grief-stricken Grace was avenging her mother, or Minnie Harrison was engineering an escape from the house.

The Harrisons moved out of Teesdale Street on Saturday 19 February, just as the Thornton Heath poltergeist first struck. The International Institute's investigators had been unable to determine the cause of the disturbance, nor even whether it was a hoax or a haunting, but Fodor was confident that it was over. The Reverend Nicolle confirmed that all was now quiet in Bethnal Green.

In the first methodical study of poltergeist attacks, in 1896, Frank Podmore of the Society for Psychical Research concluded that all of them were hoaxes, often perpetrated by mischievous, unstable working-class girls. But in 1911 the physicist William Barrett, also of the SPR, proposed that poltergeists were otherworldly forces working through a 'radiant human centre'. Some researchers argued that they were the spirits of the dead, and others that they were 'elementals', primitive beings from a lower astral plane.

The psychical researcher Hereward Carrington had another theory, as he explained in a historical survey of poltergeist cases in 1935. Carrington argued that poltergeists were neither ghosts nor hoaxes. Rather, they were kinetic energies spontaneously projected by psychic individuals, typically adolescent girls. Fodor had investigated cases that seemed to bear this out, such as the mysterious bell-ringing at Aldborough Manor in Yorkshire in 1936, which he traced to a sixteen-year-old housemaid, and the dull raps in a doctor's house in Chelsea in 1937, which seemed to emanate from a seventeen-year-old servant girl. But he speculated that the maids' kinetic force was psychological rather than biological, the product of feelings more than hormones. Unlike Carrington, he suspected that suppressed emotion always underlay the violence of a ghost.

By evening the Fieldings were less anxious. Fodor had created a carnival atmosphere, as if the family, the investigators and the poltergeist were larking about together. He had come to Thornton Heath that Thursday for proof of the otherworldly, but also for action, laughter, adventure. His copious notes on the happenings were punctuated, like a comic strip, with dramatic noises. Ping! Smash! Crash! Bang!

In a photograph taken for the Institute's records, Les held a broken vase up to the electric light, a cigarette tucked behind his ear, and gave the cracked china a wide, confiding smile. Alma had relaxed, too. She suggested to Fodor that George's tumble down the stairs on Tuesday might have been caused by the whisky that he had consumed while playing darts in the dining room with the *Advertiser* men.

Fodor left Beverstone Road just before ten that night, making Alma promise to visit his office in South Kensington the next afternoon. He hoped against hope that her poltergeist powers would manifest again in the controlled conditions of the International Institute's seance room, and that objects there might be floated, toppled, cracked.

THREE

Things are not that simple after you die

Fodor was born Nandor Friedlander in the Hungarian town of Beregszász on 13 May 1895, the sixteenth of eighteen children. Both of his younger brothers died in childhood, leaving him the baby of the family and, he said, his father's favourite. The Friedlanders were part of a thriving Jewish community, several thousand strong, who had built a grand synagogue in the centre of Beregszász, a cemetery, an elementary school, a religious court, a bath house, ritual slaughterhouses, butchers and bakeries. The town lay in the foothills of the Carpathian mountains, in wine and timber country 200 miles east of Budapest. Nandor loved to hunt beetles and butterflies in the woods, orchards and meadows near his home. His best friends were a small, hunchbacked child and a mischievous boy who regaled his companions with tales of huge penises and giant vaginas.

Nandor's first supernatural experience took place when he was seven. His grandfather was being buried, and he was playing on a ladder propped against the cemetery wall. He felt happy and free, and was looking forward to inheriting the long muslin sheet that the old man liked to drape over his head as protection against flies – Nandor planned to use it as a butterfly net. But when the coffin was opened for a final blessing, the boy heard his grandfather's voice issuing from the box. He could not tell what the spirit said, because it spoke in Hebrew, but he was frightened, and felt rebuked for his irreverence.

Nandor narrowly missed conscription in the war of 1914 to 1918, when he was studying law in Budapest. He worked in the city through both the Red Terror (a short period of Communist rule in 1919) and the White Terror (an ultra-nationalist backlash from 1919 to 1921, in which thousands of Jews and Communists were imprisoned and killed). In 1921, he left a staff job at *Az Est*, the leading Hungarian daily, to try his luck as a journalist in America. By then the family had adopted the surname Fodor, in place of the more obviously Jewish Friedlander, and it seemed a good time for a young Jew to get out of the country. His father wept as they parted at Budapest railway station: 'I know I will never see you again,' he told his son.

Fodor also left behind him a rosy-cheeked, elfin young woman, Irene Lichter, with whom he had fallen in love. He begged her to accompany him, but she refused: she was promised to a banker, she said.

In New York City Fodor became a reporter and feature writer for the Hungarian-American press, which catered to the hundreds of thousands of rural

Hungarians who had moved to the US before 1914 and the smaller number of urban intelligentsia, many of them Jewish, who had arrived since the war. He read avidly, partly to improve his English, and, having loved fantastical stories since childhood, he developed a passion for true tales of the supernatural. His first purchase was Hereward Carrington's *Modern Psychical Phenomena* (1919), which he found on a bookstall on Fourth Avenue. 'This work was a revelation to me,' he wrote. 'From then on I spent my lunch money on books, feasting on psychic knowledge in preference to the nourishing food of the Hungarian restaurants near my work.' He read about spiritualism, a religion that emerged in upstate New York in the middle of the nineteenth century, and about the Society for Psychical Research, founded in England in 1882 to establish a science of the 'supernormal'. Spiritualists held that the dead survived in another world, and could communicate with the living. Psychical researchers investigated weird experiences to find out whether they were governed by spirits or by natural laws that were not yet understood.

Fodor befriended Carrington, who lived in New York City, and he arranged to interview other men whose work intrigued him, such as the Hungarian-born magician Harry Houdini, the Hungarian psychoanalyst Sándor Ferenczi and the British author Arthur Conan Doyle. Houdini and Conan Doyle had once been friends, but they fell out over the supernatural: Houdini was a zealous exposer of phoney mediums, and Conan Doyle a great champion of spiritualism. Fodor asked Conan Doyle if he would write Sherlock Holmes stories from another planet after his death. The question was typical of Fodor, at once wide-eyed and playful. 'Things are not that simple after you die,' said Conan Doyle sternly. 'You cannot move to this or that planet.'

In the summer of 1922 Irene Lichter followed Fodor to America, her parents having persuaded her to accept his marriage proposal. As soon as they were married Irene became pregnant, to her distress, and she tried to induce a miscarriage with hot baths and roller skating. In April 1923 she endured a feverish, two-day labour before giving birth to a daughter, Andrea.

Fodor's father died in Hungary in 1924. Three years later Fodor called out to him in Hungarian in the darkness of a Manhattan seance room – '*Apam? Apam?*' – and heard his father respond with the words he had used at their parting: '*Édes fiam*' – 'sweet son'. When Fodor walked home from the sitting that night, the coloured lights of Broadway seemed to glow richer and brighter; the stars sparkled overhead. The spiritualists must be right, he thought: the dead survived and could speak to the living.

In 1928 Fodor conducted an interview with the British newspaper mogul Lord Rothermere, who was emerging as an unlikely champion of the Hungarian people. The press baron agreed with Fodor that far too much land had been stripped from Hungary after the war – two-thirds of its territory, including Fodor's home town, had been ceded to other nations – and that religious and racial intolerance was harming the country's reputation.

Once the interview was published, Rothermere offered Fodor a job as his adviser on Hungarian affairs, with a generous annual salary of £1,000 and a comfortable berth in the Associated Newspapers offices in Fleet Street. Fodor moved to England with Irene and their five-year-old daughter Andrea, and began to campaign on Rothermere's behalf for the restoration of Hungarian land surrendered in the Treaty of Trianon. His new boss was the third richest man in Britain, and the owner of a newspaper empire unrivalled in reach and influence.

Fodor also threw himself into the London psychical scene. He joined the Ghost Club and the London Spiritualist Alliance, befriended members of the Faery Investigation Society, contributed articles to the spiritualist weekly *Light*. Spiritualism was big business in Britain. Three-quarters of a million Britons had been killed in the Great War, and another quarter of a million in the influenza pandemic that followed. Thousands of spiritualist seance circles were established by the wives and husbands and sweethearts of the dead, their mothers and fathers and children. The faith offered 'something tremendous', said Conan Doyle, 'a breaking down of the walls between two worlds... a call of hope and of guidance to the human race at the time of its deepest affliction.' In effect, a seance was a voluntary haunting, a summoning of ghosts, at which the dead would speak through trumpets or through mediums, rap on tables and blow cold breezes, sometimes even let themselves be touched, smelt or seen. These forms of contact seemed hardly more outlandish than the other means of communication that had become familiar since the war. Nineteenth-century inventions such as the radio, the electric telegraph, the telephone, the camera and the gramophone player were now commonplace. Soon, predicted Fodor, 'the mechanism of psychic communication will be understood and used with the same facility as the wireless and the telephone'.

Scores of seances and private consultations were advertised in the psychic press, along with books and lectures on all aspects of the occult. Some spiritualists believed that there was so much supernormal activity because the dead were straining to come closer. 'The boundary between the two states – the known and the unknown – is still substantial,' wrote the renowned physicist and radio pioneer Sir Oliver Lodge, who had lost a son in the war, 'but it is wearing thin in places, and like excavators engaged in boring a tunnel from opposite ends, amid the roar of water and other noises, we are beginning to hear now and again the strokes of the pickaxes of our comrades on the other side.'

Fodor was amazed by what he witnessed in the seance rooms of London. He leapt to his feet, crying out with pleasure, upon first seeing a medium produce ectoplasm. When he discussed psychic affairs, said his friend Mercy Phillimore of the London Spiritualist Alliance, 'his words gushed forth, indeed, splashed forth – in torrents at terrific speed, and in the whirl of sounds were many amusing mistakes. He was quite willing to learn about his errors of speech, and joined in the fun.' A *Daily Express* reporter who interviewed Fodor about his supernatural inquiries in 1930 found him both lively and sensible: 'vital, vivacious', and 'eminently practical and matter-of-fact'.

While in Budapest for a journalism conference in 1933, Fodor attended a seance with Lajos Pap, a slender and lugubrious carpenter whose sittings were organised by a retired chemist called Chengery Pap (no relation). Before the seance, Fodor was invited to search the room (he examined the clock, chairs and table), the medium (he checked his mouth and ears, combed his fingers through his hair and beard) and the other sitters. Lajos then donned a one-piece boiler suit with tight luminous bands at the wrists and ankles so that he could be seen in the dark, and he slipped luminous spats over his shoes. Once the session was in progress, two sitters held his wrists lightly, to prevent trickery. Lajos made peculiar scooping motions with his hands, then climbed on a chair and started to snatch at the air: 'Take it!' he cried as he dropped an iridescent green beetle, an inch long, into Fodor's palm. Fodor enjoyed the jabbing in his flesh as he closed his fist around the creature, a sensation that he remembered from his beetle-hunting days. Over the next hour Lajos sprinkled fifty-nine green-backed beetles on the sitters, as well as a cluster of rosebuds, a squashed butterfly and a flowering acacia twig.

When Fodor returned to London, Chengery wrote to keep him up to date with Lajos's 'apports' (the word was derived from the French *apporter*, to bring). In July 1933: twelve dragonflies, thirteen caterpillars, a goldfish, fifteen stag beetles. Over the winter: a tortoise, a lizard, a bullet, black crickets, a quantity of acacia honey, dirty snowballs, a sparrowhawk. Fodor was keen to get the Paps over to London for controlled demonstrations, and lobbied the London Spiritualist Alliance to sponsor a trip.

Fodor wrote articles on famous hauntings for Associated Newspapers, and he hoped that Rothermere would let him oversee his newspapers' coverage of the supernormal – the public seemed fascinated by the haunting of Borley Rectory, as described in the *Daily Mirror* in 1929, and by sightings of the Loch Ness monster, widely reported in 1933. But the mogul showed little interest in the subject, even when Fodor sent him a sample of messages that the spirit of Rothermere's late brother Lord Northcliffe had supposedly relayed to him at a seance. 'If they are nonsense, I crave your pardon,' wrote Fodor. 'If not, may I send you the rest?' Rothermere's response was furious and derisive. 'Dear Fodor,' he wrote, 'I have a great mind to send your letter to a mental specialist. You are certainly not sane.' He ridiculed the seance messages, concluding: 'I should advise you to stop this nonsense forthwith, otherwise there will be very serious trouble for you.'

Fodor was mortified at his own lack of judgement, and alarmed at the possible consequences. He could not afford to lose his job. Rothermere, meanwhile, was consorting with anti-Semitic politicians. In 1934 the mogul travelled to Germany to meet Hitler, who had become Chancellor the previous year, and he declared his support for Oswald Mosley's British Union of Fascists. Oswald Mosley was a slick, charismatic figure, a former Member of Parliament for both the Conservative and Labour parties, who had been inspired by European fascism to found an authoritarian movement of his own. 'Hurrah for the Blackshirts' Rothermere wrote in the *Daily Mail*; and 'Give the Blackshirts a Helping Hand' he encouraged readers of the *Daily Mirror*.

Fodor tried to find other employment, working so intensely on compiling a guide to supernatural research that he came close to nervous collapse. When his definitive, 500,000-word *Encyclopaedia of Psychic Science* was published in 1934, with a foreword by Sir Oliver Lodge, he at once applied for a post at the new International Institute for Psychical Research in South Kensington.

The International Institute aimed to combine the spiritualist and scientific approaches to the supernormal. In theory, the two were compatible, as seances were designed to elicit proof of survival after death, but in practice, the alliance between science and religion proved difficult to sustain. Within weeks of the Institute's foundation almost all of the scientists on its board had resigned. When Fodor was appointed chief research officer in June, he replaced a professor of physiology who had objected to being provided with a seance room rather than a laboratory.

Fodor tried from the start to find a middle way: he was less reverent towards weird phenomena than the spiritualist church, less severe than the Society for Psychical Research, which he described as 'rather stuffy' – it had adopted such a high-minded attitude that its membership halved after the war. Fodor took pride in cultivating a relaxed atmosphere at the Institute. 'You know, we are quite a nice crowd,' he assured one prospective subject. In a guide to the experimental seances, he wrote: 'Light conversation, laughter and mirth is encouraged. In conversation, sitters should stimulate the medium by kindness, sympathy and appreciation.'

Spiritualism was a predominantly working-class faith, but the Institute, as a research establishment with an annual membership fee of a guinea, attracted many educated, affluent types. Its few hundred members included lawyers, doctors, stage magicians, businessmen and businesswomen, writers, artists, clergymen, psychoanalysts, cinematographers, linguists, philanthropists and engineers. Fodor raised a third of the Institute's yearly costs of £1,000 from subscriptions. He tried to make up the difference by selling tickets to lectures, public seances and screenings, and by soliciting donations from rich patrons. In his first year, as he was still being paid a £300 retainer by Rothermere, he agreed to work for the Institute for free. After that, his annual salary was £300, double the average national income but less than a third of what he had earned on moving to England.

Fodor lived in a modern estate in Chiswick, south-west London, with Irene, Andrea and a dog, Cadet, who chewed up his books ('He's searching for know-ledge,' said Fodor indulgently). He was known as Dr Fodor in the press – he had a doctorate in law, and the title lent him an air of authority – and as Nandi to his friends. He was so open and friendly, said Andrea, that it drove his wife crazy. Irene accused him of flirting with the family's maid, Magda, whose Hungarian cooking he adored. He, in turn, worried about Irene's volatile temperament. He discouraged her from developing her psychic gifts, warning her that all mediums were unhappy. Just as he had turned to spiritualism after the death of his father, Irene went to seances in the hope of making contact with her beloved younger brother, who had been killed in the war.

Fodor travelled the country to investigate hauntings, levitations, automatic writing and drawing, spirit possession, glossolalia (speaking in tongues), telepathy (the reading of minds), psychometry (the reading of objects), materialisations (the production of objects) and spirit photography (images with ghostly 'extras'). He was alerted to strange phenomena by news-paper reports and by individuals who approached the Institute for help. His chief rival was the well-known ghost hunter Harry Price, a ruthless self-publicist who had been chasing spooks and cultivating mediums since the 1920s.

At weekends Fodor sometimes took Irene and Andrea on ghost hunts. They stayed overnight in haunted houses, surrounded by cameras, flashbulbs, switches and timers. Andrea looked forward to these trips, partly because she hoped to see a spook, but chiefly because she adored her clever, good-looking, sociable father. Fodor delighted in his work. He modelled himself, he said, on the boy in a Hungarian folk tale who plays games in a haunted house, throwing skulls to the resident ghost, whooping with joy as his bed flies up and down the stairs. He enjoyed ghost stories as well as psychical studies, and secretly gave Andrea collections by the British horror writer Algernon Blackwood ('Don't tell your mother!' he warned). He only regretted that he was not more psychically sensitive himself. In an attempt to enhance his receptivity, he arranged for a doctor at the Maudsley Hospital in London to inject him with mescaline, and experienced sensations of colour, light and movement so stupendous that he felt bereft when the drug wore off.

Fodor advertised for subjects to submit to similar experiments. Ronald Cockersell, aged twenty, the son of a convict from west London, took nitrous oxide at one International Institute seance to see if it improved his extrasensory powers. In a trim three-piece suit and a pair of round spectacles, his hair oiled smooth to his scalp, Ronnie went into trance and allowed his spirit guide 'Cosma' to speak through him. 'You married because you wanted to,' Cosma informed Irene Fodor, 'and did not have parental consent.' Irene replied, 'Yes, that is true.' On the transcript of this exchange, Fodor drew an arrow to his wife's 'Yes' and wrote 'No!' At another seance Ronnie took Benzedrine, with similarly negative effects. Cosma told the widowed Dorothy de Gernon that her husband had been very humble. 'No,' said Mrs de Gernon. 'He was very conceited.'

In 1935 Fodor and Irene attended an evening seance with the twenty-four-year-old 'flower medium' Hylda Lewis at the British College of Psychic Science in South Kensington. Hylda, a plumber's daughter from north London, was slightly built and wore her dark hair in a crimped bob. During the sitting, her spirit guide 'Robin' spoke through her, in a high, lisping voice, to tell the Fodors that their daughter had just moved to a new school, and remained very friendly with a girl called Pamela. 'All these statements were hits in the bull's-eye,' said Fodor. 'My daughter changed her school the day before.' A profusion of flowers then began to swell from beneath the left lapel of Hylda's jacket, damp and gleaming: pink and red roses, grape hyacinths, lily of the valley, snowdrops, violets.

At Fodor's invitation, Hylda and her friend Miss Evans visited the International Institute for an experimental seance. To show that she had nothing concealed on her body, Hylda undressed in front of two female members of the Institute. She warned them not to touch her, showing them burns on her abdomen that she claimed had been caused by human contact. The lights were turned off during the sitting. Hylda bent double in her chair, her chin to her knees, her body heaving as seventeen roses and cornflowers splayed slowly from her hair and shoulders. Robin, her spirit guide, asked the sitters to notice that the flowers were breathing as they came. Hylda handed the wet plants to Fodor. She always felt labour pains as she gave birth to the flowers, she told him.

A few days later Hylda produced ten roses, all hanging head down, with warm buds and flattened, dewy leaves. 'I asked the Medium if her blouse was not wet underneath,' wrote Fodor in his report. 'She promptly took my hand to feel. I went around her back, up to her elbow and in front all around under her breasts. There was not the slightest trace of moisture. She took her coatee off, then the blouse. I suggested that we film this.' A seance room was a permissive place – mystical, tactile, erotically charged – in which convention often fell away.

Fodor was also introduced that year to Harry Brown, an eighteen-stone house painter from east London who claimed that he could levitate. Harry was tall, moustachioed, barrel-chested. Under his suit jacket he wore a soft striped shirt and tie, and a knitted tank top that rode up his belly. At Harry's first sitting, Fodor sat directly to his left and held his hand – Harry said that he liked to hold hands with those to either side of him, for fear that he would otherwise float clean through the ceiling. Once the lights were turned off, Fodor felt his hand gently lift with the bigger man's. Soon he could sense Harry bobbing above him, as a cork might bob in water. He felt one of Harry's dangling legs bump against him. In the blindness of the seance room, the other senses came to the fore: sometimes sharper, sometimes more malleable. Harry seemed to be twirling, tethered only by his neighbours. The Institute's photographer was in position in the corner, waiting for Harry to give the signal for him to take an infrared picture. 'Go!' Harry shouted. As the camera shutter came down, Fodor felt his arm jerk upwards, as if Harry was jumping.

When the photograph was printed, it seemed to show that Harry had staged a levitation by leaping from the chair as the shutter fell: his feet pointed down as they would if he had just pushed off. And yet, oddly, the hem of his coat was hanging perfectly straight, unruffled. Fodor tried to imitate a faked levitation by standing on a chair and jumping; though he weighed just twelve stone – six fewer than Harry – he could not control his descent, and the chair toppled onto him as he fell to the ground.

Harry became a regular at the Institute. One night a child spoke through him. On another night he produced a symphony of raps in the darkness: loud, small, clear, liquid, crisp, metallic; raps that cracked, scraped, rang. Some were swallowed by the muffled rush of the underground trains passing every few minutes beneath the seance-room floor.

Fodor's friend Wilfred Becker, the director of a photography company, would reel and faint during Harry's seances, lurch forward and fall off his seat. It was as if Harry were sucking the energy from him, so that one man fell as the other rose. Becker's skin turned clammy in Harry's presence; he felt sick when touched by him. During the session of 5 November, Becker slumped in his chair and slid onto the floor, deaf to the crackle and burst of Guy Fawkes' Night fireworks in the street outside, and the clanging of fire-engine bells.

Fodor enjoyed Harry's visits regardless of whether they provided proof of the supernormal. They were occasions for wonder and levity, a kind of vaudeville, in which the atmosphere rolled from eeriness to hilarity, suspense to relief. The sitters sometimes broke into song ('Good King Wenceslas' just before Christmas) or fell about with laughter. 'Next Weds we have the levitation man,' Fodor wrote to a physicist friend, 'and hope to get him in the air. It starts at 8.30.' He relished the improbability, the bravura of this hulking labourer who claimed to float like a feather.

Now that he had his own research budget, Fodor was able to bring the Hungarian medium Lajos Pap and his minder to England for experimental seances. He put Lajos and Chengery up in a hotel in South Kensington, provided them with expenses and a daily Hungarian newspaper, and alerted the press to their visit. 'Watch your goldfish tonight!' the *Evening Standard* cautioned its readers on the day of Lajos's first London seance: 'If your canary disappears tonight, or your goldfish bowl is emptied, Lajos Pap will probably be responsible.' That evening Lajos produced nothing. If anyone's goldfish had gone missing, Fodor noted ruefully, they should probably blame the cat. But at the second seance Fodor's faith and perseverance were rewarded. Lajos showered the sitters with trinkets, gravel and rosebuds, and materialised two legal documents issued by the

Orphan Board of Budapest along with a pebble and a snake ('twenty-eight inches long' noted Fodor; 'quite soft, and dead') before kicking over the table and falling like a log to the floor.

Fodor had to prove himself as a scientist as well as a showman. In his first laboratory experiment at the Institute, he tried to recreate a recent study in which Dr R. A. Watters of Reno, Nevada, claimed to have photographed astral bodies escaping from dying animals. Fodor commissioned B. J. Hopper, a young physics teacher from west London, to build a 'cloud chamber' that could detect ionising particles. Hopper assembled an elaborate contraption of rubber tubes, metal cylinders, glass jars, lamps, pumps, wires and switches. Fodor applied to the Home Office for a licence to experiment on living creatures, and purchased nineteen white mice, three linnets and a collection of frogs and American cockroaches.

Fodor and Hopper anaesthetised the animals with ether-soaked cotton wool, then transferred each one to a tube in the chamber, where its throat was encircled with a blade. The cinematograph was rolling as the guillotine came down on the slender, sweet-voiced linnets, the long, stinking roaches, the frogs, the mice.

Though the cockroaches continued to twitch for half an hour after being decapitated, the researchers saw no vapours rise from any of the bodies, no souls slipping away. Fodor took a photograph of Hopper peering into the misted box: 'Mr B. J. Hopper, MSc.,' ran Fodor's caption, 'watching for the ghost of an American cockroach.'

When Fodor published his results, he pointed out flaws in Dr Watters' original experiment and concluded that the phantoms in his pictures must have been particles of dust. Watters retaliated, writing to the British spiritualist press from Nevada to denounce Fodor and his associates and threatening to sue the International Institute for libel. A bitter correspondence ensued.

Some of the researchers who studied the cloud chamber footage thought that they detected faint forms rising from the tiny corpses, but Fodor was cautious. 'This phenomenon,' he wrote, 'is akin to watching for the appearance of fantastic figures in the burning coals in a fire or sky-gazing to find shapes in the clouds.' If you looked for long enough, your eyes would find things to see.

With the cloud chamber experiment, Fodor established the Institute's scientific credibility, and he embarked on his war with the more fervent devotees of spiritualism. He yearned as much as they did for proof that the dead lived, but he had to be true to the evidence.

FOUR

Where the facts are fantastic

In the summer of 1935 Fodor learnt that a private detective had exposed Hylda Lewis, the flower medium, as a fraud. On the instructions of the Society for Psychical Research, Edgar Wright of Wright's Detective Agency had followed Hylda to the seance that Fodor and Irene attended in January. Wright shadowed her by bus to Oxford Circus from her office in the City, watched her buy flowers from a series of shops and stalls and then slip into a side street to bite the stalks off a bunch of roses. Hylda stashed the roses in an attaché case, bought more flowers, and stopped again, outside a Lyons restaurant, to slide several stems of lily of the valley into her coat. Finally she proceeded by bus to the British College of Psychic Science in South Kensington.

In the darkened room, Fodor realised, Hylda had made it appear that the flowers were pressing out of her body by secretly prising them out of her clothes. He also discovered how she had acquired her eerily accurate information about his daughter's life: as a switchboard operator for a City firm, Hylda was able to eavesdrop on the telephone calls of people due to attend her seances.

Fodor felt betrayed by Hylda Lewis, whose phenomena had so impressed him and the other investigators at the Institute. He was learning that the golden age of psychical study was also the heyday of supernatural hustle, and that to verify his subjects' claims he would have to turn sleuth himself.

When Lajos Pap materialised a snake and other apports at the International Institute in 1935, Fodor tried to work out whether he could have produced them by normal means. The staff of the Natural History Museum in South Kensington identified the snake as a Central European dice snake, about two years old and not long dead. Fodor rang reptile shops listed in the London telephone directory and found that though the species was available in stores in Merton and Islington, neither outlet remembered serving a man of Lajos or Chengery's descriptions. He arranged for Irene to be given access to Lajos's hotel room, where she found a suitcase with a double lining, and he tried to establish whether Lajos really had a medical reason for wearing a whalebone belt beneath his clothing. Fodor hid a pebble on his body, and challenged his colleagues to find it. He put folded sheets of paper in his shoes. On completing his experiments, he concluded that Lajos Pap could have smuggled a live snake over from Hungary in the lining of his suitcase, drowned it in the hotel washbasin and zipped it into his belt. Before the seance he might also have pressed the orphanage documents into the soles of his shoes; lodged a stone in his navel; tucked trinkets behind his false teeth; stored rosebuds in his cheeks; and stuffed a gold coin up his nose. 'Our verdict is "Not Proven",' Fodor told the Institute's members when the Paps returned to Budapest.

Fodor unmasked other hoaxers with infrared photography, a new technology that made it possible to record images in the dark. His pictures of a ghostly form in the home of the Dundee railway engineer Charles Stewart revealed the railwayman himself, dressed in a white sheet. Fodor sent Mr Stewart copies of the photographs without comment. Infrared photos of the well-known trance medium Agnes Abbott showed that she was impersonating an ethereal visitor by waggling a luminous spirit trumpet on her thumb. 'Mrs Abbott, the game is up,' said Fodor, dramatic as a movie detective. But he was careful not publicly to shame her. He reminded his team that they should be kind to mediums even when they caught them cheating. Fake psychics were only trying to earn a living, after all. 'Never at any time must a bullying attitude be adopted,' Fodor wrote, 'and the whole business must be carried through with dignity… and with gentleness and consideration.' It would, in any case, be bad business to be rude. If word got around that the Institute treated its subjects roughly, it would have no one with whom to experiment.

In 1935 Fodor and Irene befriended an American couple called the Woodwards who lived in a neighbouring apartment block in Chiswick. Dick Woodward was a tall, good-looking man in the film business, with whom Fodor would sit up until one in the morning, playing canasta and drinking whisky.

One evening in June, the Fodors and the Woodwards were playing bridge at the flat of another couple when Dick Woodward announced that he was able to levitate flowers. Fodor ran up to his own flat, on the fifth floor, to fetch a potted geranium about two feet tall. He returned to his friends' fourth-floor apartment, and switched off the electric lights. The sky was clear, and by the light of the moon Fodor could see his companions' faces, the furniture, the pattern of the carpet, the luminous dial of the wireless set. He put the geranium in the middle of the room and sat against a wall.

Woodward stood about three yards from the pot, his arms outstretched. 'His breathing became heavy,' recalled Fodor, 'he snapped with his fingers, as one snaps to a dog; his breath came faster and faster, and suddenly the branches of the geranium swayed and twisted.' Woodward fell back on the sofa, his arms out wide, his head thrown back. Then he stood up and began again. This time 'a storm broke loose among the branches and leaves of the geranium. First there was a faint rustle; then, in silence but with the force of an explosion, a shower of leaves and flowers shot up in the air.' Fodor counted seven leaves and eight flowering twigs strewn around the room, along with a bud and a scatter of petals. He was staggered. 'You are one in a million!' he told his friend.

Woodward produced no further phenomena that year, but in September 1936 he was roused to action after reading an interview that Fodor gave to *Psychic News*. 'At present, in England,' Fodor told the magazine, 'there is no contemporary scientific evidence for the reality of materialisation.' Woodward told Fodor that he would prove him wrong by producing just such evidence. He made Fodor promise him dinner at the Hungaria – a top-notch Hungarian restaurant in Regent Street – if he got him photographic proof of flower levitation.

At the first attempt, in the Fodors' flat, Woodward consumed a large quantity of whisky. Fodor heard him hiss and pant, and saw the green and white carnations tremble violently. But none of the photos registered any movement among the flowers.

They tried again a week later. Fodor got in supplies of alcohol for Woodward, who turned up at 10.45 p.m. He already seemed to have had more whisky than was ideal for psychic experiments, said Fodor. 'Nevertheless, he fell greedily on what I had for him.' In the Fodors' living room, Woodward put his carnations in a vase, which he placed in front of a bookcase on a carpet on the parquet floor. Woodward was soon very drunk. By midnight he was dancing alone to gramophone records while muttering what sounded like: 'I am afraid you will catch me in what I do. I want to talk. Whisky is darkness itself.' At 1.10 a.m. he succeeded in creating a shudder among the flowers, but then Fodor noticed the glint of a safety pin on the carpet, and a cluster of black threads stretching from the pin to the carnations.

'So,' Fodor asked, pointing to the thread, 'is this how the flowers moved?'

'Yes,' replied Woodward carelessly. 'What else did you think?'

'That is why you needed the background of the books. It was so the thread would not be visible.'

'Yes, of course.'

Woodward had moved the flowers by pulling on threads that he had looped round their stems. Fodor told him that he found his conduct despicable. He could not trust him again. Woodward said that he had only been trying to help him by providing physical phenomena. 'I showed him the door,' wrote Fodor, 'and he left.'

A few days later, Woodward begged for a reprieve. He said that his phenomena were genuine, and that he had pretended to be a fraud in order to test Fodor: many people on the block said that the 'spooky' business was a racket, and he wanted to see whether Fodor was sincere in his belief in the supernatural. He said that he would try again to lift flowers, under any conditions that Fodor imposed. He agreed to be filmed at the Institute by infrared light.

At the International Institute on 11 December, Woodward drank a bottle of cheap whisky, provided by Fodor. He stood on a platform in a dark suit and red shirt, his features twisted in a diabolic grimace, and waved his fingers at a bunch of white carnations until they shook in their vase. The session broke up at 9 p.m. so that the sitters could tune in to Edward VIII's radio broadcast: the king announced that he was giving up the throne in order to marry the American divorcée Wallis Simpson.

The filming resumed the next evening, by which time George VI was King of England, and at Woodward's bidding one white carnation leapt from the vase, rising eleven inches into the air. Afterwards, Fodor examined stills from the film. Woodward's palms, wrists, fingers vibrated and blurred as the stalk of the flower bent and spun away from him, its head a shining haze. With the help of a floor plan, Fodor made calculations about the speed and trajectory of the carnation and how it corresponded to the quivering of Woodward's hands. He magnified the images to check for thread.

But back in Chiswick, Fodor heard that Woodward was boasting about how he had duped him. When confronted, Woodward denied fraud but was then defiant: 'Why shouldn't I go about pulling threads?' Fodor denounced him as a scoundrel and a liar.

Fodor had been humiliated in front of his neighbours as well as his colleagues. To have given Woodward a second chance after the original discovery of the thread now seemed helplessly gullible. And there were rumours that Dick Woodward had betrayed him more intimately, by having an affair with Irene. Soon afterwards, Fodor left Chiswick with his family. He would not be so credulous again.

The Fodors moved to Park West, a new complex on the Edgware Road within walking distance of Marble Arch and Hyde Park. The block was decked out in marble, wood and brass, and fitted with elevators, a

gymnasium, squash courts, a swimming pool and a sol-
arium; each flat had gas central heating, a refrigerator
and a telephone. The rent, at £250 a year, accounted
for much of Fodor's salary, while Irene's expensive
clothes, Andrea's schooling and the maid Magda's pay
used up most of the rest. Fodor's anxiety about money
brought his relationship with Irene under further
strain. The fourteen-year-old Andrea, now at ballet
school, worried about their marriage. 'Is Daddy going
to divorce us?' she asked Irene.

After two years as a ghost hunter, Fodor was also
losing his faith in spiritualism. He no longer believed
that the dead communicated with the living or infested
old houses, and he knew that most self-professed
mediums were fakes. But he still believed that some
individuals had supernatural powers. He guessed that
a few people suffered from mental abnormalities that
allowed them to detach from their conscious selves
and tune in to others' moods and thoughts, and that
a very few were so dissociated that they radiated kinetic energy. He wondered whether this energy might
stem from suppressed feelings. If unconscious desires
found ways to reveal themselves in slips of the tongue,
dreams, jokes and tics, as Freud described, perhaps they
could manifest themselves beyond the body too.

Freud's work had been published in English in the
1920s, and the press now referred regularly (if satiric-
ally) to neuroses and fixations, inhibitions and inferiority complexes, sublimation and repression, the ego,
the id, the libido, the talking cure and the unconscious

mind. Fodor was entranced by the idea that individuals contained secret worlds, hidden from themselves, and that supernatural events might be stories to interpret, symbols to decode. He talked about his new psychological theories with friends such as Eileen Garrett, one of the most famous clairvoyants in England. Eileen agreed that her gifts might be psychological rather than spiritual and that her spirit guides – Uvani, an Arab warrior, and Abdul Latif, a Persian physician – might not be mystic revenants but parts of her subconscious self.

An imposing woman with sleek, cropped hair, Eileen started to assist Fodor on ghost hunts. When he was invited to investigate a haunting at Ash Manor in Surrey in the summer of 1936, he asked the owners if he could bring Eileen with him. 'Mrs Garrett is an extremely intelligent and vivacious woman,' he assured Maurice and Katherine Kelly. 'You will love her. She has more sense than all other mediums lumped together. And, curiously, she is still a sceptic. She does not believe in spirits.'

The Kellys had been disturbed by bangs, raps and ghostly footsteps ever since they bought Ash Manor in 1934, and they had both seen the figure of a small man at their bedroom doors. He wore a smock, leggings and a cloth hat, they said, and his eyes glittered malevolently in a round, red face. He would tip back his head to show his throat, which had been slashed from ear to ear. The couple had turned to the International Institute only when a Church of England priest failed to drive out the ghost.

On arrival at Ash Manor, Eileen sensed discord. She went into trance and addressed the Kellys in the voice of her Arab control, Uvani. 'Haven't you discovered that these things only happen to you when you are in a bad emotional state?' asked Uvani. 'Don't you realise that you yourself vivify this memory?' Uvani told the family that their unhappiness was animating the phantom: it was a 'spectral automaton', he said, 'living on life borrowed from human wrecks'.

To dispel the ghost, Eileen first let it occupy her. She convulsed, stiffened, grabbed Fodor's hand so tightly that it went numb, and allowed herself to be possessed by 'Henley', a sixteenth-century nobleman determined to revenge himself on a rival. Fodor urged Henley to leave the earthly sphere and let God bring his enemy to justice. 'You prate to me of God!' shouted Henley, through Eileen. 'I want my vengeance.'

Back in London, Fodor held a private sitting with Eileen, at which Uvani disclosed further facts that he had picked up at Ash Manor: Maurice Kelly was a homosexual 'debauchee' and an alcoholic, and his wife Katherine – a beautiful half-Russian woman who had trained as a lawyer – was sexually frustrated and addicted to morphine. Fodor sent a transcript of Uvani's revelations to Mr Kelly, who admitted that the information was accurate. Fodor felt sorry for the couple: 'I realized how the ghost had been used as a distracting element, a sort of tranquillizer, which helped hold the family together without bringing their true frustrations into the open.'

A few weeks later Maurice Kelly wrote to tell Fodor that the haunting had worsened: 'It is no longer in the house alone but is in me too.' Fodor assured him that this would pass – 'the fear of one's own desire often leads to persecutory delusions', he said, encouraging Maurice to be more forgiving of his sexual impulses. The case confirmed Fodor's hunch that supernormal phenomena could be caused by forbidden feelings.

At the end of 1936 Fodor had to lobby for donations to make up a £400 shortfall at the Institute. He worried for his future. Rothermere had axed his retainer, and even with the proceeds of freelance journalism (£250 in 1936 for a nine-part supernatural series for *Empire News*), he was struggling to make ends meet. He feared that he would be forced to leave England if he lost his job as a psychical researcher. To raise the Institute's profile, and his own, he decided to tackle one of the most famous stories of the day, the mystery of Gef the talking mongoose.

Gef (pronounced 'Jeff') was said to live in a remote farmhouse on the Isle of Man with James Irving, a piano-salesman-turned-farmer, his wife Margaret and their adolescent daughter Voirrey. Several islanders claimed to have seen or heard Gef over the years, but he was especially attached to Voirrey, while the fullest account of his antics was a log kept by James since 1932. Though Gef took animal form, he was a classic poltergeist: unruly, elusive and rude. On one occasion he described himself as 'an earthbound spirit', though on another he told the Irvings: 'I am not a spirit. I am just a little extra-clever mongoose.' Gef threw objects at the family, spat at them, jeered at them, killed rabbits for them, roamed the island gathering gossip by day and returned to raid the larder by night. He was partial to butter and chocolate. The mongoose could speak several languages, according to James Irving's log, and was proud of his intellectual prowess.

'I'll split the atom!' declared Gef. 'I am the Fifth Dimension! I am the Eighth Wonder of the World!'

Fodor's fellow ghost hunter Harry Price failed to flush Gef out when he spent three days with the Irvings in 1936. Fodor, hoping to get the better of Price, arranged with James Irving to stay for a week. He promised that he would be no trouble: 'I would willingly pay you £5 for the week's board,' he wrote to him. 'Considering that I am a vegetarian and eat only vegetables cooked in water for 10 minutes, I do not think that Mrs Irving would have too much trouble looking after me.' At night, he said, he would be happy to 'rough it' anywhere in the house.

'I hope that Gef will bear with me and will not throw things at me or spit at me in the night!' added Fodor. 'He has my admiration. He is certainly the cleverest thing far and wide... Tell him also that I shall bring him chocolates and biscuits.'

James Irving later told Fodor that while he was reading this letter to himself in the cottage, Gef screamed down from the attic: 'Read it out, you fat-headed gnome!'

The Irvings put Fodor up for a week in February 1937. Though he did not manage to communicate with Gef, he was able to verify statements that the mongoose had made about the interior of Ballamooar, a grand Manx house which the Irvings claimed never to have visited. When Fodor left the Irvings' cottage, he installed a contraption to take automatic photographs of Gef, and he left a note for him:

Dear Gef,

I am very disappointed that you did not speak to me during the whole week which I spent here. I came from a long way and took a lot of trouble in collecting all your clever sayings, and I shall lecture about you in my institute where people are extremely interested in your doings. I hoped that you would be kind and generous. I believe you to be a very good and generous mongoose, I brought you chocolates and biscuits and I would have been happy if you had done something for me... Will you send me a message? Or will you write a letter to me? I should be very pleased if you gave a definite promise that you would speak to me. I would come again in the Summer. Congratulations on Ballamooare [sic]. You scored there, Gef.

With best wishes,
Your friend,
Nandor Fodor

On his way back to London from the Isle of Man, Fodor called on a physician in Leeds who was interested in psychoanalysis and the supernatural. They discussed

Gef. Fodor told Dr Maxwell Telling that he thought that James Irving's unhappiness somehow lay behind the Gef phenomena. Irving had failed in life, he observed, and the mongoose may have been a means to express his unconscious desires. The Leeds doctor was sympathetic to Fodor's views. 'Where the facts are fantastic,' advised Dr Telling, 'you should never be afraid of fantastic theories.' He suggested that Gef could be a detached part of Mr Irving's personality that had taken up residence in an actual mongoose.

In the year after the Gef adventure, Fodor had more bad luck with mediums. Rudi Schneider of Austria, Lára Agústsdóttir of Iceland and Anna Rasmussen of Denmark all turned out to be clumsy frauds. Arthur Findlay, the Institute's chairman, admitted to the members, 'So far our efforts to establish supernormal physical phenomena have been unsuccessful. It gives us no satisfaction to expose fraudulent so-called mediums but in work such as is ours we must be prepared for all kinds of experiences.'

Fodor passed some of the Institute's evidence of fraud to the spiritualist weekly *Psychic News*, which happened to be owned by Findlay, but the journal chose not to publish any of it. Instead, it ran scornful articles about Fodor himself. 'Fodor still attacks mediums,' ran one headline: 'Sneers at England's materialisation evidence.' The journal claimed that Fodor was harsh towards his experimental subjects, excessively sceptical, and obsessed with sexual theories and technological gadgets. Fodor suspected that the magazine's editor, Maurice Barbanell, bore him a grudge because he had not given him an entry in his *Encyclopaedia*.

'Fodor Finds Sex in Mediumship', *Psychic News* announced in December 1937, reporting the 'unblushing audacity' of Fodor's 'repugnant' claim, in an American publication, that supernatural events were exciting to mediums. According to Fodor, the famous Italian psychic Eusapia Paladino used to tremble, convulse and moan during seances, entering 'a state of voluptuous-erotic ecstasy which was followed by true orgasm'. The journal declared that Dr Fodor was disgusting, insensitive and incompetent.

When Fodor sued *Psychic News* in January for publishing malicious falsehoods about him, Arthur Findlay, as the journal's owner, immediately resigned his chairmanship of the International Institute and his membership of its council. Fodor now needed urgently to prove himself to the rest of the board.

FIVE

Something is moving

F odor spent much of the morning of Friday 25 February 1938 on the telephone, excitedly inviting friends and colleagues to meet Alma Fielding at the International Institute for Psychical Research. Dr Wills picked Alma up from home at two o'clock, and an hour later showed her in to the Institute's premises at Walton House, a detached, five-storey Arts and Crafts building on a cobbled mews behind Harrods department store. The property belonged to a rich young widow called Mary Dundas, who lived in the upper storeys and accommodated the International Institute on the first two floors. It was the most imposing and capacious of the several psychic-research establishments in South Kensington. Other supernormal institutions lay in neighbouring districts: the Psychic Bookshop, founded by Arthur Conan Doyle in 1925, was next to Westminster Abbey, two miles to the east, while the seance halls and occultist societies of Marylebone were two miles to the north.

Fodor welcomed Alma to Walton House. She looked well. Her hair was waved and lustrous, her eyebrows neatly plucked. She was wearing a cloche hat, a dark wool coat with a fur collar, a sheer, calf-length dress, glossy stockings and dark shoes with a modest heel. Once she had hung her hat and coat in the ladies' cloak-room on the ground floor, Fodor took her up to his office and introduced her to his secretary, Elyne Tufnell, the Institute's only other salaried member of staff.

Fodor asked Alma whether there had been any trouble since he left her the previous evening. There had, she said. That morning, she and Rose had been at the Welcome Café in Thornton Heath high street when her teacup and saucer were smashed out of her hand and a glass of milk crashed to the floor. Their friend Mabel, who ran the café, brought Alma a cup of Bovril. 'I dared not drink it,' Alma told Fodor. 'I sat for some time spooning it. But while talking, I forgot about my fears and lifted it to my lip. It immediately flew off.'

Dr Wills, who was sitting in on the interview, added that when he called to collect Alma from Beverstone Road, she was followed out of the bathroom by a scrubbing brush and a soap tray. She was in full view, he said, as they came rattling down the stairs behind her.

Fodor often found it hard to persuade mediums to take part in scientific seances – 'They are all scared stiff of psychical research,' he told a friend, 'so we have to go very gently' – but Alma seemed remarkably unfazed by the idea of being monitored. She suggested that Fodor search her before she went into the seance room. He, Dr Wills and Miss Tufnell rifled through her pockets and handbag, making a note of the odds and ends that they found. The group was joined by Dr Frayworth, the Croydon physician who had called at the Fieldings' house the previous day.

Fodor showed everyone in to an airy, light-flooded room on the first floor, originally designed as an artist's studio. The studio was twice the height of a normal room, sparsely furnished, with a bare wooden floor and tall mullioned windows – Fodor described it as having the proportions of a cathedral. On one side, a small staircase led to a gallery. On another, a door opened on to a chamber in which Fodor kept his recording devices. Next to a giant carved fireplace in the main room was the curtained cabinet in which visiting mediums often sat. Fodor had placed five cut-glass tumblers on a folding table in the cabinet, in the hope that they would be smashed by Alma's ghost; a flashbulb was nestled in one of them and a rattle in another. He had put saucers and cups on chairs around the room for the same purpose, and had trained cameras on the chair inside the cabinet and on the armchair in front of it.

Most experimental subjects liked to sit in the dark, but Alma chose to walk around in the light. Fodor, Dr Wills and Dr Frayworth accompanied her as she paced the room clasping a tall, dimpled glass. At 3.30 p.m. they heard a bang and saw that a brass-bound brush, three inches long, had fallen about twelve feet away. Fodor was sure that Alma had still been holding the glass with both hands when the brush landed. He picked it up and found that it was warm. Alma recognised it as her own: she had last seen it in her bedroom, she said.

The group broke for tea at 3.50 p.m. to allow nine new arrivals to join the party. These included Fodor's brother Henry, who was visiting from Budapest, and Countess Nora Wydenbruck, an Austrian author of forty-four who had been a member of the Institute's council since its inception. The Countess was a serious, sensitive woman, tall and very thin, who smoked heavily and dressed soberly, in tweeds and pearls. She and Fodor – Nora and Nandi, as they called one another – both spoke German, and had been fellow citizens of Austria-Hungary until the state was dissolved in 1918. The Countess had published an English translation of poems by Rainer Maria Rilke, whom she had known in Austria, and had written several novels. She claimed to have composed *Woman Astride* while in trance, taking automatic dictation from a seventeenth-century ancestor who had disguised herself as a boy to fight in the Thirty Years War. The Countess, unlike Fodor, was still convinced of the survival of the personality and the reality of spirit return. She was excited to meet Alma. 'Whenever I sit with a new medium,' she said, 'I do so with a feeling of happy, childlike anticipation.'

After tea, Alma again paced the room. She was walking with Fodor and Dr Frayworth at 4.15 p.m., clutching a glass with both hands, when a small circular tin of Carter's Little Liver Pills – a popular over-the-counter laxative – fell with a clatter behind her. Alma identified it as a tin from her dressing table. Fodor picked up the container and found that, like the brush, it was warm to the touch. Apports were usually warm on arrival: the heat, it was supposed, was generated by the energy expended when an item undid and reconstituted itself as it passed from one plane to another.

At 4.45 p.m. Alma was invited to sit inside the cabinet on a wooden chair, with the curtains draped over her back so that she could still be seen by those ranged in the seats before her. She was given a cup of tea on a saucer, which she held with both hands. She sat quietly, the black fabric rising and falling with her breathing, until after almost half an hour she said: 'Something is moving behind me underneath the chair.' A few moments later: 'Something is still there. I feel as if I were sitting on it. I think it is something solid.' The Countess felt sick.

Fodor came forward and reached behind Alma to pull a glass dome, about two inches in diameter, from the back of her seat. Alma recognised it as an ornamental dust cover from Don's bedroom.

As Miss Tufnell came into the seance room at 5.30 p.m., Alma's teacup and saucer flew out of her hands with a 'ping!', drenching the Countess and splashing Fodor. He, Miss Tufnell and two other witnesses testified that they had seen the saucer in mid-air, already split; a fifth observer was sure that it had been whole as it left Alma's hands. It was as if it had been hit in flight, said Fodor, by an invisible hammer.

At 5.40 p.m. Alma was still visible in the cabinet, her hands in her lap, when the sitters heard a bump in the box. Fodor looked in and found on the floor the flash-bulb that he had stowed in one of the tumblers. The bulb was intact: a thin shell of blown glass encasing a thread of filament and a shiny crush of foil. The tumbler had seemingly tipped it out, then returned to a standing position. This, said Fodor, was the best phenomenon of the day.

Before Alma left Walton House, Fodor took a flash-lit photograph of her in the armchair, with five of the sitters, including the Countess, assembled around her. The suspense of the seance had dissolved. Alma, already in her hat and coat, looked straight at the camera with a trusting smile.

The events of the afternoon had been even better than Fodor had hoped. Alma's poltergeist had managed not only to move things but to produce them from thin air. For the Countess, who had been raised as a Roman Catholic, Alma's apports were spiritualist miracles, reminiscent of the wonders produced by 'the highest type of medium', the Catholic saints. For Fodor, as a secular Jew, they were precious scientific evidence, proofs of the poltergeist force that could make objects travel through space, vanish and reappear. He measured, weighed and catalogued each of the items that had arrived in the studio that day.

Fodor had promised to return Alma to Beverstone Road by seven, so they set out at six o'clock in Dr Wills's car. Alma seemed excited by the events of the day. She sat on the back seat, next to the remains of the crockery that Fodor had taken to Thornton Heath on Thursday; by her feet was an old amplifier that he planned to give to Don as a gift, having learnt that he and the boy shared an enthusiasm for electrical apparatus. Fodor sat in the front next to Dr Wills.

Ten minutes into the journey, a saucer flew up from the back seat and snapped loudly into four pieces, and the amplifier lid twice banged open. Fodor asked Dr Wills to stop the car so that he could move to the back. He sat next to the amplifier, placing one of his feet between it and Alma's leg. The phenomena continued: Alma's bag smacked into his face; her shoe disappeared, then her hat and her diamanté clip.

Fodor shifted towards Alma and held her from behind, his left hand clutching her left hand, his right arm resting on her right wrist. Alma was wearing a fur glove on her right hand, which reached almost to the elbow, but she had misplaced the other glove, leaving her left hand bare. Somehow, the glove on her right hand removed itself while Fodor was holding her. He didn't notice it slide off but felt it emerge beneath her left wrist: 'It was the soft, empty tip that was touching my fingers.' When he next looked down he saw that the glove had crept back on to her right hand, and a few minutes later was encasing her lower arm. It seemed impossible that Alma could have pulled it on without his noticing. The incident, Fodor said, filled him with 'a sense of the marvellous': it was like being in *Alice in Wonderland*. He took both her hands and held them tight.

Fodor and Dr Wills followed Alma into her house in Beverstone Road at 7 p.m. Alma's friend Rose Saunders had called round, so Fodor asked her about the incident in Mabel's café that morning. Rose confirmed Alma's account, adding that a few of their fellow customers had dismissed the tale of the poltergeist as 'a put-up job', but when they saw Alma's mug of Bovril fly off and soak Rose's coat they had hurried out of the shop in fright.

Dr Frayworth, who lived nearby, came over to help Fodor and Dr Wills conduct further experiments. The sitting room was cold and Alma was wearing a thin frock, so Fodor encouraged her to put on Dr Wills's big overcoat. The investigators emptied the coat's deep, flap-covered pockets in readiness for apports. Alma sat with her arms folded.

'Something is moving by this side of my arm,' said Alma at 9.15 p.m., gesturing to her right.

'It is still moving on my hip,' she said two minutes later.

'I feel shivery,' she added, and after a few minutes: 'It is still moving, almost like a hand in my pocket.'

Fodor lifted the right-hand pocket flap, reached in, and found the diamanté clip.

Fodor planted his wristwatch in the left-hand pocket to see if it would disappear. Dr Wills followed Alma, watching closely, as she walked upstairs and back down, her hands clasped in front of her. Fodor felt inside the pocket: the watch was gone. She went to the kitchen, walked upstairs, went to the kitchen again. She came back to the sitting room and sat in the armchair.

'Something is moving near the side of my leg,' said Alma. 'Still moving. Still moving. Now it's stopped.' Fodor reached into the pocket and pulled out the watch.

Fodor returned the watch to the left-hand pocket.
Dr Wills put a penknife in the right-hand pocket. Dr
Frayworth gave Alma a golden pencil, which she clasped
under the lapel of the coat. She wandered around the
house again. The knife vanished; reappeared. Dr Wills
felt the outside of the pocket move.

By the end of the night, said Fodor, 'We were quite
inured to these crazy happenings. We laughed heartily
and our laughter did Mrs Fielding good.' Alma was
becoming playful, even flirtatious. Her guests were
watching her, touching her, teasing her. The poltergeist, instead of terrorising her, was serving her. Les
and George kept out of the way.

The intimate manoeuvrings of the 'magic taxi ride',
as Fodor described their drive to Thornton Heath, had
evolved into this skittish 'vanishing game'. In the car,
Alma's foot had slipped out of her shoe, her hand into
her glove, and Fodor had checked her movements by
wrapping himself around her. In the house, Alma had
slipped into Dr Wills's big coat, and then let the men's
hands and their belongings – the watch, the knife, the
golden pencil – slip in and out of her pockets, moving
against her hip and leg as they came, making her shiver.

Fodor tended to talk up his psychic subjects. By nature
and by necessity, he was an enthusiast, more likely
to advance possibilities than to voice doubts. But his
excitement about Alma was real. Through her, he
hoped to show – before his libel suit came to court –
that *Psychic News* had been wrong to mock and malign

him. Her case, he believed, might not only restore his good name as a ghost hunter but revolutionise the study of psychic science.

'There has not been a greater or truer ghost story than this one for many years,' Fodor announced in the *Journal of the American Society for Psychical Research.* 'I always wanted to meet a Poltergeist. Now I have met one, a Poltergeist which is certainly destructive, yet not malevolent, in fact, to a certain degree, amenable to experimental suggestions.' He informed the *Sunday Pictorial* that the Thornton Heath haunting was 'a genuine and amazing case of the supernormal'. The paper remarked: 'There are, it is plain, strange forces about us of which we know practically nothing, just as once we knew nothing of electricity.'

So far, Alma had proved an excellent subject. She operated in the light, without a companion or chaperone. She had volunteered to be searched, and she let the investigators touch and hold her as she worked her wonders. Fodor wrote to congratulate her on the 'splendid spirit' in which she had submitted to observation. He was determined to keep her away from other ghost hunters. Harold Chibbett, who ran a medium-busting operation called The Probe, was pestering him for access; Harry Price had driven over to Beverstone Road when the first article about the poltergeist appeared; and C. V. C. Herbert, the austere and punctilious research officer of the SPR, had tried to sign Alma up for tests before conceding that Fodor and the IIPR had 'got in first'.

The team investigating Alma comprised Fodor, Dr Wills, Laurie Evans and the Countess. Fodor wrote to his friend Wilfred Becker, who had proved so sensitive to the levitation medium Harry Brown, asking him to join them. He knew that Becker might be reluctant, having recently taken part in the farcical six-week investigation of Lára Agústsdóttir, but he urged him to suspend his cynicism. 'I feel I can rely on you to join us in a spirit of keen anticipation instead of dark and gloomy suspicions,' Fodor wrote, enclosing the notes that he had made at Thornton Heath. 'Will you do it? Remember what it may commit you to but think also that this is the thing we have been praying for.'

Part Two

THE GHOST HUNT

'Whenever she stopped, the outdoor silence
pressed as close as suspense: you had the
sensation of a great instrument out there in
London, unstruck'

Elizabeth Bowen, 'No. 16' (1939)

Alma and Les, 1920; Don, Alma and Les, 1929; and (left) Alma, Don and George in the Sunday Pictorial, *February 1938*

SIX

Fear! We swim in it

The cold snap was over. It was mild and wet when Fodor visited Beverstone Road in the evening of Monday 28 February to interview Alma at more length.

The house was full of visitors again. The Reverend Nicolle had been there all afternoon with George and Alma, as had Dr Wills and his friend Mr Faraday. Don's former headmaster, Mr Tomkins, had called by, along with George's sister Adelaide, his sister-in-law Rose, and several children. A crowd had been hanging around outside over the weekend. 'People have been unkind,' said Alma. 'They do not try to be helpful at all. It is bad enough without people throwing stones at the windows.'

Fodor and Alma went upstairs to her bedroom, so that they could speak in private, and Fodor asked her about her past.

Alma was born on 17 August 1903 to Charles Smith, a plumber and gas fitter, and his wife Alice. Her sister Doris was born in 1900, and her brother Charles in 1915. At first the family lived near Alice's parents in Pimlico, on the north bank of the Thames. By the time war broke out they had moved south to Croydon, but

Alma and Dorrie were staying with their grandparents when Pimlico was heavily bombed by German aircraft in 1917. Alma suffered a series of childhood illnesses (measles, chicken pox, scarlatina, whooping cough, tonsillitis) and at the age of sixteen, while on holiday with her father, she careered into a wall on a hired bicycle. It took her months to recover from her injuries.

At about this time Alma met Les, who had settled in Croydon when he returned, wounded, from the Western Front. The illegitimate child of a housemaid, Les had been raised in Hertfordshire as the son of his grandparents, a coffin maker and his wife. In Thornton Heath, where he lived with an 'aunt' (actually his sister), he established himself as a builder and decorator. He took on anything from plumbing to paperhanging, and for a few years also received a disability pension from the army.

Les and Alma were married at the Croydon register office in March 1921 when he was twenty-one and she seventeen. Alma described it as a runaway marriage, contracted against her father's wishes, but it was also a shotgun wedding: she was three months pregnant with Don when she signed the register.

Since then, the family had lived in several rented properties in Thornton Heath, a working-class district built when the railway was laid to Victoria in the late nineteenth century. The suburb was served by a parade of shops, a library, a train station, and buses and trams that ran to the cinemas and department stores of central Croydon. A baker's van made daily deliveries to houses in the neighbourhood, as did a horse-drawn milk float and a coal cart.

Thanks to a house-building boom in southern England, Les's business continued to prosper even during the Depression – or Great Slump – of the early 1930s. When Don left school to work with his father in 1937, Alma tried to find employment herself. She briefly ran a snack bar in Thornton Heath, serving hot pies, Oxo beef stock, tea and coffee, but failed to cover her costs. She said that her café was frequented by too many tramps asking for free cups of hot water.

Alma was often in pain, she told Fodor. Ever since her bicycle crash in 1919, she had suffered from kidney abscesses, which had been drained seven times. In 1930, just before the Fieldings moved to Beverstone Road, an otherworldly experience alerted her to a different illness. She was playing cards with Les and some friends when she felt sleepy and lay down on a sofa. Les thought that she had fainted – her left arm was hanging limply to her side – and he and one of their friends tried to rouse her. As she lay there, half-conscious, she saw her father, who had died of tuberculosis four years earlier, tugging at one of her hands while Les pulled the other. 'My father leant across,' she recalled, 'and drew a cross with his fingers on my left breast.' When she came round she saw a mark on her breast in the shape of a cross, as if blood had been sucked through the skin. The next morning, she found a white scar where the cross had been, and beneath the scar a lump. She made an appointment with a specialist, who found a cancerous growth and removed the breast. Some time later another tumour was found, and treated with radium.

Fodor noticed that Alma's bodily failings seemed to trigger a special capacity, as if she were trading physical for psychic power. When she fell ill she entered a borderland, a zone in which she was susceptible to transcendent experience. It was unclear whether Alma's father – tussling with her husband over her body, inscribing her breast with blood – had been warning her of the cancer, or cursing her with it.

Then Alma recounted a weirder medical crisis: nine years ago, in 1929, she had suddenly lost her sight.

'I told nobody, because I could walk about, ride my bicycle and could carry on. I never had an accident.'

Fodor asked how she had managed to get about if she could not see.

'I cannot explain. It seemed to me as if a sense was given to me. I knew everything that was coming near me. I knew by the sound of the tram whether it was from London or from Thornton Heath, and I could get on the right one.'

Fodor wondered how she knew at which stop to alight.

'I had a picture in my mind,' she said, adding, 'I could play cards by the feel of the cards.'

For a while, Alma said, she managed to hide her blindness from Les, but at the cinema one day he noticed that she was not looking at the screen. 'He said nothing until we got home. He picked up a cup and saucer and handed them to me. I did not take them. Then he put his hand across my face. I did not flinch. He said, "You cannot see." I burst out crying. We went to a place in Croydon to have my eyes tested. The optician said there was no sight at all. It was a case for the hospital.'

The specialist eye hospital, Moorfields in east London, gave Les drops to put in her eyes. 'The following morning I went into the garden and ran into the lavatory edgeways. My sight came back like a shutter which opened.'

Fodor and Alma went downstairs to find that Les had come home from work. Les confirmed the details of Alma's cancer diagnosis, and asked Fodor whether the poltergeist disturbances might have been caused by the radium needles implanted in her chest. Similar upheavals, he said, had taken place in the home of a friend whose tumour had been treated in the same way.

Fodor asked Les about Alma's episode of blindness. 'Oh yes,' said Les. 'She was blind for about three weeks. It was either before she had the cut on her breast or after. She could ride her bicycle, do all her work and everything. I did not believe it.' It was a difficult idea to take in: Alma told her husband both that she was blind and that she could, while blind, somehow see.

Fodor had come across people who claimed sightless vision before. There were some who said that they could see while their eyes were covered, like his Chiswick neighbour Theodore Kolb, a plump Viennese cloth merchant who was paid £30 by the *Sunday Chronicle* to drive through the streets of London with his eyes blindfolded and filled with dough. When Kolb visited the Institute, Fodor and his colleagues realised that he was flexing his facial muscles to break the seal of the dough and peer through the chinks. Others claimed to be completely blind. In 1936 the Institute had hosted a talk by Captain Gerald Lowry, an osteopath who said that he could box, play golf and sail a yacht even though his optical nerve had been severed by a bullet in the war. Captain Lowry believed that he could see with his skin, and argued that a blind man in a kilt – that is, naked from the waist down – would detect a red pillar box much sooner than a blind man in underpants.

Fodor knew that both Captain Lowry and Alma might have been suffering from hysterical blindness, a 'conversion disorder' in which suppressed feelings bypassed conscious thought to express themselves directly through the body. Yet Alma was not obviously unstable. She seemed a capable and kind-hearted housewife and mother, on good terms with her friends and neighbours, tender towards her pets.

Fodor invited Alma to take part in further seances at the Institute. Before he left, the two of them carried out another experiment with a small object. She walked around the house holding his magnifying glass, and he followed close behind, his arms around her shoulders and a finger beneath her hands to stop the glass from sliding into the opening of her black chiffon dress. It was not until Alma sat down in an armchair that the magnifying glass vanished as they had hoped. Fodor searched her pockets and the seat, but found nothing there.

At Walton House on Thursday evening, Fodor hosted a seance with the transfiguration medium Elizabeth Bullock, a regular at the Institute. When Lizzie Bullock went into trance, her features would mutate into those of the spirits who possessed her. Her audiences used to recognise Arthur Conan Doyle (who had 'passed over' in 1930) by the giant walrus moustache that seemed to appear on her face. At other times she took on the features of 'the Chinaman', with wizened skin and a long, straggly moustache; a Zulu warrior with a ring in his nose; and a soldier with a bullet hole in his forehead. Lizzie Bullock confided to Fodor that during her transformation into the Chinaman she felt as if a hand were massaging her womb. Officially, Fodor allowed that her transfigurations might be evidence that the dead survived, but privately he noted, 'Sexual hysteria probably covers the case.'

Two hundred people had gathered to see Mrs Bullock on Thursday, among them a reporter from the *Daily Mail*. Fodor switched out the lights and trained a red-filtered lamp on Mrs Bullock as her features twisted. She relayed a series of spirit messages to her audience, finishing with an address by the Reverend Dick Sheppard, a famous pacifist who had died in November. The *Daily Mail* correspondent noticed that Mrs Bullock tucked her thumbs into her armpits, just as Sheppard used to tuck his thumbs into the armholes of his waistcoat, while his spirit assured the gathering that he was campaigning for peace from the other side. Like most ethereal visitors, he brought a message of comfort to the circle.

Many Britons had turned to spiritualism in the 1920s because of the losses of war, and many were turning to it now for fear of a conflict to come. Spiritualist seances offered a sense of wonder and intimacy rarely found in the Church of England, where attendances were falling so fast that the Archbishop of Canterbury had appointed a committee to investigate the allure of the rival faith. The national anxiety was also fuelling a boom in supernatural swindles, as *Reynolds News* pointed out in January: 'Never have fortune-tellers, horoscope-casters, crystal-gazers, teacup-twisters and fakers had so many mugs or made so much money.' The 'futurity racket', *Reynolds* observed, was typical of societies on the brink of chaos and destruction: the Italian magician Count Cagliostro flourished in Paris before the revolution of 1789, much as the faith healer Grigori Rasputin thrived in St Petersburg before 1917. Even the popular press was at it, the paper complained: since the publication of the first newspaper horoscope in 1930, astrology had become a national craze.

'Fear!' observes the narrator of Orwell's *Coming Up For Air*. 'We swim in it. It's our element. Everyone that isn't scared stiff of losing his job is scared stiff of war, or Fascism, or Communism, or something. Jews sweating when they think of Hitler.' London, he says, feels like 'one great big bull's-eye'.

The Thornton Heath haunting tapped into the fear of attack. 'We are puzzled by mysterious crashes,' Alma told the *Croydon Times*. 'We hear a tremendous crash that shakes the house, and when we rush upstairs we find everything in place.' Her home shuddered as if in anticipation of a bombing.

Fodor hoped that Alma would produce supernatural phenomena under tighter controls. Before Friday's sitting, he and Dr Wills checked for hidden objects by patting her body from top to toe, as did two female members of the Institute: Helen Russell Scott, a Scotswoman of fifty-eight, and Florence Hall, a younger, married woman who had agreed to take notes on the seances. During the war, both Dr Wills and Miss Scott had served on the Western Front, he as a physician (he was awarded the Military Cross) and she as a nurse.

Fodor asked Alma to put on the one-piece silver jumpsuit that Lajos Pap had worn on his visit to London three years earlier. She slipped the suit over her short-sleeved dress. The fabric ballooned around her, so her attendants bound it at the ankles and wrists with elastic bands and at the waist with a belt. They used a safety pin, wrapped with adhesive tape, to secure the zip at the back. Dr Wills took off Alma's shoes and shook them. Fodor photographed her from the front and from behind.

Fodor suggested to Alma that she try table-turning, a method of communicating with the dead established by the founders of spiritualism, Kate and Maggie Fox, when their home in upstate New York was invaded by a poltergeist in 1848. In the small seance room on the ground floor of Walton House, the lights were dimmed as Alma and the investigators placed their hands on an illuminated three-legged table, their fingertips touching. They hoped that the table would respond to their questions with coded raps, indicating 'yes' and 'no' answers or even letters of the alphabet.

The table rotated, tilted, lifted on one leg, clacked and snapped, but these were effects that were often achieved with unconscious movements of the knees, thumbs or toes. To Fodor's disappointment, it failed to provide coherent responses to the investigators' questions.

As Alma was leaving Walton House that afternoon, two halves of a 'trick penny' fell on the stairs behind her. She said that she recognised it as belonging to George, who confirmed when telephoned by Dr Wills that a trick penny had disappeared from his trouser pocket. In fact, said George, he had been showing his sister-in-law Rose and his fourteen-year-old niece Jean how the trick worked at about 3 p.m. This was after Dr Wills had met Alma's train at Victoria and driven her the last mile to Walton House.

The next day Dr Wills motored down to Thornton Heath to get signed statements from George, Rose and Jean about the bogus penny, which George said that he had bought from an acquaintance in a snack bar. A trick penny was a filed-down coin slotted into the recess of a matching, hollowed-out coin; the 'trick' was that an apparently normal penny had two heads or two tails. Having secured the signatures, Dr Wills went to the Welcome Café in the high street to ask Mabel to verify the story of the smashed cups. Mabel attested to the commotion in her café. It seemed unlikely that Alma had persuaded all these friends to lie for her, but the value of their testimony was limited. Besides, it was possible that she had dropped a double of the trick penny down the Institute's stairs, and that she had sent Mabel's cups flying with flicks of the wrist.

Alma told Fodor that she was meeting with resistance at home. She and Les had been sitting by the fire in the dining room, with Don, George and George's niece Jean, when Les told her that he wanted her to stop going to the Institute. Alma argued at first, but Les when opposed could be stubborn and unyielding.

'Very well,' she said. 'I won't go to Walton House any more.'

At this, she told Fodor, they heard a crash in the kitchen: a plate and a tumbler had been broken, crushed almost to powder.

Alma headed for her bedroom.

'I had just got into bed when the bed jolted three times at the foot and then went up in the air,' she said. 'When it dropped, it shook the house because it is a heavy oak bed. I thought there was someone under the bed and screamed and Les came running up. He said he would come to bed and had just got in when the bed lifted again, then a chair at my side turned a somersault three times across the room.' Fodor didn't know how to account for this story: as a hallucination, a lie, or evidence of supernormal energy.

George had hurried up on his crutch when he heard the noise, said Alma. He knocked on the door and asked if he could come in. As soon as he entered, everything was quiet.

'Oh, nothing happens while I'm about,' said George. 'I'll go outside the door and listen.'

Once he had closed the bedroom door behind him, she said, the chair tilted on two legs, moved towards the door and wedged itself under the panel. When George tried to get back in he had to push until the chair tipped over.

The room again fell quiet, and George went to his own bed. Alma's pillow sailed across the bedroom and her head banged down on the bolster. Les's shoes hurtled into the fireplace.

'You'd better give in,' said Les.

'All right,' said Alma. 'I'll go up next Wednesday.'

There was silence in the house.

Before Wednesday's seance Alma was asked to undress completely in the presence of Miss Scott and Mrs Hall. The women watched her take off her frock, petticoat, knickers, corset, shoes and stockings, and then put back on her own corset along with a set of clothes provided by the Institute.

The Countess joined them for the table-turning experiments. The table was more agitated today, but again produced no intelligible raps. Fodor then walked round the studio with Alma. In the gallery overlooking the room, he spotted a grey sock with a hole in the heel, partly mended with blue wool. Alma said that it might be a sock that she had started darning for George and had then thrown in the dustbin at home. But George, when telephoned by Dr Wills, could remember no such sock. The Institute's caretaker – Mr Creedy – later identified it as his polishing rag.

The same afternoon, Fodor threw objects into the air, hoping that they would vanish, and he fired a toy pistol behind Alma's back to see if the shock might trigger an apport. Neither strategy was effective.

Fodor received a discouraging response from his friend Wilfred Becker, to whom he had sent his notes on Alma. 'My general impression from the notes,' Becker wrote, 'is that a lunatic obsessed with the idea that she was possessed by a poltergeist, might have caused all the happenings.' The apports, he said, were 'due either to great artfulness or great supernormality! Unless something happens sometime which is *manifestly* beyond normal human power, the odds are on the former.' He declined Fodor's invitation to join the investigative team.

Fodor was affronted. 'Mrs Fielding is not a lunatic,' he told Becker. He knew that many of Alma's marvels looked like conjuring tricks, but for some of them he could find no natural explanation. He had seen objects fly in her house. He had seen the glove move in the car and the brush materialise in the seance room. And he believed in Alma's terror. He had felt her tremble and start.

Fodor worried that the poltergeist's powers were already spent, but he would not give up on Alma yet. He knew that even the great mediums were inconsistent and that psychic research was often slow, dull, contradictory and ambiguous. Amid the stretches of boredom and the welter of nonsense, the investigators had to hold out for the transcendent nugget, the surplus that could not be explained. He decided to take Alma to the seaside. He hoped that in a new setting the poltergeist would come back to life.

SEVEN

If there are devils

On Friday 11 March, Dr Wills and his wife Hilda drove Fodor and Alma to Bognor Regis, a resort fifty-five miles south-west of Thornton Heath, where they planned to meet Laurie Evans and his girlfriend in the afternoon. Fodor sat in the back seat with Alma, clasping both her hands between his, and asked her more about her life. He was hoping not only to substantiate her phenomena but to unravel their psychological origins. If she could move objects with her mind, he needed to locate the fierce feeling that empowered her.

The poltergeist had started to pilfer on her behalf, Alma told him. She had taken the tram into Croydon with Rose the previous day, a penny ride on a lumbering double-decker that clanked and shrieked its way down the London Road. The two women called at British Home Stores, where Alma tried on a ring and then returned it to the assistant, saying it was too 'common'. When she glanced at her hand in the fishmonger's shop, she saw that the ring had magically appeared on one of her fingers. Rose cheekily suggested that Alma get her a string of pearls. 'I said I would not,' said Alma, 'but we went to Woolworth's and I looked at one. I was careful not to touch it.' She feared that the poltergeist was waiting on her whims, like a genie: she hardly dared wish. 'We came out,' she continued, 'and as I put my foot on the tram the pearl necklace was fastened around my neck. I did not know how to undo the clasp and told Rose, "Take the damn thing, I don't want it."'

Whether the theft was supernormal or not, Fodor was curious about what it indicated. Alma had no obvious need to steal. Les earned at least £200 a year, £50 more than the average British family, and the house at Beverstone Road was chock-a-block with inessential items: Don's collections of model trains and aeroplanes and postage stamps, Les's hoard of old coins, all the ornaments on the sideboards and tables, chests and mantels. Alma could afford jewellery, make-up, perfume, visits to the hairdresser and the theatre. Compared to most women of her class, she was well-off. But Fodor knew that the poltergeist's stealing could represent something other than financial need: the Freudian analyst Wilhelm Stekel argued that compulsive theft, being the secret taking of forbidden objects, was an expression of suppressed sexual desire.

Alma mentioned that her dentures had vanished from the glass by her bed overnight, and then appeared suddenly in her mouth. Fodor asked when she had lost her natural teeth. She told him that at twenty-three she had contracted anthrax poisoning from a Woolworth's toothbrush that scratched her gum – anthrax was, very rarely, transmitted through animal bristles. Alma said that her gums turned black and she became delirious, slipping in and out of consciousness. She woke up one day when Les was in the kitchen making a cup of tea. 'I went downstairs and picked up a big carving knife. He had his back to me. I was just going to stab him when he whipped around and caught my hand. Then I started screaming, "Murder! Fire!" and ran into the street in my nightdress. They got me back to bed and sent for the doctor.' As part of her treatment, a dentist removed all of her teeth. Fodor was struck by Alma's account of her attack on Les. It sounded like a psychotic episode, and a foreshadowing of the poltergeist violence. Perhaps the removal of Les's teeth in February had revived this memory.

Alma also told Fodor a peculiar, apparently unrelated story about something that happened when she was sixteen. She was living in Maplethorpe Road, Thornton Heath, with her father Charles, her mother Alice, her sister Dorrie, then nineteen, and her four-year-old brother Charlie. While lying in bed one afternoon with a headache, she saw a long-faced man step out from her bedroom cupboard. She had seen him before, she said. Usually he came at night, and vanished as soon as he emerged from the wardrobe's double doors. But this time he walked right over to her. She didn't recall what happened next: she fell asleep, or passed out. When she came to, she found a piece of paper beside the bed, marked with some sort of writing in smudged soot or charcoal. She showed her mother the obscure message, and her mother threw it on the fire.

Fodor noticed that both these stories hinged on a break in consciousness. In each case Alma had become unmoored, detached from herself. He wondered if at times like this her buried life surged to the surface and broke out. 'There is a door which leads from the mind we know to the mind we do not know,' he told the *Daily Mirror* in March. 'Now and again that door is opened. Strange things happen. There are manifestations, queer phenomena, transfigurations. Who or what opens that door? The mind itself? Or some outside agency?' As the door to the unconscious swung open, a suppressed feeling might escape its human host in the form of a cold wind or a warm clothes brush, a spinning teacup or a figure from the past.

Fodor did not know how this transmission worked: in his *Encyclopaedia* he speculated that mediums might discharge electromagnetic rays from their fingers and toes, or extrude invisible, semi-metallic psychic rods, or ectoplasmic threads like cobwebs. He had tested the theory of mental radiation by asking the young medium Ronnie Cockersell to carry photographic plates in his pockets, in case he could project his thoughts, as black shapes, onto the silvered sheets of glass. The Hampstead medium Madge Donohoe claimed to have produced hundreds of 'skotographs' in this manner. Though Fodor's experiment with Ronnie was unsuccessful, it was not ridiculous: the Austrian physicist Victor Franz Hess, who won a Nobel Prize in 1936, had discovered cosmic radiation by laying photographic plates on mountaintops and sending others three miles into the sky in the basket of a hot-air balloon.

Fodor told Alma that her poltergeist seemed angry: a psychoanalyst might describe the shattering of glasses and other objects in her house as a protest from her unconscious self against 'things whole'. She ignored the suggestion, replying only that Les was dull, but she liked fun, adventure, risks and danger. Alma no longer seemed the fragile, frightened woman who had called the reporters to Beverstone Road. She was in a holiday mood.

At midday they stopped for coffee at the village of Billingshurst, halfway between London and the sea. Fodor picked two books off the shelf in the coffee shop and gave them to Alma to hold, in case 'Jimmy', as he christened the poltergeist, could summon them later as apports. The books were Professor Hoffman's *Modern Magic*, a nineteenth-century compendium of conjuring tricks, and a recent publication about how to predict one's fate. He seemed to be teasing her with the titles – one a manual for stage magicians, the other a guide to fortune telling.

Alma, in turn, was tickled by Fodor's naming of the poltergeist. It so happened, she told him, that her maternal grandfather was known as Jimmy. A wheelwright-turned-house-painter, James Bannister had died in 1927. He had been something of a poltergeist himself, Alma said: he used to plague his family with practical jokes. He was forever putting tacks on chairs, pulling the linen and blankets off freshly made beds, shaming his relatives in front of strangers. As if to make a connection with Fodor, she remarked that Jimmy Bannister had been partly Jewish.

They continued towards the coast. At one point on the journey Fodor let go of Alma and a few minutes later noticed a new ring on her right hand. She expressed surprise: her wedding and diamond rings had been joined by a band inset with a large, artificial blue stone. Fodor was uneasy. He thought that he had noticed her right hand slip out of view just before the ring's arrival.

At 1.45 p.m. the group reached Bognor Regis. As well as the usual seaside fixtures – an arcade, a pier, a beach, an esplanade – the town boasted an amusement park and zoo and a branch of the British Union of Fascists, which ran an annual summer camp nearby. The fascist party had been weakened by the passing of a Public Order Act in 1936, which banned political uniforms and unauthorised marches, but had started to gain ground again in the south of England. Three weeks earlier its leader, Oswald Mosley, had urged an audience in the Bognor Theatre Royal to show friendship to Italy and Germany.

Over lunch in a small Bognor restaurant, Dr Wills remarked that it would be nice if Alma's diamanté clip, which she had left at home, were to appear on her frock. While Alma was leaning forward, her elbows on the table and her hands clasped in front of her, Mrs Wills cried out and pointed at her dress. The clip had come. 'I was looking at Mrs Fielding's rings,' she explained afterwards, 'then at her hair, which she herself had permed. Suddenly there was a bright flash. It must have been the moment of the clip's arrival.'

After lunch they met Laurie and his girlfriend on the Bognor seafront, as arranged, and Fodor took a few snaps of the company with his Leica. There was Alma, slight, smiling, hunched against the breeze in her ruffled cretonne frock, fur-collared coat and brown hat; Gerald Wills, skinny and self-assured, leaning proprietorially towards Alma to his left, with the stockier Hilda Wills in a pale matching jacket, skirt and hat to his right. Gerald and Hilda Wills had married in the 1920s, after the death of his first wife. Towering above them was Laurie, fair and moustachioed in a double-breasted checked suit, bow tie and felt fedora, and his statuesque, dark-haired companion, the film actress Barbara Waring, in a fitted suit and round sunglasses.

Dr and Mrs Wills, Fodor and Alma made a side trip to Pagham, a suburb of Bognor in which Alma wanted to visit some bungalows available for summer rental. In one of the bungalows, Dr Wills laughingly picked up a tumbler and placed it in front of Alma to see if 'Jimmy' would smash it. As they were walking along a road next to the shingle beach a few minutes later, a tumbler crashed to the ground behind them. Fodor collected the fragments as evidence.

Back in Bognor they joined Laurie and Barbara, and hatched a plan over tea: they would visit Woolworth's and see if Alma could psychically transport a piece of jewellery out of the shop, as she had done in Croydon. Alma said it would be fun if something turned up in

Fodor's Kodak film canister, so he lent it to her. As they were walking to the local Woolworth's, which was some distance away, they passed a branch of the Marks & Spencer department store and Alma suggested that they go there instead. It turned out to have no jewellery counter, so they reverted to the original plan and made for the Bognor 'Woolie's', on the London Road.

The Woolworth's shopfront was bright and inviting, with a bold red sign and a busy window display. Inside, maroon-clad shop girls stood at the counters. Fodor and his party stopped at the jewellery stand and watched as Alma selected a ring with two stones on a curved bridge, examined it, then returned it to the assistant; it was the nicest ring there, Alma said, but she did not want to buy it today. The shop girl eyed them suspiciously as they moved away. 'It looked fishy to her,' wrote Fodor. 'She followed us. We began to feel uncomfortable. We were afraid we would get in trouble if the ring which Mrs Fielding had handled suddenly appeared on her finger.' Barbara stopped to buy something at another counter. The others left the store, and saw a policeman across the street. 'I thought we had better hurry,' said Fodor. As the group turned into a road a few hundred yards from Woolworth's, Alma said that she heard a rattle in the film container. Fodor took the box from her, opened it, and found inside the ring that she had handled. 'My flesh creeped,' he said.

Everyone was staggered by the arrival of the ring. All swore that they had seen it still on the jewellery counter as they left.

'The experience was rather alarming,' said Fodor. 'We had committed psychic shoplifting! We were in possession of stolen property.'

He checked Alma's dress and the lining of her coat for secret pockets but found none.

Back in London, Fodor gathered signed statements from Laurie, Barbara and Dr and Mrs Wills about the Woolworth's incident, and put the 'Bognor apports' on display: the base of the broken glass, the rings, the diamanté clip, a tiny black elephant that Alma had magically acquired in a knick-knack shop. In the photograph that Fodor took of the Bognor booty, the objects were bathed in a dusty glow. The stolen ring glinted, naughtily.

The poltergeist had started as a hooligan, chucking objects around the Fieldings' house. It had then played conjuror, magicking things into pockets, plucking them from the air. In this latest phase, it was a sneak-thief, and Fodor and his fellow investigators were bound to Alma now by a crime. They had willed Jimmy on, plotting the psychic robbery, hoping for its success. No one suggested returning the ring to Woolworth's.

Fodor was still troubled by the surreptitious movement that he had noticed in the car in the morning. But if Alma had tricked that first ring onto her finger, she might have done so only because she felt under pressure to provide an apport and feared that her poltergeist would fail her. In the event, the Bognor trip had resulted in her most impressive phenomena yet.

Fodor accepted that Alma might be both truthful and dishonest, gifted and fraudulent. He rarely dealt with snow-white, morally upright individuals, but rather with people who were damaged and divided. It was well known that when mediums found their powers fading, they would compensate, invent, create illusions to please their admirers or protect themselves. Psychics were natural transgressors, crossing all kinds of boundaries, from waking to trance, from the earthly to the spirit world. Their weaknesses – moral, physical, emotional – were the fissures through which the phantoms came. 'If there are devils,' said the American philosopher and psychical researcher William James in a lecture of 1896, 'if there are supernormal powers, it is through the cracked and fragmented self that they enter.' In psychic science, one fraudulent act did not invalidate all of a medium's claims. The transcendent and the tawdry were often united in one psyche.

Fodor had become familiar with the consumerist, aspirational working-class culture of post-war Britain. A few of the hauntings that he investigated took place in crumbling old manor houses with creaking stairs and hidden priest holes, but most were in ordinary towns and suburbs like Bognor and Croydon. 'This is the England of arterial and by-pass roads,' wrote J. B. Priestley in *English Journey* in 1933, 'of filling stations and factories that look like exhibition buildings, of giant cinemas and dance-halls and cafés, bungalows with tiny garages, cocktail bars, Woolworths, motor-coaches, wireless, hiking, factory girls looking like actresses, greyhound racing and dirt tracks, swimming pools, and everything given away for cigarette coupons.'

'You need money in this England,' Priestley added, 'but you do not need much money. It is a large-scale, mass-production job with cut prices.' He proposed that J. W. Woolworth, an American chain, was the best symbol of the nation. Thirty years after opening its first British store, the company was the biggest retailer in the country, and it still managed to price everything at sixpence or less. 'The very modern things,' observed Priestley, 'like the films and the wireless and the six-penny stores, are absolutely democratic, making no distinction between their patrons.' But England had become 'a bit too cheap', he warned. 'That is, it is also cheap in the other sense of the term. Too much of it is simply a trumpery imitation of something not very good even in the original.' In the Woolworth's world, goods were closely mimicked, profusely reproduced, easily acquired. The chain could sell gramophone records at half the price of its rivals because it made cover versions: Flanagan and Allen's 'Underneath the Arches' was performed for Woolie's Eclipse label by Cavan O'Connor and Bobby Sanders, who used the pseudonyms Hardy & Hudson because they were under contract to other companies. The recording was an impersonation wrapped up in a disguise: doubly inauthentic.

In Britain, even supernormal phenomena were social markers. Fodor's fellow ghost hunter Maude ffoulkes declared in *True Ghost Stories* (1936) that she longed for spooks in the same way that she yearned for the 'unspoilt country of yesteryear', a land untainted by roadhouse pubs and electricity pylons. Traditional ghosts were relics of a romantic, aristocratic past. Poltergeists, by contrast, were a Woolie's brand of phantom, vulgar copies of the ethereal apparitions of old. The *Daily Mail* described them as 'altogether different from the honest, upright ghosts of decaying castles and ancient halls'. They were characterised by 'low cunning and nasty intention' and 'mean, underhand ways'. The *Hull Daily Mail* lamented that the 'old-fashioned family ghost' was giving way to spirits 'right at the other end of the social scale'. Poltergeists were domestic hoodlums: destructive, subversive, uncouth. 'Not that being a ghost can be much fun,' admitted the paper, 'in this age of service flats and arterial roads and psycho-analysts.'

But Fodor was not bound by the snobbery or nostalgia of his adopted country. He enjoyed the comfort and convenience of his modern apartment; he was fascinated by the wilder ideas of psychoanalysis; and far from sneering at poltergeists, he liked them. Where others might see Alma as typical of her class and gender – irrational, opportunistic, sly – to Fodor she was ingenious, complex and fun. He understood why an imaginative working-class woman might be drawn to the supernatural, whether by opening herself to spirit possession, to supernormal hoaxing or to kinetic projections of her stifled yearnings. She might find release in her poltergeist just as James Irving might have found release in Gef the talking mongoose.

Alma's days were a repetitive round of domestic chores, relieved only by forays to the shops and cups of tea with friends. She had to dust and polish the many objects in her house, to darn, sew and knit, launder and iron, cook meals for her family, sweep hearths and floors, fetch coal and lay fires, scrub dishes, pots and pans. British women had enjoyed a spell of freedom during and immediately after the war, when many of them went out to work, but the popular press now encouraged them to keep to the home. They were urged to tend to their appearance ('What men hate about your hair' the *Mirror* revealed in March) and their family's health. The *Daily Mail* warned female readers against having too lively a relationship even with their belongings. 'Don't wear a necklace if you're tempted to twiddle it,' advised the paper. 'Keep your hankie in your bag; it's not meant to be twisted.' The ideal woman was contained, composed, restrained.

But for a woman with psychic powers, different rules applied. A medium could undertake extravagant feats of mobility – astral projection, transfiguration, time travel, levitation – and in doing so escape the constraints of her gender and her class. Alma's poltergeist not only twiddled necklaces but sprang them from shop counters; it whipped saucers across rooms, upended eiderdowns, spun rings onto fingers. It took gifts to the researchers at the Institute, as if to charm or trade its way into their world. And when Les tried to stop Alma from going to Walton House, her poltergeist leapt back into action, enabling her to defy her husband, to follow her own path, to break free of her home.

EIGHT

The face in the mirror

Hitler violated the terms of the Versailles peace accord on Friday 11 March by marching his troops into Austria. 'The continent thunders with the tramp of armed men,' reported the *Pictorial*, acknowledging that its readers must be worried to death about what lay ahead. There were already wars between the republicans and the fascists in Spain, noted the paper, and between the 'Little Yellow Men' (Japanese and Chinese) in the Far East. The prime minister called an emergency Cabinet meeting to discuss the international crisis.

Many in Britain, especially on the Left, believed that Hitler and Mussolini must be stopped by force. Others, like Chamberlain, hoped to avert or delay a conflict by acceding to some of their demands. Others still, including Mosley and his confederates, held that Communist Russia and 'international Jewry' posed more of a threat than the fascist dictators. As audiences poured out of the West End theatres on Saturday 19 March, 600 young men clambered onto the running boards of taxis and motor-cars in Piccadilly Circus, shouting, 'Down with the Jewish warmongers!', 'British cars for British people!' and 'Britain for the Britons!' Beneath the giant shining signs for Guinness and Gordon's, Bovril and Schweppes, the rioters singled out foreign vehicles for attack. The police tried to restore order, throwing a protective cordon around the delicate figure of Eros at the heart of the roundabout.

The mediums in Britain's seance rooms, meanwhile, were channelling the elders of other races: Abyssinian tribesmen, Egyptian pharaohs, Persian warriors, Chinese sages and, especially, Indian chiefs. In Queen's Hall, off Oxford Street, more than 2,000 people gathered in March to hear the prophecies of White Hawk, the spirit guide of the well-known medium Stella Hughes. 'There will be no war,' the chieftain assured his anxious audience.

About a dozen members of the Institute attended Alma's next two seances at Walton House. She was strip-searched before each session, and monitored throughout. Female supervisors accompanied her to the ladies' room in the tea break, keeping an eye on her even when she was in the lavatory cubicle. In the seance room she produced a silver charm in the shape of a hawk, a silver disc inscribed with the signs of the zodiac, a sweet-scented nut, a polished stone, a locket, a penny. When the apports were slow to arrive, Fodor would chivvy the poltergeist in cheerful impatience – 'Come on, Jimmy!' Some of the sitters shook as Alma materialised her treasures. Helen Russell Scott's head spun. The Countess's face tickled. Fodor's friend

Wilfred Becker, who had been reluctant to join the investigation, smelt something rotten, sweet, funereal in the room. The Irish writer Shaw Desmond reacted the most strongly of all: he felt sick, his heart raced, his face poured with sweat. Shaw Desmond was a well-known journalist, the author of a weekly column for the *Sunday Graphic* and of spiritualist tracts such as *We Do Not Die* (later to be outdone by *Nobody Has Ever Died!*). Like many members of the Institute, he had suffered a great loss – his ten-year-old son had died in the 1920s.

Fodor was struggling to make sense of Alma's phenomena. At a tea party at the Countess's house in west Kensington, he asked the advice of Elizabeth Severn, an American psychoanalyst who had been a member of the Institute since 1934. Alma was horrified to overhear part of this conversation, and informed Fodor afterwards that she and Les had taken a violent dislike to 'that woman' and did not want her to play any part in the inquiry. Fodor assured her that he would not invite Mrs Severn to the sittings. Freudian ideas were in any case not popular with his colleagues. Shaw Desmond described psychoanalysis as 'a sex-ridden science', 'a gross instrument for gross minds'.

Privately, Fodor continued to discuss Alma's case with Elizabeth Severn, whom he greatly admired. In the 1920s Mrs Severn had been treated in Budapest by the pioneering psychoanalyst Sándor Ferenczi, and she was one of the few members of the Institute open to the idea that supernatural phenomena were products of mental disturbance. She believed that people emanated 'etheric waves', like radium, with which they could unconsciously disrupt the world around them, and she agreed with Fodor that Alma's poltergeist might be a projection of her submerged emotions. 'We are all constant receiving-and-sending stations,' said Elizabeth Severn, 'and under the influence of intense feelings the dynamism is greatly increased; so that if the emanations are accelerated and of a violent nature, they may do much harm.'

Fodor learnt in March of a poltergeist attack in east London with resemblances to the Thornton Heath case. Mr Gilmore, a twenty-five-year-old tobacconist, reported that he and his lodgers – Mr and Mrs Bradley, who had been married for twenty-seven years – had been troubled for a fortnight in February by flying crockery, wandering bedclothes, lights turning on and off, stopped clocks. Mr Gilmore said that he did not believe in spirits, but when Mr and Mrs Bradley moved in he had started to faint and to fall into trances. The poltergeist attacks took place, he said, only when he and Mrs Bradley were alone together. At the end of February, Mrs Bradley fled the house and Mr Bradley took to barricading himself in the dining room in case his landlord, under the influence of the poltergeist, tried to attack him. Finally he too moved out.

Having spoken to both men, Fodor concluded that Mr Gilmore's manifestations sprang from his obsession with Mrs Bradley. Under pressure of his inner torment, the young man fell into amnesic, dissociated states, in which one part of him acted without the knowledge of the other. The protagonist of Patrick Hamilton's novel *Hangover Square* switches between personalities in a similar way: he is helplessly besotted with a woman who spurns him, and at a '*click!*' in his head ('or would the word "*snap*" or "*crack*" describe it better?' he wonders), his yearning, humiliated self is replaced with a numb, implacable avenger. In a poltergeist case, thought Fodor, a suppressed personality might act independently even of the body.

Fodor knew that Alma had a history of episodes in which she was half-there, present and absent, inside and outside herself, like the time that she collapsed on the couch and saw her father's hand mark her breast, or the time that she attacked Les with a knife. Her blanks and lapses seemed intrinsic to her strange experiences, and keys to their cause. Perhaps Alma, like Mr Gilmore, had a psyche that had split under pressure of a forbidden desire. Fodor wondered if her estranged alter ego was now escaping her body altogether, snapping and cracking itself into being. Ping!

To discourage more attention from her neighbours, Alma told the *Croydon Advertiser* that all was quiet in her house. But to Fodor she confided that it seemed still to be haunted. Les and George confirmed that there had been further incidents.

One night in March, Les heard shouting from George's bedroom. 'Don't touch me!' yelled George. 'Don't come near me! Get away!'

In the morning Les asked: 'What was wrong with you last night?'

George said that he had woken to his own shouts, and as he sat up in bed had seen Alma enter the room and switch on the light. 'She asked what was wrong with me, grinning in a horrible way. She was wearing a red dressing gown.' He yelled at her to leave him alone.

Les told George that he must have dreamt it, as he had seen Alma asleep beside him when he heard his cries. But George insisted that it wasn't a dream: he had found the light still on when he woke in the morning.

Alma said that she had no memory of going to George's room. Anyway, she had given her red dressing gown to her mother.

The next Saturday, Alma told Fodor, a shower of violets fell on her as she leant over her bed to wake Les from a nap. They were 'big as pansies', said Alma, 'fresh and wet'. She had carried a bouquet of violets on her wedding day, exactly seventeen years earlier. Later on Saturday afternoon, she noticed a nasty smell in the house, like decomposing meat or fish. Les smelt it too. The clean, sweet scent of the violets had given way to a rotten stench. Alma and Les searched but could find no source.

Don, who had moved back in to the family home, told his parents on Sunday morning that the light in his room had been switching itself on and off all night. Though frightened, he had not called out but instead buried his head under the bedclothes to escape the flaring of the electric bulb.

The haunting at Beverstone Road had started with a bulb removing itself from the lamp in Les and Alma's bedroom. Now the light in George's room had switched on in the middle of the night, and Don's light had flashed on and off, as if in warning. On Sunday, George said, he saw the sideboard in the dining room tip forward. When he reached out to stop it crashing down on the table, the dresser pulled back into place against the wall.

Fodor wondered whether the poltergeist was drawing on Alma's feelings for her lodger, much as Mr Gilmore's poltergeist had drawn on his illicit longing for Mrs Bradley, or as the ghost at Ash Manor had drawn on Maurice Kelly's secret attraction to men. At Beverstone Road, the poltergeist's antics often brought George to Alma's bedroom door, even across the threshold. In George's dream or vision, Alma had approached him like a predator.

Alma seemed to be haunting herself, too. While lying in bed one evening, she told Fodor, she looked over at the fireplace and saw her face in the mirror above the mantel. It was impossible, she knew, that she should see her own reflection from this angle.

'What are you staring at?' said Les.

The face vanished.

Fodor and the Countess discussed how to proceed. The Countess was worried about the effect that the investigation was having on Alma, and Fodor agreed that they should be careful not to exhaust or alarm her. They decided to suspend the physical searches and instead set up a 'development circle', a series of relaxed, undemanding seances at which a spirit – or, as Fodor believed, an unconscious, poltergeist self – might speak through her. The Countess suggested that Fodor sit out the seances for now, since his pragmatic manner might be alienating the spirits. He accepted the suggestion. He needed to retain the support of the Countess and the rest of the council, and a circle led by spiritualists might in any case get better results. He could continue to experiment with Alma outside the seance room.

Fodor drew up a contract to guarantee that Alma would attend the Institute exclusively for the next two months. 'The Institute will call upon her services twice a week,' read the document, 'for periods not exceeding 3 hours and will pay a retaining fee of £2 per week.' He told Alma about the plan to hold smaller, private sessions, led by the Countess, to stabilise and develop her phenomena, and he informed the readers of his column in the *Journal of the American Society for Psychical Research* that he was taking steps 'to prevent too much drain on Mrs Fielding's delicate organism'.

Countess Wydenbruck felt attuned to Alma, and hoped that she could help her. She too had undergone dislocating episodes, snaps in consciousness that were like a stepping between worlds.

Nora Wydenbruck was born in London in 1894, the daughter of an Austrian diplomat who had been posted to the city.

'What a big nose she has,' said her father.

'She has indeed,' said her mother, Marie Fugger von Babenhausen. 'She's as ugly as a monkey.'

Her parents had hoped for a boy. They already had a daughter, a pretty one.

Nora grew up in a baroque schloss in an Austrian valley, her mother's ancestral estate. The house was pale pink and gold. Vines and roses climbed its frescoed walls, and firs darkened the encircling mountains. As Nora lay in bed in this fairy-tale castle, she had nightmares: her papa, or his friend the English aristocrat Baron Rothschild, would transform into a huge orangutan and bear down on her with a smile, opening a yellow-toothed maw to devour her. In other dreams Nora's bedroom door would swing open and fill with a dense black shadow that pressed towards her, a vast darkness with a gaping mouth of fire.

Walter von Rothschild liked to take photographs of Nora, for which he insisted, to her distress, that she remove her shoes and socks.

Nora's older sister and her mother were inseparable. They would dress up together for the high-society parties and soirées that they attended in Vienna each winter. But Nora was a gawky child. Her mother persuaded her that she was too plain to be coquettish, so she adopted a grave demeanour.

Nora's parents became estranged, and her father spent most of his time abroad. He was moody and bitter, and drank a lot. When Nora was ten she went on holiday with him to the Alps. As they took the narrow road up the mountains, Nora felt suddenly terrified, as if she were losing her identity and turning into an unreal being in a raw and menacing universe. The moment passed.

When Nora was thirteen her father visited the hotel in Vienna where she was spending the winter with her mother, her sister, and an English governess who had become her closest friend. He said that he was going to dismiss the governess and send Nora to boarding school. They were standing at the top of the hotel staircase. Nora thought: 'I must do everything in my power to prevent this.' She screamed as loud as she could. She made to throw herself over the banisters. Her father grabbed her, tried to gag her and stifle her cries. They struggled. Nora sobbed and foamed at the mouth. The outburst, which had begun as a performance of suffering, now engulfed her. Her mind seemed to have split. One part of herself was watching from a great distance. The other was convulsing like a mad creature.

Nora's father sent her to a sanatorium. The governess went with her but after three weeks was taken aside and told to leave. She ran screaming back to Nora and threw her arms around her, refusing to let go. The director of the sanatorium dragged the Englishwoman away by force.

In the absence of her beloved governess, Nora refused to eat; she refused to speak; she tried to strangle herself with her long, heavy pigtail. She was a lanky girl: only fourteen years old and five feet eight inches tall. Food was pushed into her through a tube in her nose. Eventually she was treated by a psychotherapist who was versed in Freudian theory. Nora mentioned to him that she could not remember the face of the man who had torn the governess from her. 'That shows how right Freud is,' the therapist remarked. 'Unpleasant memories are pushed away and vanish!' He persuaded Nora to eat, encouraged her to write and to draw.

Nora was discharged from the sanatorium and sent to boarding school. Her mother warned her never to speak about her spell of madness.

In 1919, against her mother's wishes, Nora married a handsome artist called Alfons Purtscher, who specialised in making portraits of animals. She came close to another breakdown a year later when she gave birth to their first child. Bearing a baby, she said, was an experience 'so extraordinary and terrifying that it is one of the great marvels of nature that millions of women survive it year by year without suffering a fatal dissociation of personality'. She and Alfons called their daughter Nina, after a dog of which they had been fond. Nora hoped that nursing the baby would be a mystical joy. Instead it made her feel like a cow. They had a son, Christopher, two years later.

Seances were all the rage in Austria, as in England, and Nora and Alfons started to dabble in the super-normal. 'We were like children at a party when a magician is performing,' recalled Nora, 'expecting magic and hardly surprised when the most incredible things took place before our very eyes – as when, by the light of the street-lamp outside the uncurtained window, which was intensified by the snow, we saw a pair of snow-boots that had been left in the hall climb up, one after the other, on to the table.'

In the economic crisis of the early 1920s, Nora parted with her pearls and her diamonds for next to nothing. She sold her father's fine silver dishes by weight, for melting. Few people in Austria had horses any more, let alone the funds to commission Alfons to paint their animals. In 1926 he went to England to find work. Nora missed him desperately, and as soon as she could she followed him there. The children were dispatched, separately, to relatives. Nora's mother berated her for abandoning Nina and Christopher. 'If one brings children into the world,' she said, 'it is one's duty to look after them.' Nora could not see that she had any choice.

In a down-at-heel hotel in Bayswater, west London, Alfons and Nora scratched a living by decorating silk lampshades (each took three days, and was sold for a guinea) until he received a few orders for paintings of dogs and cats. They graduated to a furnished room where, since neither of them knew how to cook, they lived on bread and cheese. Nora took a job as a waitress at a Lyons tea shop and pawned all her remaining jewellery, including her wedding ring. Gradually they made money – she as a writer, he as a painter – and moved to Holland Park, west Kensington. Alfons decorated the drawing room in bruised greens, browns and greys, the colours of an Austrian forest at twilight.

In the seances and experiments at Walton House, as in her writing, the Countess found expression for the rebellious, passionate self that had briefly broken out when she was a girl. At the Institute she hoped to experience moments as intense and transcendent as those that she once shared with her English governess.

NINE

Knocks in the cupboard

Alma arrived at Walton House half an hour late on Friday 25 March, the day assigned for the first sitting with the Countess's circle, claiming that she had no recollection of anything that happened between 1.35 p.m. and 2.15 p.m. She had recovered consciousness in a railway carriage on the train to Victoria, she said, to hear a woman exclaim, 'Fancy, bringing white mice into a train!' She felt something on her arm and glanced down to see a white mouse creeping towards her hand. She snatched it up and put it in her bag.

In Fodor's office at 3.30 p.m., Alma lifted the mouse out of her handbag. The creature scampered about in excitement. Helen Russell Scott fetched it some morsels of biscuit and Fodor found a cardboard box in which to house it. He punched a few holes in the lid. Very rarely, mediums did materialise living creatures – the Australian psychic Charles Bailey was said to have produced an eighteen-inch shark – but Fodor thought it more likely that Alma had purchased the mouse during the lost forty minutes, whether on purpose or in a state of trance. In an 'ambulatory amnesia', as in a spell of sickness, a person could undergo time warps, in which seconds seemed to last for hours and minutes to go in a flash.

Alma showed Fodor and the Countess a cross scratched on her forehead. George had noticed it the previous morning, she said, when he came into the dining room as she was sweeping the hearth. 'What's that on your forehead?' he asked. She went to the mirror, pushed back her hair and saw the mark. She recalled having a vision of her father in the dining-room armchair. His ghost must have scratched her head, she supposed, just as it had once scratched her breast.

Fodor took a picture of Alma with her hair pinned back so that the scratches were visible. She lowered her eyelids as he clicked the shutter.

Alma headed downstairs with the Countess, leaving Fodor in his office, and took her place in an armchair at a small, four-legged table with the other sitters in the development circle: the Countess, her husband Alfons, Dr Wills and Helen Russell Scott. Florence Hall sat to the side in an armchair, making notes for Fodor.

Alma's poltergeist guide 'Jimmy', as Fodor had named him, began to communicate with the sitters by tilts of the table. The Countess slowly recited the alphabet and the guide rapped for her to stop at individual letters. By this method, he informed them that Alma's father had scratched the cross on her forehead so that she would know that he was near. Dr Wills and the Countess put in requests for supernormal phenomena. 'I have a black elephant on my mantelpiece,' said the doctor. 'Will you try to take it away?' Jimmy rapped once, for 'yes'. 'I want a bullfinch,' said the Countess. 'Will you try to bring one?' The poltergeist rapped on the table again.

Fodor was sitting out the sessions, as agreed, and following the proceedings in Mrs Hall's notes, but Alma seemed keen to keep him involved. First she had turned up with the mouse and the scratch, and then, on Wednesday 30 March, she telephoned him at the Institute to report her most startling feat yet.

Just before eight o'clock on Tuesday evening, Alma said, she had been to the Picture Palace in Thornton Heath to watch a Hollywood movie about an aviator, starring Joan Fontaine and John Beal. She referred to the film as *The Man Who Lost Himself*, though it was in fact *The Man Who Found Himself* – a meaningful slip, Fodor thought, in the light of what happened that night.

In the cinema Alma was wearing her fur-trimmed coat and a hat with orange ribbons. An old lady was sitting to one side of her, and the seat to the other side was empty. At about 9.15 p.m., she said, she lost consciousness and found herself standing in Walton Street near the blue lamp of the police station opposite Walton House. All nine members of the council were due to attend the Institute's fourth Annual General Meeting that night, among them the Countess, Miss Scott, Mrs Dundas, Dr Wills, Shaw Desmond and Mr and Mrs Becker. Fodor planned to address the council about the previous year's work. Alma, being a research subject, had not been invited to the meeting.

Alma saw a chauffeur in a dark blue uniform and cap outside Walton House, looking at her. She saw two saloon cars near him in the mews, one of them a blue sedan. She was surprised, she said, that there was no sign of Dr Wills's car. She wanted to cross the road to the Institute, so that she could knock on the door and check that she was really there, but something stopped her. She was wondering how she would get to Victoria station when she suddenly found herself back in her seat in the cinema in Croydon.

Fodor checked out Alma's story. She had been right to say that Dr Wills's car had not been in the mews: it had developed engine trouble at Putney Bridge, and the doctor had missed the meeting. By making enquiries of the other Institute members, Fodor learnt that a chauffeur had been waiting outside Walton House on Tuesday night. He invited him to the Institute.

At Walton House on Friday, the chauffeur confirmed that during the AGM he had noticed a 'Spanish-looking' lady with very dark hair and a small round hat on the other side of the road, staring at him intently. The hat, he said, was decorated with something red or orange. He saw the lady walk towards the police station, turn, walk back, cross at the red pillar box and turn into Pont Street. He thought that she was acting strangely. Then a policeman stopped to chat to him and he paid her no further attention. The car he drove, he said, was a cream Rolls-Royce. Also in the mews, Fodor learnt, were Mrs Becker's black-and-cream Hillman and a smaller, blue Austin, one behind the other. It was possible that a passer-by might have seen only two of the three cars.

Alma was downstairs with the Countess's development circle while Fodor was interviewing the chauffeur in the library. She came up at 6 p.m., and stopped when she saw the visitor. Fodor whispered to him to put on his cap. He did so, and Alma identified him as the man outside Walton House on Tuesday. The chauffeur recognised her as the woman he had seen. Alma's account had been verified.

Many members of the Institute, the Countess among them, thought that Alma might have undergone an astral projection from the cinema, her spirit flying to Kensington while her body remained in Croydon. Spiritualists believed that each person had an etheric self that survived death and could, in rare cases, detach itself from the body even in life. This capacity explained the 'out of body' experience of looking down on one's own physical being. New theories of quantum mechanics made astral projection seem all the more plausible: some physicists proposed that a subatomic particle could be in more than one place at a time and could know about another particle's state even when separated by a great distance. 'Matter has been wiped out of existence,' declared the ghost-story writer Algernon Blackwood in 1938, welcoming the 'rapprochement between Modern Physics and so-called psychical and mystical phenomena'. The physical world had been revealed as ghostly, spectral, no longer solid, and the invisible world full of secret force.

Fodor, though he was open to the possibility that Alma had projected herself, considered other explanations. Alma probably knew that the Institute was shortly to host a talk on astral projection by the Honourable Ralph Shirley, editor of *Occult Review* and author of *The Mystery of the Human Double*. Perhaps she had deliberately staged the projection episode in a bid to keep Fodor's attention. Or perhaps she was so suggestible that she had unconsciously mimicked a projection. She might have fallen into a trance at the Picture Palace, walked out of the building and taken a train to London, regained her normal awareness for a few minutes when she reached Walton House, then zoned out again and returned to the cinema, becoming conscious only when she was back in her seat. The event might even have been triggered by her setting: a cinema, after all, was a place in which speaking, moving phantoms were magically projected onto a screen. For now, Fodor thought that ambulatory amnesia was the likeliest explanation for Alma's journey.

That Wednesday, *Psychic News* submitted its libel defence to the King's Bench of the High Court of Justice. Fodor had attacked spiritualism and mediums, its lawyers argued, and by implication the journal itself. *Psychic News* had been entitled to criticise him, and its articles had been factual and fair.

At the end of March, Fodor was invited to the home of a young couple in Putney who said that their dining table was making unexplained movements. Clive Richardson, twenty-eight years old and six feet nine inches tall, was a composer for Gaumont Films. His wife Eileen was an Irish-born opera singer of twenty-two. She believed that their furniture was being manipulated by the spirit of her former fiancé Douglas, who had been killed in a car accident after she broke off with him to marry Clive. When Fodor visited the Richardsons, he saw the oak table jerk across their dining room in the dark, lit dimly by the embers of the fire and the rays of a street lamp. The table seemed to move even when he climbed on top of it, and again when he crouched on a stretcher beam between its legs. Fodor invited his hosts for experiments at Walton House. He told them about the poltergeist activity at Beverstone Road, and promised Eileen Richardson that he would introduce her to Alma.

All over Britain domestic furniture seemed to be bristling into life. The previous June, Fodor and Eileen Garrett had investigated a haunted bed in Essex, in which two sisters had felt themselves being strangled, while a third sister reported feeling something furry when she slept there. Fodor spent a night in the bed. He woke abruptly, but with a feeling of 'glowing happiness' rather than disquiet. The same month, an Oxfordshire woman advertised her haunted wardrobe for sale in the *Morning Post*, claiming that an elderly man in a deer-stalker hat emerged from it each evening, marched downstairs and out of the front door. A more sinister wardrobe featured in the February 1938 issue of *Two Worlds*. One night in September 1937, according to the medium Horace Leaf, an oak cupboard launched itself at a friend of his while she lay in bed, its locked double doors flying open and its screws tearing free as it crashed down beside her. The wardrobe had done the same in 1908, on the last occasion that this woman slept in the room in which it stood, and had seriously injured her. 'Now what kind of grudge had the wardrobe cherished for twenty-nine years?' asked *Two Worlds*. 'Why did the wardrobe show such passionate resentment of one person, and one person alone?'

Perhaps a poltergeist or a discarnate spirit could invade a piece of furniture, speculated the journal, imbuing it with malevolence in the same way that the Egyptian pharaoh Tutankhamun imbued the objects looted from his tomb in the 1920s. As recently as January 1938 a jinx had befallen Sir Alexander and Lady Seton when they removed a bone from its burial ground on the banks of the Nile. Back home in Scotland, the couple were plagued by illness and supernormal visions until – on the advice of a medium – they returned their souvenir to its original resting place. Again, the curse seemed rooted in the anger of the dead.

But Fodor thought that haunted objects, like the golems of Jewish folklore, might be animated by the emotions of the living. He guessed that Eileen Richardson's table was not being moved by the spirit of her former boyfriend, but by the strength of her feeling for him. He wondered if Alma's objects, too, had been forced into life by her guilt or desire. On the drive to Bognor, she had told Fodor about the faceless ghost that stepped from the wardrobe in her childhood home. In Beverstone Road, Don's wardrobe had thrown itself on the empty bed. A cupboard that came to life, pitching forward or swinging open, might mark a resurgence of feelings that had been shut away.

Fodor observed that Alma was acquiring a kind of radiance. Her eyes shone and her skin glowed. She relished the attention of the educated ladies and gentlemen at the Institute. In the Countess she had found a passionate, sympathetic ally, and in Fodor a stimulating, attentive admirer. Where once she had been alone with her strange experiences, now they brought her friends. After the Picture Palace incident she reported further projections – to Mabel's café, to her mother's house, to Rose's kitchen. She said that two mice materialised at Beverstone Road, one in the fur collar of her coat, and that she found a goldfish in her vest; while she was sitting in the dining room, a stick of rhubarb landed in her lap, on top of her dog Judy, and in Croydon high street a butterfly brooch attached itself to her scarf, as if it had sailed out of the jeweller's window. Sometimes it seemed that reality slipped and shifted even as Alma described it. She kept hearing cheeps and chirps, she said. At the Countess's twice-weekly seances, the table rocked violently and everyone felt sick. Alma remarked that the table's aggression was typical of her grandfather Jimmy. 'He played tricks', she said, 'and when not sober could be very nasty indeed'. Once the table was calm, Alfons fell asleep on it, as if the whole thing was a dream; or unconscionable.

Fodor devised further tests outside the seance room. Before Alma sat with the Countess on 1 April, he and Dr Wills took her to the Victoria & Albert Museum in South Kensington to see whether she could remove an artefact from a locked cabinet. An official checked her bag before their tour of the collection.

Back at the Institute, Fodor searched Alma. 'She allowed me to feel all over her body,' he noted. 'I went right over. I felt her corset under which nothing bulked. I went down her legs. She took off her hat and allowed us to go through her hair.' These acts of surveillance could be exciting. Intense observation, close physical checks, even suspicion could feel like desire.

Upstairs in the library, Alma sat down on the lea-ther Chesterfield sofa and let out a cry of surprise: on her lap was an ancient terracotta oil lamp, delicate in shape and rough in texture. Fodor took the lamp to be weighed and measured. He could swear that it had not been concealed in her clothes.

On Saturday morning, George telephoned Fodor at home, highly agitated, to say that a burning-hot neck-lace had appeared on Alma's neck. She thought that it came from the museum. She had collapsed in an arm-chair, George said, her heart beating wildly.

Fodor asked Dr Wills to drive him down to Thornton Heath, along with Eileen Richardson, the young opera singer whose table he had ridden in Putney, and Irene and Andrea, who were also eager to see Alma's latest apport. When Alma had visited the Fodors' flat in Park West, Irene and Andrea had both seen a jar jump off a windowsill in the bathroom, five feet behind her.

At Beverstone Road, Alma showed her guests the necklace, a choker hung with five long chains, six shorter chains, fifteen silver coins and a Byzantine cross. Fodor, Dr Wills, Eileen, Irene and Andrea saw the weals and blisters where the hot metal collar had touched her neck.

Alma said that she had developed marks on her skin even before the object arrived. She and George had been having tea and biscuits in the kitchen – the two of them were, as usual, alone at home while Les and Don were out at work – when she suddenly felt something tighten around her throat. George saw two red bands slowly appear. 'I took no notice,' Alma said, 'covered them up and went out to the butcher.' As she walked along Thornton Heath high street, she saw an Indian chief walking by her side. 'He had a shawl thrown across the shoulder and lots of beads. His headdress was falling back.' All the time he was with her, Alma said, she could hear a jingling sound. She got home about an hour later and went upstairs. 'As I was coming out of the bathroom something hot was clasped around my neck. It was tight and heavy. I shouted: "George! George!" and ran down.'

Some of Alma's marvels resembled the bizarre juxtapositions of the surrealist artists, who, like Fodor, were fascinated by Freudian ideas. The Belgian painter

René Magritte explained in 1938 that he aimed 'to show everyday objects in situations in which we never encounter them', 'to make them shriek aloud'. His daft, unsettling inversions crossed the comic with the creepy, the familiar with the weird. Alma conjured up similar images. An Indian chieftain jingled along beside her as she made her way to the butcher's shop; a stick of rhubarb perched on her dog; a mouse issued from her arm; a soap dish chased her down the stairs. Her apports were not only mysterious in their means of production, observed Fodor, but in their meaning and intent. They seemed senseless. 'They are not capable of normal explanation,' he told the spiritualist journal *Light*. 'Perhaps that is their main purpose.' Fodor had started by attributing her poltergeist's actions to frustration, but this did not seem enough to explain their extravagance and peculiarity.

Surrealist art was condemned by the Nazis as 'degenerate', but it was popular in London. Magritte's first solo British show had opened in Mayfair at midnight on 1 April. The guests were greeted by a man in a pith helmet, scarlet gloves and huge mirrored spectacles, holding a sign that read 'Totally Blind'. He declared the show 'an exhibition of people' rather than art: the pictures in the gallery, he said, were anxiously awaiting their first view of the humans now arriving. In *Portrait*, one of the forty-six paintings on display, an eye stared out from a slice of ham. In *Reproduction Forbidden* a man stood before a mirror that instead of his face showed the back of his head. In *The Black Flag* a window and a coat hook flew like bomber aircraft through a darkening sky. In *The Rape* a female torso was rendered as a terrorised face: the breasts were staring eyes, the navel a nose, the triangle of pubic hair a muffled mouth.

TEN

Mrs Fielding's mouth was a round O

On Tuesday 5 April Fodor photographed Alma in the necklace. She wore a black tunic, so that the chains and coins lay bright against her body, and the thick metal band circled her neck like a yoke. She gazed into the distance, composed and aloof. Fodor compared the necklace to a 'slave ring'. The branching chains seemed to imprison Alma, as well as to shield and exalt her.

Nearly all the sitters in the Countess's circle detected cold breezes that day: the Countess herself, Alma, Helen Russell Scott, Alfons, Florence Hall. Only Dr Wills seemed immune. After the seance Fodor was developing photographs in the darkroom, with Alma and the Countess, when a bottle fell from the shelf to the floor with a 'ping'. Alma shivered and the Countess took hold of her hands in the dark. Fodor felt a rush of cold air. In case Alma was blowing on him, he pulled her head onto his shoulder and covered her mouth with his hands. The three of them held still. The breezes stopped.

In the library a little later, Fodor saw Alma turn towards Florence Hall, who was sitting next to her on the settee, and blow on her neck. He caught Alma's eye. She knew that he had seen her. 'Mrs Fielding's mouth,' he noted, 'was a round O.'

Fodor kept quiet. He reflected that Alma might, mischievously, have been checking whether her investigators could distinguish between natural and supernatural wafts of air. 'It is very difficult to suppress the urge of experimenting in blowing when breezes are claimed,' he wrote. 'The fact that she blew need not necessarily rule out a psychic breeze or mean that she tried to deceive us.' He and Wilfred Becker had fooled each other with puffs of air during one of Harry Brown's sittings. But Fodor knew that he was struggling to excuse Alma's trick. He instructed Florence Hall to watch Alma for suspicious movements when she was next at the Institute.

Until recently, reflected the *Evening Standard*, everyone had thought that war was about to engulf England – such was the 'panic-stricken refrain' in 'the mad March days'. Now it was April, and there was no war. On the contrary, said the paper, the country was enjoying a 'summer-in-spring', an unusual and welcome warmth. The daffodils had come early, and so had the birds: the chiffchaffs, the sand martins and the willow warblers.

To some readers, this sort of chirpy editorialising only confirmed how bad things really were. 'Funny how we keep thinking about bombs,' says the narrator in Orwell's *Coming Up For Air*. 'Of course there's no question that it's coming soon. You can tell how close it is by the cheer-up stuff they're talking in the newspapers.'

At Walton House on Friday 8 April, Alma took off her coat and hat in the ladies' room, as usual, then went up to the library in a thin frock and a brown woollen cardigan to join Fodor, Mrs Taylor and Florence Hall while she waited for the Countess's table sitting. Mrs Hall kept a close eye on her hands.

Alma said that her head hurt and she could hear a chirping sound again. As she rose from her seat, Fodor felt a movement at his right trouser leg; he looked down and saw a bird flutter up from Alma's skirt, fly across the room and alight on a pot of flowers on the bookcase. Mrs Taylor, the librarian, also saw the bird in flight. It was a small creature with blue-grey wings, a pink bill and pink skin around the eyes, legs and feet. Jimmy had not produced a bullfinch, as the Countess requested, but something very similar; the bird was afterwards identified as a waxbill finch, a native of Indonesia.

Fodor put the finch in a makeshift cage, which he set on a table in the conservatory adjoining the upstairs studio. Alma sat down at the table with Mrs Hall, and imitated the sounds that she had heard before the bird arrived. 'She can chirp extremely well,' observed Fodor.

Helen Russell Scott, who was standing near the conservatory door, noticed a ridge beneath the fabric on Alma's thigh. She walked over and, on the pretext of leaning down to look at the finch, rested her hand on Alma's knee. Alma remarked: 'I twisted my ankle this morning and jerked my knee as well.' She had mentioned these injuries to Dr Wills when he collected her from Victoria. She lifted her dress, saying, 'I put a cold-water bandage on it and tied this handkerchief round. I may as well take it off now. I don't think it's much good.' She undid a large handkerchief that was knotted above her knee, folded it up and handed it to Miss Scott. As Miss Scott took the handkerchief, she saw something flutter to the ground. She stooped as if to look into the cage, and while doing so fumbled on the floor with her right hand. She found the object. It was a tiny feather.

Surreptitiously, Miss Scott passed Fodor the feather. He gave it to Elyne Tufnell, his secretary, to keep safe. Miss Tufnell put it in an envelope and labelled it: 'The feather that fell from Mrs Fielding's skirt after the arrival of the Javanese sparrow.'

Fodor knew that he would now have to step up his research into Alma's phenomena. There was no avoiding the fact that she had come to Walton House that afternoon with a bird tied to her thigh. His mission was confusing: he must be a dogged sleuth, working to expose Alma as an out-and-out fraud, while hoping desperately that his efforts would fail. He believed that she had strayed into trickery only to please her friends at the Institute.

Fodor began by asking the Victoria & Albert Museum whether it had lost a terracotta oil lamp or a silver coin necklace – it had not – and then took both items to the British Museum in Bloomsbury. The curator of British Antiquities told him that the lamp was an early Christian item from North Africa, and referred him to the Greek and Roman curator, who on examining the lamp said that it dated from fifth- or sixth-century Egypt or Syria. A numismatist said that the Turkish coins on the necklace were minted in about 1830, the reign of Sultan Mahmud II, and the rest was modern work; the whole was worth no more than its weight in silver.

Fodor sent Dr Wills to scour Croydon for places in which Alma might have purchased the bird or the mouse. The doctor tried three pet shops, but none of the proprietors had sold a waxbill finch that week, nor did they recognise Alma in the photograph that he showed them. He visited an antique shop, outside which Florence Hall had spotted Alma, in case it had sold her the clay lamp, the necklace or any of the stones and jewels. The owner did not recognise Alma either, but he took Dr Wills's card and promised to telephone if she paid a visit in the future.

At the Institute, Fodor, Wilfred Becker and Shaw Desmond conducted saucer-breaking experiments, and found that they were unable to crack the plates as cleanly as Alma's poltergeist.

Fodor planted the brass-bound brush outside the door of the seance room and watched Alma's reaction when she emerged from the Countess's sitting.

She seemed surprised to see the brush, but almost instantly everyone was distracted by an apport that had just fallen behind a radiator, a brooch encrusted with turquoise chips.

Fodor recorded his failed attempts to rumble Alma as if they implied her honesty. The file on the case grew bulkier – with witness statements, letters, photographs – but he still did not know whether it was a catalogue of marvels, of mental breakdown, or of pranks and petty crimes.

Fodor had put a selection of Alma's apports in a glass cabinet in Walton House, the prize exhibits in his nascent psychic museum: a silver powder compact, embossed and engraved; a T-shaped wind-up Meccano key; an art deco brooch inset with tiny paste diamonds; a miniature perfume bottle with a Bakelite stopper; the clothes brush, its stiff bristles rising from a rectangle of gleaming brass. Like the *objets trouvés* displayed as sculpture by British surrealists, these ordinary things had been endowed with uncertain meaning.

In the Countess's development circle early in April, a spirit spoke through Alma when she went into trance. 'Bremba,' Alma said, very faintly, and then, in a low voice, 'I am Bremba.' Just the day before, the medium Mrs Sharplin had told Alma that she had a spirit control, a Persian artist, who was struggling to get through to the earthly plane.

'Are you going to look after Mrs Fielding?' asked Dr Wills.

'I always look after her,' Bremba replied, through Alma.

The Countess thanked Bremba for the charming little bird he had sent. Dr Wills asked him to help Alma project herself to the library upstairs, where Fodor was working. The spirit guide refused to participate in such stunts, and advised the investigators not to do so either – 'Not unless you want to kill her.' He chided them all for the demands that they were making of Alma: 'You are children still.' They promised him that they would stop pushing her so hard.

'Her body is so weak,' Bremba told them. Alma had lost more than a stone in the course of the investigation. 'She must eat. You must make her.'

The sitters said that they would do their best.

'I am sending a present for a brave little woman,' Bremba announced. 'Will you give it to her?' The investigators looked around but could not see anything.

'It is not visible to us yet,' said the Countess.

'It is at the back of Mrs Fielding,' said Bremba. Dr Wills, who had been holding one of Alma's hands, got up and felt behind her. He couldn't find anything in the chair.

'Be careful,' said Bremba.

'Of what?' asked Dr Wills.

'Her heart. No sudden movement.' The Countess reached over and felt Alma's heart banging in her chest. Dr Wills could feel the pulse racing at her wrist. Bremba said that he would go.

'Leave her gently, Bremba,' said Miss Scott.

'Yes,' said the spirit guide. 'Goodbye, friends.'

Alma seemed to come round. She looked dazed, so Dr Wills brought her some brandy and water.

'Where have you been?' asked the Countess.

Alma said that she could not remember anything. Dr Wills searched her chair again and behind the left-hand cushion found a silver locket on a heavy chain.

After the sitting the Countess was delighted to tell Fodor that an articulate spirit had emerged to supervise Alma's development and to communicate with her circle. Fodor was excited. He did not believe that Bremba was the spirit of a dead Persian, but he hoped that he was a new element of Alma's unconscious self. Perhaps he would prove a civilised, protective personality, the superego to Jimmy's id, and might even collaborate in the quest to untangle Alma's inner life.

Frederic Myers, a founder of the Society for Psychical Research, had proposed in the 1880s that a medium's trance voices issued not from the spirit world but from a shifting, multiple, subliminal layer of the mind. Similarly, the Swiss philosopher Théodore Flournoy argued in 1899 that the trance personalities of the French medium Hélène Smith – which included a Hindu, a Martian and the French queen Marie Antoinette – were dissociated impersonations. Fodor loved Flournoy's book about Madame Smith and longed to develop a muse-medium with selves as rich and various. He had already studied Eileen Garrett's secondary personalities, Uvani and Abdul Latif, and he remained fascinated by the alter egos of Lajos Pap even after he discovered that his apports were fake. Lajos's two selves were Isaac, a fourteenth-century rabbi, and Saol, who at one seance had punched Fodor in the mouth.

At least Bremba seemed to be on Fodor's side. A few days after his emergence, Alma told Fodor that though Les and her mother opposed her trips to Walton House, her new guide was in favour of the investigation. 'I am right behind U,' Bremba spelt out at a table-turning session at Beverstone Road on 11 April. 'Go to Institute, do not give in.'

ELEVEN

A push, a punch, a kiss

Fodor suggested that Alma attempt another astral projection from a cinema on Tuesday 12 April, in the company of Dr Wills's wife Hilda. Seven weeks into the inquiry, he was getting impatient for verifiable phenomena or evidence of dissociation. If Alma was observed in the picture house and the Institute at the same time, he would have proof that she could project herself. If she tried any tricks or left the cinema in a trance, Mrs Wills would let him know.

In the afternoon, during the Countess's seance, Fodor asked Miss Tufnell to go through Alma's bag and make a list of the contents. She found just under twenty shillings (£1) in cash, as well as a green handkerchief, a Betty Lou disposable velour powder puff, a tube of Tattoo lipstick ('for glamorous, amorous, transparent redness'), and a pair of brown kid gloves.

After the sitting Alma went to the library with Mrs Taylor, the librarian, while the others convened in Fodor's office. As Alma sat down, Mrs Taylor saw a heavy wooden armchair on the other side of the room topple onto its back. The investigators heard the bang and hurried in. They could smell violets. Mrs Taylor insisted that Alma had been nine feet from the chair as it fell.

When Alma left for the cinema, Dr Wills told her that he would put out a pencil and a piece of paper for her in the seance room in case she could write a message during her astral return. He and Fodor would be working late at Walton House, hosting a table-turning seance with Clive and Eileen Richardson.

Hilda Wills and Alma had tea at a café in South Kensington, then took the Tube two stops to Victoria. Directly opposite the station was the New Victoria, a 2,000-seat 'super cinema' built in 1930 with a stark, Germanic art deco façade. A woman was selling roses near the entrance. 'I do love roses,' said Alma.

At 7.45 p.m. Hilda Wills bought two half-crown tickets and took Alma in to find seats in the stalls. The auditorium of the New Victoria was styled as a fantastical underwater world, a luscious mermaid's grotto in pale blues and sea greens. Rays of ruby light washed over the silvery dolphins carved on the walls, and shone up sculpted columns that burst like fountains against the scallop-fringed ceiling. Long lamps spiralled down from the dome.

Alma went to find the ladies' cloakroom, telling Hilda Wills that she thought that her period was coming on. She was back five minutes later. She had needed some sanitary napkins, she told Mrs Wills, and since there were none in the cinema she had gone out to the street to buy some. She was still in time for the start of *Second*

Honeymoon, a romantic comedy starring Tyrone Power and Loretta Young.

At 8.30 p.m., Alma said that she felt sick. Mrs Wills looked over and saw a bunch of roses in Alma's lap, fresh and wet.

'Did you feel them come?' she asked in amazement.

'I only felt a slight touch on my hand,' Alma replied.

At 9.25 p.m., while the feature was still playing, Alma seemed to go into trance for a few minutes, and on returning to consciousness told Mrs Wills that she had tried to visit the Institute astrally, as planned. 'I had great difficulty in knocking,' she said, 'but I managed to knock very gently and Dr Fodor looked up.'

Clive and Eileen Richardson, the couple at whose house Fodor had taken the magic table ride, arrived at the International Institute at 8.15 p.m. Fodor invited them to join him at a three-legged table in the big seance room, along with Dr Wills and Helen Russell Scott. Florence Hall made notes. When the light was turned off, the sitters placed their hands flat on the table, and it started to tilt. One of the table legs pressed on Eileen's shoe. 'Get off, Douglas!' said Eileen, apparently addressing her dead fiancé. Clive jovially remarked that he wouldn't stand for such rudeness if he were a spirit, at which the table thumped three times.

For the next half-hour the table continued to tremble and tip, directing itself at Eileen. The sitters could see its shape in the darkness. Each time Eileen changed her place, the table changed the direction of its tilts. Fodor was sure that he saw it move twice when everyone removed their hands, and soon after nine o'clock it pushed so fiercely at Eileen that she shrieked. Florence Hall switched on the electric light. When Eileen was calmer the seance resumed, but at 9.55 p.m. she started screaming as the table banged frantically at her. Florence Hall rushed to the light switch. Eileen was found on the floor with the capsized table. It had flown at her, she said, and wrapped its legs around her neck.

Alma and Hilda Wills arrived at Walton House twenty minutes later. While they were sitting on the first-floor landing, waiting for Clive and Eileen to leave, Alma 'went off' again, reported Mrs Wills. As she came round, she said that she had just been handed a ticket at the cinema. She rummaged in her bag and found a stub, numbered 85425.

When Fodor and Dr Wills joined them, Alma showed them the roses and the ticket stub. Mrs Wills produced the stubs of the two that she had bought – 85383 and 85384 – and recounted the events of the evening. Alma confirmed that she had tried to project herself to Walton House.

'You didn't put out the paper and pencil for me?' she asked Dr Wills. He admitted that he had forgotten.

Fodor thought that he might have been faintly aware of Alma's presence during the sitting with the Richardsons. 'I definitely heard a knock on the door some time after 9,' he recorded in his notes. 'The thought came to my mind that it might be Mrs Fielding but then

it seemed so preposterous that I put the thought away.'
For a moment, still wanting to believe, he wondered
whether she really had been hovering at the door while
the researchers were distracted by Douglas.

Alma telephoned Fodor the next morning, very miser-
able. Les had met her off the train the previous night,
she said, having waited at Thornton Heath station for
an hour. He told her that he didn't like her visits to the
Institute: the experiments were damaging her health
and he wanted her back home. They argued again that
morning, she said, and she agreed to withdraw from the
investigation. Straight away, a plate in the dining room
fell on the fender and broke. A rolling pin flew at her.
Les gave in.

Fodor asked Alma how much money she had in her
bag. She counted: ten shillings, half a crown and three
or four sixpences, she said. Fodor calculated that the
difference between this and the twenty shillings that
Miss Tufnell had found would almost exactly cover the
cost of a bunch of roses and a cinema ticket. It seemed
very likely that Alma had pretended to be shopping for
sanitary napkins near the New Victoria while she was in
fact buying roses outside the entrance. When Dr Wills
telephoned the cinema, the manager confirmed that the
ticket in Alma's bag was issued within five minutes of
the two that Mrs Wills had bought.

Fodor realised that the New Victoria episode had
been a stunt, but he refused to dismiss all of Alma's
stories. The question of her authenticity had become

a question of his own credibility. Besides, he feared that any discussion of fraud would be dangerous to her health. When Alma first visited the Institute, he had recorded her weight at 9 stone 5 lbs. She now weighed 7 stone 12 lbs, a loss of 21 lbs in seven weeks, and she seemed to be in a reckless state of mind. He could not risk distressing her. For his own sake and for hers, he dared not let the case fail.

Fodor resolved to manage Alma's behaviour more closely. He persuaded the Countess to let him join the development circle, and he took advice from Eric Cuddon, a barrister and amateur magician on the Institute's council who had written a guide to hypnosis.

In the seance room on 14 April Alma lay back in the armchair. Fodor faced her, held both her hands, and in a quiet monotone directed her to look into his eyes and do just as he told her. A hypnotic trance was almost identical to a mediumistic trance, but placed the subject under the hypnotist's control.

'You are asleep,' he said. 'Do you know that you are asleep? Answer me.'

'Yes.'

'You are going away for a holiday for the Easter,' he told her. The Fieldings were planning a trip to the coast. 'It will be a glorious holiday. You will leave all care and worry behind. Nothing will disturb you. Nothing will upset your happiness. You will eat plenty. You will be hungry. You will have a tremendous appetite and you are going to gain weight… Nothing will fly at you. No apports will come. You will not wander… Your body will not be in two places at the same time. Repeat after me: "I shall eat plenty. I shall have a tremendous appetite. I shall put on weight. I shall not have any psychic experiences during the holidays. I shall not have any phenomena except at the Institute." '

Alma repeated his words sentence by sentence.

'You will wake up when I count ten,' Fodor told her. 'One, two, three...'

The Fieldings took regular seaside holidays, often cycling to the coast overnight and sending their luggage ahead to a guesthouse by train. The family photograph albums were filled with pictures of these jaunts: an infant Don digging in the wet, rippled sand at Ramsgate; Les larking about on Canvey Island in a one-piece costume and a rubber ring; Alma reclining on the pebbled beach at Shoreham in a white-belted swimsuit, her skin tanned and her hair wild.

This bank holiday weekend the family visited Whitstable, a fishing village in Kent known for its weatherboard houses, its shingle beach and its oysters. The weather was mild and the international situation stable. 'No bad news – official!' announced the *Pictorial*, which in the absence of any momentous world events ran a picture of a topless 'spring nymph', an Eve-like figure plucking an apple from a tree, and a piece about the Duchess of Kent's visit to a branch of Woolworth's in Slough (she bought a toy windmill, a card of hair curlers, several chocolate Easter eggs, a packet of cheese, a set of cooking tins and a green salt shaker).

Alma returned to Walton House on Wednesday. She, Les and Don had stayed in a hotel in Whitstable, she told Fodor. She had eaten voraciously. Fodor weighed her and found that she had gained one and a half pounds. She seemed 'puckish', he noted, full of devilry.

Fodor checked Alma's armchair before she sat down for the afternoon seance, putting his hands down the sides of the seat and shaking out each cushion. He hypnotised her again. 'Your eyelids are heavy,' he intoned, 'very heavy...'

Fodor repeated his instructions to Alma about looking after herself, and then — supposedly to test the effectiveness of the hypnotic trance — took a needle from Dr Wills.

'I am taking a cigarette,' he said. 'It is burning. I will touch your hand with it. It will burn you, but very slightly. It won't hurt you but will discolour your skin.' He pressed the needle into the back of her hand. 'I am now touching the skin. Tell me what do you feel?'

'Nothing,' said Alma. She did not flinch.

'Here is the cigarette,' said Fodor, pressing again, 'a red-hot cigarette.'

Still she claimed to feel nothing. This was confusing: if she was genuinely hypnotised, she should have felt the burn of a cigarette and if not, the prick of a needle.

Alma reported that she could see Bremba standing beside her, that he was placing something next to her, near her elbow. Fodor reached behind her and found a piece of pottery on the chair, with a small, weathered label marked 'Carthage'.

Alma returned slowly to consciousness. She said that she had a vague memory of being at the East End docks with Bremba, next to a cargo boat, with a lot of 'coloured gentlemen' walking about.

There was a knock at the door and Dr Wills crossed the room to unlock it. As he admitted Eric Cuddon, the young barrister who had written a guide to hypnosis, Alma cried out, 'What's this?' and lifted something to the light. It was a small mushroom-shaped object apparently covered with tiger skin; to Fodor, it looked like an African drumstick, or gong-beater. Alma unscrewed the shaft from the head and tipped out some fine black powder. The Countess was alarmed. It might be poisonous, she said. She and Miss Scott took Alma to the ladies' cloakroom to wash her hands.

As they were coming back up the stairs to the studio, Alma asked the other women if they could smell something. They could: a horrible, animal-like smell, said the Countess; the smell of bear, said Miss Scott. 'Tiger!' cried Alma, and rolled up her right sleeve to reveal three long marks like the scratches of a giant claw.

In conversation with Fodor after the seance, Alma mentioned that she came from a family of performers. In 1902, she said, a year before her birth, her mother took part in the 'Paris in London' fair at Earl's Court, appearing both as the Half Lady Alive (the lower part of her body concealed by a black curtain) and as the

Mermaid at the Bottom of the Sea (reclining between two glass tanks in the Palais des Illusions). According to Alma, her mother also wrote a number of short plays, including one – *Rolling Passion* – about a group of people who abducted a wealthy woman. 'They got her into this house,' explained Alma, 'tied her up and whipped her into submission and made her leave her money to someone else.' It was a kind of revenge drama, in which the poor tortured the rich.

As a girl, Alma told Fodor, she had herself been trained by her uncle George to be a tightrope walker, trapeze artist, acrobat and dancer. She hoped to become an actress, and had a set of professional photographs taken to this end. Her training was interrupted first by a bad fall from the tightrope, then by her bicycle accident. Soon afterwards pregnancy and marriage put paid to her ambitions altogether. Instead of joining the rackety, shimmery world of the circus or the stage, she submitted to life as a housewife.

Fodor had thought that Alma's circumstances were workaday: she was the daughter of a plumber, the wife of a builder, and had briefly run a snack bar in Croydon. But she had now – voluntarily – revealed that the wish to tease, alarm and delight an audience was part of her inheritance. She was trained in dexterity. It seemed suddenly more likely that the whole supernatural adventure had been an act.

And yet the next evening Alma reported an incident that revived Fodor's curiosity and concern. 'I hardly know how to tell you,' she said, 'but I feel I *must* tell you that I had a very frightening experience last night.'

She had felt herself pressed hard to her bed, she told him, unable to move or speak. Les was asleep by her side. A cold weight began to push against her. She described her helplessness and the heft of her phantom assailant.

'Did this man come to you as a husband?' asked Fodor.

'Yes. I struggled, but I was quite powerless. I could not shake him off.' The ghost had forced himself on her, she said, yet she remembered not just her fear but her physical pleasure: a feeling of ecstasy. 'I hope it cannot lead to trouble,' said Alma.

Fodor hastily assured her that it was impossible that the phantom had impregnated her, and advised her to do everything she could to resist any further encounters. In truth, he did not know what this visit could mean, or how to avoid a recurrence. Alma made Fodor promise to keep the information to himself. He sealed his report of their conversation in an envelope, which he kept separate from the main log of the case.

On Saturday Alma told Fodor over the telephone that she felt tired and lifeless. He asked her whether she had been visited by the ghost again.

'Yes,' she admitted. 'I was awake most of the time. But I could not help myself. I felt paralysed.'

Fodor asked for a description of her attacker. 'It was a man with a broad head,' said Alma. 'I know nothing about him. I have never seen him. He stayed quite a long time. He paid two visits.'

Later that night, Alma added, she felt someone bite her neck and when she woke at 5.45 a.m. she saw her late uncle George approach her. After this she dressed, went downstairs and sketched his image from memory. George Bannister, who had died in 1924 aged forty-six, was the younger of Alma's mother's brothers. It was he who had trained Alma when she was a girl. Perhaps there was a connection between her disclosure of her family history and the arrival of the phantom lover.

Alma told Fodor that she had first seen the ghost of her uncle just a few days ago, at a variety show at the London Palladium. At the end of Thursday's matinée performance of *London Rhapsody*, which featured the popular comedy act the Crazy Gang and the Welsh conjuror Cardini, she claimed to have seen George appear between the stage curtains. He bowed and smiled and was gone.

Of all her experiences, Fodor could tell that the night visits scared Alma the most. He wondered what they were. Returning memories? Visits from the dead? Fantasies about a man who, like Fodor himself, was both attractive and dangerous to her? Alma's encounter had been pitched between pleasure and revulsion – she described the icy, insistent press on her body, her answering pulse of excitement.

A predatory erotic demon was known in psychical circles as an incubus or – if female – a succubus. These figures were sometimes the former lovers of those they assaulted. In May Sinclair's short story 'The Nature of the Evidence', a dead woman thrusts herself between her widowed husband and his new wife as they lie naked in bed, ensnaring him in 'terrible and exquisite contact' so thrilling that he abandons his flesh-and-blood bride. Alma had recently heard real-life stories of vengeful, envious ghosts: just a week ago, Eileen Richardson was seemingly assaulted in Walton House by her former fiancé Douglas, in the guise of a three-legged table, and a few weeks before that the spectre of Mrs Davis was said to have driven her love rival Minnie Harrison from their home in Bethnal Green. In both cases, the dead were animated by sexual jealousy.

In Alma's phenomena, said Fodor, 'the genuine and the fraudulent marched in queer procession. It was too dangerous to conclude from one to the other.'

Now that Fodor had joined the sittings again, he wanted to test Alma in front of a larger audience. He organised a public seance on 22 April, and made sure that she was not left alone for a second that afternoon. Dr Wills met her at Victoria. Miss Scott took over at the door of Walton House. Fodor himself searched the ladies' room, the upstairs seance room and the armchairs in the library.

Alma stood in the middle of the library and undressed, revealing the scars from her mastectomy and from the operations to drain her kidney abscesses. She passed her clothes to the searchers to place on the Chesterfield sofa by the window and stepped onto the Institute's scales: she had lost a pound since the last sitting. When Alma was naked, the Countess ran her fingers through her hair, looked into her ears, up her nose, under her arms and in her mouth. Alma removed her false teeth for inspection. She dressed herself in her corset, two baggy woollen vests, a pair of long, loose bloomers and a pair of stockings. Miss Scott sewed the tops of the stockings to the legs of the knickers. Alma pulled on the one-piece silver jumpsuit, which her attendants zipped up the back, cinched at the waist with a narrow suede belt and tied with tape at the neck, ankles and elbows. The women checked Alma's hands – 'the two hands should be examined simultaneously by two examiners and the fingers spreadeagled', specified Dr Wills's written instructions – before putting her arms into a pair of custom-made gloves: these were silk stockings with the feet cut off and the ends tied in a knot. Miss Scott sewed the open ends of the gloves to the arms of the one-piece suit, and the library door was unlocked to admit Dr Wills, who tied bandages around Alma's arms. She was led to the adjoining seance room, her hands held all the while.

Among the nineteen sitters in the large studio were Will Goldston, an English stage magician whose publications included *Will Goldston's Card System of Exclusive Magical Secrets* (1920), *More Exclusive Magical Secrets* (1921) and *Further Exclusive Magical Secrets* (1927), and Horace Goldin, an American magician who claimed to have devised the illusion of sawing a woman in half. Fodor had invited them to assess whether Alma, under cover of feminine passivity, was using tricks like their own. Mediums and conjurors both dealt in magic, but a medium aspired to be a conduit for real supernatural forces, whereas a conjuror was a master of illusion. As Harry Houdini, the most famous exposer of fake mediums, liked to say, 'It takes a flim-flammer to catch a flimflammer.'

While Alma was walking around after the tea break, she complained of sharp pains in her stomach. She jerked, twitched, collapsed into a chair, seemed to lose consciousness as her head fell forward: a small glass vase was found in her hand beneath the stocking-glove. Five minutes later she shook, blanched, faltered; trembled all over and again fell into a chair: a dogtooth quartz crystal appeared, this time outside the stocking. An hour later, she started to give way for a third time. Fodor rushed forward and caught her. He and Will Goldston held her up, clasped her flinching hands and felt the sinews pulse. She subsided into a chair, shaking from head to foot as she opened her palm: there, out-side the stocking, was a small piece of pottery with a faded label inscribed with tiny writing. On examining it through a microscope, the investigators made out the word 'TIMGAD', the name of an ancient Roman city in Algeria.

The magicians were amazed. 'It was the most won-derful thing I have ever seen,' said Horace Goldin afterwards. 'I am absolutely convinced.' Will Goldston said that he had heard and read many stories about apports, but had never believed that they were truly supernormal: seeing Alma's phenomena had changed his mind.

Alma lay on a sofa in the conservatory while Dr Wills brought her brandy. She then went to the library to dress in her own clothes, under the supervision of six women. Just as she was about to pull on her cardigan, 'Oh, my arm!' she cried. 'That tiger again!' Her right arm was bright red from elbow to shoulder with four livid weals, as if raked by claws.

As she was buttoning the cardigan, 'Oh, my back!' she exclaimed. She took off the cardigan and lifted her blouse: red scratches reached from one shoulder blade to the other, and down her spine from neck to waist. All the women in the library felt sick, and some detected a foetid smell. Miss Scott had a violent headache. Everyone sensed something alien in the room with them. Alma cried out again: there were marks on her left arm now, and more on her back, and two minutes later a thick red band appeared on her neck from her left ear to her throat.

Alma's bodily manifestations fascinated Fodor. He had rarely experienced supernatural sensations himself, but in his *Encyclopaedia* he dwelt almost longingly on them. Sometimes a supernormal touch was yielding, he wrote, 'like a rubber ball or an animal's paw', and sometimes light, like 'feathers, gloves, fur, powderpuff, cobwebs, flowers, fingers etc'. It could be rough or tender: 'a tap, a caress, a stroke, a slap, a kick, a prick, a push, a punch, a kiss'. He noticed that Alma's sensations had become increasingly intense. To begin with, she had been tickled and chilled by breezes, bumped and bruised by airborne objects. Now she claimed that her body had been penetrated by a spirit. She had been cut, blistered, pricked, scored on the arms and back and neck. She kept lifting her clothes to show the researchers her wounds, as if to impress her damage upon them.

Alma's tiger scratches reminded Fodor of the marks found on the skin of Eleonore Zugun, a thirteen-year-old Romanian girl whose visit to London in 1926 had popularised the term 'poltergeist'. Eleonore was a square-faced child with a short, dark bob, in whose presence toys twirled in the air and knives flung themselves at doors. When she was tested at Harry Price's Laboratory of Psychical Research, the investigators saw red discs bloom on her hands and red stripes rise on her cheeks and chest, hardening as they faded to white. Long ridges ran along her arms, like the welts left by a whip, and dents appeared in her flesh, as if she had been bitten. Eleonore blamed her stigmatic wounds on 'Dracu', the Devil. Traditionally, stigmata and poltergeist disturbances were signs of witchcraft. The *Daily News* described the manifestations of the 'Poltergeist Girl' as 'one of the most bewildering problems, psychical and psychological, of this generation'.

The American writer Charles Fort noted that poltergeists often emanated from those who had no direct power – women, servants, adolescents, children. In the event of a world war, Fort suggested in *Wild Talents* (1932), a squad of poltergeist girls might be deployed against enemy troops. He imagined the scene – both futuristic and archaic – in which the girls combined their violent gifts: 'A regiment bursts into flames, and the soldiers are torches. Horses snort smoke from the combustion of their entrails.'

Eleonore Zugun was accompanied to London by Zoe Wassilko-Serecki, a twenty-nine-year-old Romanian countess with an interest in psychical and psychoanalytic theory. Countess Wassilko-Serecki, like Fodor, believed that inner conflicts could manifest as supernormal events: if a surviving part of a dead person's soul could haunt the physical world, she asked, why not a repressed part of the living self? This might happen, she speculated, when a strong desire co-existed with a strong sanction against that desire. Sometimes, wrote Countess Wassilko-Serecki in the *British Journal of Psychical Research*, 'Dracu' spoke through Eleonore, 'in a manner which seemed to prove that in the child's soul a great conflict, caused by sexual affairs, had taken place'. The Countess believed that this conflict was connected to Eleonore's father. Fodor wondered if Alma had an equally disturbed history. Perhaps her poltergeist was a chunk of her self so damaged that it had been torn off and expelled.

TWELVE

The potato-wine projection

On 26 April, in the biggest peacetime Budget in British history, the Chancellor of the Exchequer announced that he planned to fund a rearmament programme by substantially raising taxes on income, petrol and tea. For the past three months, he revealed, the government had been buying in large reserves of wheat and other supplies in case of war.

At Walton House, Fodor again joined the Countess's circle. Bremba, frustratingly, had so far not uttered a word in his presence. Fodor let the Countess lead the conversation.

Bremba's voice came through soon after the seance began. He told the sitters that he had 'passed over' eighteen years ago, in 1920, while studying art in England. The Countess asked him where he had studied.

'Why are you so impatient?' Bremba retorted.

'We are not impatient, Bremba,' said the Countess. 'We are only interested.'

'You shall know all soon.'

'We don't want to hurt your feelings, Bremba. Don't take it that way.'

The Countess asked Bremba if he would help them with an experiment in astral projection. 'That lies with my medium,' he said. 'It can only be done by her will.'

'We don't want to exhaust your medium,' the Countess assured him, 'or do anything contrary to your laws. Are there any suggestions you would like to make? Are we doing anything wrong?'

'You don't seem to trust her,' said Bremba.

'We do trust her,' said the Countess, earnestly. 'It is the outside world. We want to establish a case. We trust her, but you know what the outside world is.'

'That is good,' said Bremba.

Laurie Evans chipped in: 'There is no mistrust. We believe in her absolutely, but we have to take all these precautions to convince other people. We have to convince outsiders that such things do exist.'

'Bremba,' said the Countess, 'could you explain why I always feel sick when your medium gets apports?'

'You are a great help,' said Bremba. 'She is drawing from you.'

'Bremba,' asked Florence Hall, 'what caused the scratches on your medium last Friday?'

'That was my pet. It did not do her any harm.'

The Countess asked him what kind of animal it was.

'It is a tiger,' said Bremba, 'a fully grown one.'

The Countess asked Bremba about the waxbill finch, which had died within days of materialising at the Institute. 'Do you know whether the little bird died a natural death?'

'It was not a little bird,' said Bremba, 'not a real bird... it was a little child, an unborn baby that was not wanted.'

The Countess wondered if the finch was the spirit of an unwanted baby of her own. She sometimes experienced pulsations when one of Alma's apports arrived, as if she was herself giving birth.

Fodor asked Bremba: 'Was it because the bird was a child it had to arrive under such peculiar circumstances?'

'Yes. From her right instep.'

'We don't quite follow that, I'm afraid,' said Fodor, who suspected that Bremba was trying to account for the fact that the bird had been seen flying out of Alma's skirt. Bremba seemed more set on protecting Alma from the investigators than in helping them to explore her psyche.

'It is very hard to make you understand.'

'When you brought those mice,' asked Dr Wills, 'were they real mice or little souls?'

'They were real mice. They still live.'

'Where did they come from, actually?' asked the doctor.

'They were just pets belonging to anybody.'

'You couldn't tell us where they came from?' persisted the doctor. 'It would be interesting to go and see if they had been missed.' Dr Wills was eager as ever to match Alma's supernormal claims to verifiable facts.

'No,' said Bremba.

Alma's spirit guide seemed prickly and defensive.

The sitters broke for tea at 4.45 p.m. They were joined in the library by Mrs Kelly, the treasurer, Mrs Taylor, the librarian, and Mrs Dundas, the young widow who owned Walton House. When Alma was handed a cup of tea, it flew out of her hands.

The group sensed strange forces in the room. Laurie and Dr Wills heard a ping. The Countess said that her head ached on one side. Alma said that she heard a cracking noise in her chair. Fodor lay on the floor and listened: it sounded like something stretching, he said, in the left front leg.

Mrs Dundas saw a light on the cushion just by Fodor's shoulder, and heard a ticking sound. Mrs Taylor – who had seen the chair topple over in the library a fort-night earlier – said that she too could hear ticks, quite distinctly.

Fodor, still recumbent, heard a crackling in the chair's left leg. Alma saw something flash past. Fodor got to his feet and sat on the arm of her chair. The Countess, sitting on the other arm and holding Alma's clasped hands, sensed a soft object like a cushion pushing against her.

Suddenly Mrs Taylor, who was sitting opposite, started jerking in her chair, her eyes shut, clasping and unclasping her hands and crying, 'I don't want it! I don't want it! Take it away!' She thrust her hands towards Alma. 'You have it! You have it!'

The Countess went over to Mrs Taylor, but she shouted, 'Don't touch me! Don't touch me! Leave me alone!' The Countess stepped back. Again Mrs Taylor started: 'I don't want it. You take it!'

Alma went up to her, took her hands, and soothed her: 'It's all right, Mrs Taylor, I'll take it. I'll take it. You are all right.' Mrs Taylor sank back in the chair and opened her eyes.

The atmosphere in the seance room was more febrile than ever. Alma's uneasy sensations were washing through the other sitters like waves: sounds and smells, cold, heat, jolts and shudders, lurches in the head and the gut. Solid edges seemed to melt, objects to quiver and press. The sitters flinched at the metamorphoses, the breaching of boundaries, the spillage.

Fodor was worried by the panic that had seized Mrs Taylor, and Alma seemed unsettled too. At the next session, as if to regain control, she performed a tightly managed projection.

At 3.20 p.m. on Friday, she leant back in her armchair and closed her eyes. 'Hello, George,' she said. 'I have forgotten to give Rose that recipe. Give me a pen and paper. Anything will do, George. I feel giddy, George.'

Fodor put a sheet of paper in front of her and a pencil in her right hand. Her eyes still closed, she wrote out a list of ingredients for potato wine:

1 lb Potatoes
1 lb Wheat
1 lb Raisins
½ lb Dem. Sugar
½ oz Yeast

Since Alma seemed to be enacting a projection to Beverstone Road, Fodor urged her to bring something back to the Institute: the trick penny, or a dart, an egg cup, a brass ashtray, anything at all.

Alma said that George was trying to get through on the telephone, and she wanted Fodor to speak to him.

Fodor pretended to comply. 'Hello, George,' he said. 'What has happened? I see. Yes, you mean you have seen her. That is very interesting, George. You are quite positive? Yes, she is here all right, George. Goodbye. Thank you very much.'

But then Mrs Kelly, the Institute's treasurer, appeared at the glass door of the conservatory to announce that George had just telephoned to say that Mrs Fielding was at home. Alma had been right to report that he was trying to get through.

'Will you leave George and bring something?' Fodor asked Alma.

'I cannot,' said Alma. 'He is holding my arm.'

Laurie left the seance room to telephone George.

'George has given me something,' cried Alma. 'I cannot hold it.'

'Try to hold it and bring it,' said Fodor.

'I cannot bring it,' she said, 'but it will come as an apport.'

'Can you describe what it is?'

'It is a compass off his watch chain.'

Alma said that George had released her now, but she was struggling to return to the Institute. 'I cannot get back. I want to come back. I'm outside and I can't get in.'

'It's all right,' said Fodor. 'We'll let you in.' Dr Wills went downstairs to the front door, in case Alma's etheric self was outside, but found no one there.

Alma opened her eyes. She said that she had projected herself to the house and found George polishing some shoes. She had left a recipe for Rose by the telephone.

Laurie came back into the seance room and told the gathering about his phone call: George said that he was holding Alma's arm. Laurie encouraged him to let go and put Alma on the phone. He heard George say, 'Come along, they want to speak to you,' before the call was cut off. When Laurie called back, George said that Alma had left the house with his compass. He read out the list that she had written. Laurie asked him to post it to the Institute as soon as possible.

The ingredients that George listed were the same as those that Alma had written in the seance room, except the abbreviation 'Dem.' (for demerara) was missing, and the quantity of sugar was given as 1 lb rather than ½ lb.

'Did he say where she wrote it?' asked Fodor.

'On the dining-room table,' said Laurie.

After tea, Alma produced several apports, including the compass from George's watch chain. As she dressed in the library, 'My arm!' she cried. She pushed up her sleeves, lifted her cardigan to show the researchers the fresh scratches on her arms and back.

Fodor was struck by the daring of Alma's projection to Beverstone Road. 'If she frauds,' he wrote, 'she does it very coolly.' This was the most elaborate self-transportation yet. It was obvious that she could have manufactured it only with George's collusion. Fodor arranged to go to Thornton Heath to interview him the next day.

Alma telephoned Fodor at home before his visit on Saturday to ask him not to mention the latest astral projection to Les. She said that Les was already worried that something might happen to her. Fodor thought that Les might be worried about Alma's increasingly wild deceptions rather than about her capacity to project herself across town.

Alma had endured another difficult night, she confided to Fodor: the incubus had visited again. She had been wide awake throughout his assault and with an effort of will managed to free herself from his clutches 'before anything happened'. She still seemed very frightened by these phantom sexual encounters, Fodor observed, and yet quite unfazed by the recipe incident, an astral projection in three dimensions which, as far as he knew, was unprecedented in the psychic literature. He suspected that this was because the night visits were genuine episodes of dissociation, while the story of astral travel was a complicated piece of nonsense that she had cooked up with George.

Irene Fodor was curious about the latest developments in the case, so Fodor agreed to take her along to Beverstone Road on Saturday afternoon. He also invited

Eric Cuddon, the barrister on the Institute's council. Fodor interviewed George in their presence.

'I was repairing boots in the shed at the bottom of the garden,' said George. 'About 3.30 p.m. I brought the shoes up into the kitchen to finish them up by the gas stove, as I had no methylated lamp.' While he was working, he said, 'I felt as if somebody was beside me.' He turned to see Alma, who had left for the Institute an hour and a half earlier. He had not heard her come in. 'I said, "Hello, what are you doing here?" She said, "I have just come back. I have forgotten the recipe."'

Believing that she had projected herself from Walton House, George said, he pulled the compass off his watch chain and gave it to her, saying: 'Take this little thing.' He then went to the front room to telephone the Institute while Alma wrote out the recipe on the sideboard. George tried to get Alma to speak to Laurie, but the call was cut off. When Laurie rang back, George grasped Alma by the left elbow, holding the telephone's mouthpiece towards her. The phone was one of the older, candlestick models, with a mouthpiece at the top of the stand and a rotary dial in the base. Alma ignored George, he said.

'Did she seem quite solid?' asked Fodor.

'She looked slightly dazed,' said George, 'but her normal self.' He let go of her arm, Dr Wills having warned him that a person could be injured if forcibly detained while in a projected state, and she headed out of the front door.

Fodor asked him what he made of Alma's visit.

'I was flabbergasted,' said George.

George and Alma must have rehearsed all the details of this episode, thought Fodor: what he would say that he was doing when she arrived, how he held her, the choice of apport. Though Alma was not wearing a watch during the seance, she had timed her account to match George's live telephonic description of her movements. George had posted the recipe before Alma got home (the postmark was 6.15 p.m., and Alma left the Institute at six). Fodor spotted only one inconsistency. On Friday, George had said that Alma wrote the recipe on the dining table in the back room; today he said that she had written it on the sideboard in the front room. And there were the differences in the lists of ingredients.

Alma rolled up the arm of her sweater to show her guests the claw marks from the previous day. The scratches had broken the skin and formed scabs, as if the tiger was becoming rougher and more demanding.

Once the interviews were over, Alma's son Don took Eric up to the loft to see his train set. Mischievously, Alma suggested to Fodor that they remove the ladder and let Don and Eric think that the poltergeist had done it. Fodor helped Alma shift the steps away from the trapdoor. He and she had 'a good laugh', he said, at her dark and complicated joke.

Supernatural episodes were diversions from more concrete fears, but sometimes stagings of them, too. The unease in the International Institute seance room mimicked wider anxieties about the dissolving borders in Europe, the alien forces within Britain, the dangers of sedition, infiltration and invasion. On Sunday 1 May thousands of young fascists gathered outside the Houses of Parliament for a May Day march to southeast London, while tens of thousands of members of the labour movement assembled for a procession to Hyde Park. The left-wing marchers raised their clenched fists in solidarity as they set off from Westminster; Oswald Mosley's followers gave the fascist salute, their right arms extended and raised, palms down, fingers closed. In Bermondsey, where the fascist march ended, Mosley addressed his followers. He praised Chamberlain's decision to appease Mussolini, and urged a similar accommodation with Hitler. Britain had no reason to fear a fascist dictatorship, he said: after all, the country was already in thrall to 'the alien Jewish money power'. In Hyde Park the leftist speakers decried the concessions that the prime minister had made to Hitler and Mussolini, and his refusal to support the republicans against General Franco in Spain. 'Down with the fascists', read their placards; 'Arms for Spain'; 'Chamberlain must go'.

THIRTEEN

I want to be nasty

Fodor was unnerved by Alma's hint that he was in on her poltergeist pranks. Perhaps, like his flower-lifting neighbour Dick Woodward, she was pandering to him, or testing him, or both. He knew that the Institute bore some responsibility for her confabulations. 'We have been encouraging the development of abnormal tendencies,' he admitted. 'We have been rearing a strange plant.' He described Alma's phenomena as 'hybrid flowers', rooted in her unconscious but nourished by the investigators' hopes and wishes. Fearing that he was becoming complicit in her inventions, he determined to crack down on her opportunities for fraud.

Fodor wondered whether Alma might be managing during the tea break to retrieve small objects from inside her underwear or her body. Perhaps Miss Scott sometimes neglected her surveillance duties in the lavatory cubicle. At the preliminary session of 3 May he asked Bremba to help Alma produce apports before she visited the ladies' room, and to try to curb Jimmy's practical jokes.

Bremba replied that his first responsibility was to his medium rather than to them. He told Fodor that Alma felt under great pressure at the Institute, and did not like so many people staring at her. She was also under strain at home, he said, as Les objected to her visiting Walton House at all.

'Yes,' said Fodor, 'what is the particular reason for that?'

'He doesn't like the idea of her being searched because he says if you are not convinced now, you never will be.'

'It is because we are bringing in people who will not accept our word,' said Fodor.

'Then he would say stop trying to tell them.'

'Well, then science would make no progress.'

'He is not interested in science.'

The Countess intervened: 'Couldn't you do something about Mr Fielding to make him interested?'

'Nothing.'

Fodor was annoyed with Les. 'The medium only comes two afternoons a week, when he is working,' he pointed out.

'He is a very stubborn man,' lamented Bremba.

Fodor was now having to battle both Alma's husband and her spirit guide over the right to inspect her body. To try to placate Les, Fodor improved the terms of Alma's arrangement with the Institute, doubling her fee to £2 per session. This amounted to £4 a week, almost as much as Les earned as a decorator and only £2 less than Fodor's own weekly pay. The retainer would be a significant drain on the Institute's resources but Fodor was determined to see the case through. He urged Alma to save her psychic power for the experiments and to take better care of herself.

On the telephone on Thursday, Alma told Fodor that she felt something feeding on her – 'When I eat, it does not seem to go into me' – and she kept being seized by urges to hurt her pets. 'Also, I want to be nasty with people. I have the awful feeling that I must do them harm. My husband said yesterday as I was talking to him on the landing that it was not at all me talking to him.' On Wednesday she had felt a whip strike her back, and weals had risen on her shoulders. Alma's surge of paranoia and anger may have stemmed from her feelings about Fodor. She sensed his suspicion.

On Friday 6 May Dr Wills collected Alma from Victoria station at half past two as usual. About three minutes into their car journey to South Kensington, she lifted her bag from her lap and cried out, 'What's this?' Dr Wills looked over: an inch-long terrapin was sitting on her skirt. 'Don't let it touch me!' shrieked Alma, recoiling, much as Mrs Taylor had recoiled from an invisible presence in the seance room the previous week. Dr Wills moved the tiny turtle to the back seat. Alma kept turning to look at it as they continued to Walton House: the dense, scaly flesh of the creature's head, feet and tail pushing out from the shell.

Alma told Fodor that while waiting to be served in Woolworth's the previous morning, she had the peculiar feeling of something crawling on her back. 'I said to myself that I will not turn round and tried to think what it was. Suddenly I knew. It was a tortoise. I turned around. There was a counter behind me full of live tortoises.'

Fodor tried to soothe Alma by telling her that she was so sensitive to the presence of others, living and dead, that she could feel them without seeing them. This was why she sensed the tortoise on her back. When she felt 'nasty' or empty, he told her, she might be tapping in to the experiences of spirits who had been cruel in life or who had died of starvation. She should not be alarmed by these feelings, he advised, but instead evaluate and reject them. They were not her own.

In a psychological analysis of the supernormal, external events were explained by internal turbulence; in a spiritualist analysis, the internal feelings were caused by an external agent. Fodor was trying to calm Alma with the idea that she was persecuted, not paranoid; haunted, not deranged. But privately he was convinced that her phenomena sprang from a damaged inner life, and he knew that the investigation might be making things worse.

At the International Institute that week, the horror writer Marjorie Bowen gave an evening lecture on ghosts in literature and in reality. The best spooky stories – or 'twilight tales', as she called them – existed on the cusp of fact and fiction.

On Sunday night Laurie drove Fodor down to Hampton Court, a south-western suburb of London, to meet a

medium who used a 'psychic telegraph' to communicate with the dead. Louisa Bolt and her manager, Mr
Ashdown, said that they had created this machine with
the help of her spirit guide, who in life had been an
inventor. Mr Ashdown explained to Fodor and Laurie
that the device was more efficient than the old-fashioned
spirit trumpet: it collected the messages of the dead in
spherical receptors, and then rapped them out in Morse
code. He was marketing the machine, along with the
Reflectograph and the Communigraph, in spiritualist
magazines.

Fodor and Laurie paid a guinea a head for a sitting
with Mrs Bolt and her device. As the instrument clicked
out its messages in the blue-lit room, they could sense
Mr Ashdown blowing at them, and they could dimly
see Mrs Bolt squirting them with puffs of cheap scent.
Laurie afterwards showed Fodor how easy it was to use
a magnet to make metal keys rap. The invention, they
realised, was a crude and greedy imposture.

Fodor had invited his friend Mercy Phillimore, the
general secretary of the London Spiritualist Alliance,
to supervise Alma's strip search before the session of
10 May. Alma stood naked before the searchers in the
library, her arms extended so that they could look at
her body from all sides. Miss Phillimore inspected each
piece of clothing before Alma put it on. She noticed
that some of the stitches joining the stockings to the
left leg of the knickers had come away; Mrs Taylor, the
librarian, fetched a needle and thread and sewed them

back together. Alma was menstruating, so the Countess brought her a fresh sanitary towel, which she first presented to Miss Phillimore for inspection.

The twenty sitters that afternoon included the celebrated medium Eileen Garrett, who had helped Fodor at Ash Manor and to whom he had appealed for help with Alma's case. Also present were C. V. C. Herbert, Fodor's counterpart at the Society for Psychical Research, and Sir Ernest Bennett, Labour MP for Cardiff Central and a well-known commentator on the supernormal. In 1934 Sir Ernest had made a BBC broadcast about haunted houses that elicited 1,300 letters from the public. He observed that in fiction a phantom usually had a definite purpose – it 'is bent on communicating some information, or calling attention to some tragic event, such as murder or suicide; it is quite determined to make its presence known and its demeanour is at times sinister and even menacing'. But in actual supernormal experiences, such as those relayed to him by BBC listeners, the ghost was 'a fleeing, fugitive thing', its message and meaning obscure. Sir Ernest speculated that hauntings were the dreams of the dead, communicated telepathically to the living. By this hypothesis, the poltergeist attacks in Alma's home were vivid shards of a ghost's fantasy. Fodor, by contrast, believed that Alma's phenomena were generated by her own nightmares and memories, acquiring physical energy as they spilt from her.

Miss Phillimore told the gathering that she had searched Alma thoroughly: 'I am absolutely and positively sure that she has nothing concealed about her.'

When Alma began to shudder at 4.30 p.m., Sir Ernest clasped her hands in his, and felt them throb; Miss Phillimore did the same and felt a heavy pulsing. An amethyst appeared in Alma's palm. The Countess caught Alma as she fell at 4.50 p.m., and found a copper coat button in her hand, with the profile of a woman's head picked out in enamel, turquoise and pearl. Alma became woozy at 5.50, just before a shiny insect arrived on her palm under the sheer glove. 'It's a beetle!' she cried, pulling away in horror. She was repulsed by the beetle, as she had been by the terrapin, as if she was becoming estranged from her own manifestations. Fodor fetched scissors to cut open the stocking and release a dry, dead scarab.

As usual, Alma had moved about a lot during the seance, walking with different people, climbing the stairs to the gallery, sitting and rising and turning. Fodor noticed that she had been mechanically moving her hands from her throat to her diaphragm, pressing her breast, rubbing her ribs, restlessly caressing herself, but Mercy Phillimore insisted that she could not have had anything hidden on her.

Fodor asked Eileen Garrett what she had made of Alma. Eileen said that she had detected only a weak psychic aura. She sensed that whatever supernatural force Alma possessed sprang from anger or fear. Eileen had perceived a square ceramic slab near her. 'I got it as though it were breathing,' she said, 'and she were sucking and drawing it towards her.' Alma struck her as being 'almost like a vampire'.

'She obviously receives all her power at this point,' she added, touching her diaphragm. 'I could feel the pull all the time.' She had seen the image of a baby around Alma, she said, and a zigzag of strong emotion. There was a blockage over the umbilicus that suggested a deep-seated shock. This, Eileen said, was linked to suffering over a pregnancy, and to the death of a child.

Eileen Garrett, like Fodor, believed that psychic gifts were rooted in psychological disturbance. She had her first supernormal experiences as a girl in Ireland, where she lived on a farm with her aunt and uncle. One day in about 1900, when she was seven, her Aunt Martha beat her in punishment for 'lying' about the invisible friends with whom she played. Eileen was angry. Afterwards she sat watching her aunt's ducklings paddling on the farm lake. She leant forward from the lake's edge and seized a baby duck, pushed it under the water, held it there until its wings stopped heaving against her hands. She lifted out the duckling's body, its feathers sodden with water, and laid it on the grass next to her. Then she grabbed at another duckling, pressed it down, held it below the surface of the lake. Soon all of the ducklings were dead, laid out around her, the mother duck alone on the water. As Eileen surveyed the collection of dark, soft clumps on the grass, she saw a grey tendril of smoke swirl up from each corpse.

Aunt Martha was distraught at the drowning of her ducks. She told Eileen that she was a wicked child and punished her again. When Eileen was next allowed out she found more creatures to kill: a crow, a rabbit. Suddenly she stopped, sickened by what she was doing. But she thought about what she had seen filtering into the sky after the ducklings' deaths. Had their souls lifted from their dense bodies to dissolve on the air? She had felt something like joy, she recalled, when she saw the mist rising. She wondered if grey plumes like these had issued from the bodies of her parents when they died. Her mother had drowned herself in a well in 1893, when Eileen was two weeks old, and her father had shot himself six weeks later.

Some months after the duckling incident a hunting party passed through the farm. A huntsman in a bright jacket noticed Eileen and snatched her up to his saddle. She was handed from man to laughing man. 'Their crude caresses frightened me,' she wrote later, 'and I resisted in the only way I knew – fighting with tooth and nail against rough petting – until at last they let me go.' Afterwards she lay on her bed and breathed so slowly and deeply that she felt herself move past her fingertips, above her head. She managed to numb herself, projecting her mind to a place outside her body. She felt at one with blades of grass; she inhabited the song of birds.

Eileen married young and moved to England. She had two sons, who contracted meningitis in infancy and died within five months of one another. Eileen saw the grey smoke rise, curling, from the bodies of her babies. She then had a daughter, who lived, and a third son who survived for only a few hours. After his death she found that she could see things through her bones. Her feet, her knees, the nape of her neck were weirdly wired. She heard through her skin instead of her ears. It was as if her senses had multiplied, or spread, as if her whole body was attuned to new frequencies and she could perceive beings unknown to others. Her husband, who was having an affair, was dismissive. He said that Eileen's 'visioning' was a sickness inherited from her mad parents. She left him, taking their surviving child with her, and embarked on a career as a psychic. She was able to transform the electric agony of the third bereavement, in which all her nerves seemed to see and hear, into a source of power.

Eileen had discovered – when the huntsmen groped her, when her husband betrayed her, when her sons died – that she could banish pain by forgetting and floating free. She could enter trances in which she lost herself and became a channel for other voices. On returning to consciousness she did not know what the voices had used her body to say, but she felt that this 'mechanism for diversity' liberated her from an inner life so intense that it threatened to break her apart.

Alma had managed to produce apports without visiting the ladies' room in the tea break, just as Fodor had requested, and she had impressed Sir Ernest Bennett, Mercy Phillimore and, to an extent, Eileen Garrett. She had now materialised a total of almost fifty objects at the Institute. But C. V. C. Herbert of the SPR was dubious. 'On one occasion she fell over *backwards*,' he told Fodor, 'which I have never seen except on the stage.' Herbert pointed out that the tiger scratches were all on parts of the body that Alma could reach with her hands, and that the investigators had not carried out an 'internal examination' before the sitting.

Fodor knew that he needed to prove that Alma was not hiding objects inside her body, but he dared not ask her to submit to a vaginal inspection. 'We had reason to think that Mrs Fielding would revolt at the idea,' he said, 'that her husband would put his foot down, and our experiments would come to an end before we had settled anything.' The women on the investigative team refused to countenance an internal exam. 'For reasons of delicacy, all my lady associates fought against this test. They argued that the size, shape and number of apports militated against genital concealment. They were afraid it would be the last straw to break the camel's back.' But he had an idea: with a machine that could see through solid flesh, he might obtain an image that would satisfy the spiritualists and the psychical researchers alike.

FOURTEEN

The fastest invisible rays

Rain fell on London on Friday 13 May for the first time since February. In *Two Worlds*, Horace Leaf published a rapturous piece about Alma's 'undoubtedly supernormal' phenomena and Fodor's achievement in developing her powers from the 'cruder' poltergeist phase:

> Dr Nandor Fodor is to be congratulated on the excellent way in which he deals with his mediums. He is unpretentious, sympathetic, and has a natural enthusiasm that is contagious. He shows a thorough appreciation of the intensely sensitive nature of mediumship, and the disposition and temperament of the medium. He puts everybody at ease without infringing the watchfulness demanded by science.

Leaf's article, the first detailed report of Alma's case, hailed Fodor as the mentor of a remarkable materialisation medium. The article was illustrated with a picture of Alma ('Mrs X') sitting rigid in her resplendent, many-chained silver necklace, like a warrior chief.

It was Fodor's forty-third birthday, and he had secretly arranged for two men to set up a portable X-ray machine in the small seance room adjoining the upstairs studio. Today he would learn whether Alma had played them all for fools.

Alma walked up and down naked after undressing in the library. She was handed a pair of pink woollen tights to wear in place of the usual loose knickers and silk stockings. Once dressed, she followed Fodor and Laurie to the small seance room, but she drew back when she saw the two X-ray operatives and their machine. X-rays reminded her of hospital, she said; they gave her the jitters, and left her nervous and upset for days. One of the technicians assured her that the scan was much less 'enduring' than a medical X-ray. Alma said that Les would not like it, and she must speak to him about it. Laurie suggested that he or Fodor could talk to Les, but she said no, she must discuss it with him herself.

Fodor pointed out to Alma how bad it would look to the sitters waiting for her in the next room if she refused to be X-rayed. The procedure was not designed to catch her out, he said, but to establish whether the apports were already hovering round her, as Eileen Garrett had suggested. 'It would mean a tremendous feather in your cap if a photograph by the fastest invisible rays could prove something of this sort,' said Fodor. 'You are always a sport, and you must keep up your past standard.'

By presenting the X-ray as an exploration of super-normal mechanisms rather than a test of her honesty, Fodor made it hard for Alma to refuse. She agreed to have her pelvis scanned, and lay down on a couch while the operator made an exposure. Fodor had hoped for a second X-ray, of her chest, but was afraid of agitating her too much. The technicians took the plate downstairs to be developed in a van that they had parked outside Walton House.

A large group had again convened in the main seance room, among them Eileen Garrett and the magicians Will Goldston and Maurice Goldin. Alma produced one apport before tea: a fossilised ammonite shell.

At four, while tea was being served, Fodor was told that the X-ray operators had bungled the job. He informed Alma that the men had failed to expose the film, adding that they were terribly upset about their blunder and likely to lose their jobs. To his relief, she volunteered to have another X-ray taken. Fodor ushered her into the small room and this time signalled to the scanners to make two exposures: one of her pelvic region and one of her chest.

When Alma returned to the studio, Fodor intensified the surveillance. He sat at one end of the room and posted Laurie at the other. As Alma walked towards Fodor, he saw her glance at him several times. At another point she seemed conscious of Laurie's eyes upon her. She changed direction, only to be faced by Dr Wills sitting on a small platform, watching.

One of the operatives beckoned to Fodor and Laurie, and told them that the chest X-ray had revealed two objects at Alma's left breast, shaped like a heart and a pin.

While Alma walked up and down, Fodor and Laurie noticed her clasped hands creep slowly up from her chest to her throat. She fiddled with the neck of the suit. Fodor whispered to Laurie, 'She's got it now.' They asked her to spread her hands. Alma showed them her palms, which were empty, then turned her back on Fodor and resumed her pacing. Fodor and Laurie saw tugs at the suit fabric which suggested that her hands were up at the neck again.

As Alma turned to face Fodor, she swayed and staggered. Her companions supported her as she swooned to the floor. She was breathing rapidly. After two minutes she sat up and unclasped her hands. In her palm, outside the stocking, was a small silver locket, shaped like a heart and inset with coloured stones. It promised to be a match for one of the objects revealed by the X-ray.

Florence Hall approached Laurie, who was standing by the conservatory door, and quietly asked him about the X-ray. He told her that two items had been detected at Alma's left breast and he was now waiting to see how the next one would be produced. Mrs Hall began to watch closely too.

Just after five o'clock Alma's hands dropped to her sides. She pointed to her right leg and said that she felt something brushing against it. Fodor undid the tape binding the suit at her ankle and found a small pin-shaped brooch inside the leg. He guessed that because of their scrutiny she had not dared push this final apport through the neck, and had instead dropped it down from within.

It was now 5.10 p.m., and Alma claimed to feel too unwell to continue. Fodor broke up the seance.

While Alma was undressing in the library, the searchers saw a red patch above her left breast, as if something had been pressed against it. Mary Dundas noticed her fumbling in her tights.

'Oh, those scratches again!' exclaimed Alma as she pulled on her cardigan. Her left arm was raked with five long marks from the shoulder to the elbow; blood was seeping from one.

Before leaving the Institute, Alma asked after the X-ray scan. Fodor told her that the plate would not be developed that day.

The researchers stayed at Walton House to examine the scans. The abdominal X-ray revealed nothing unusual. It showed only the sweep of Alma's hip bones, the knobs of her spine, the hooks and eyes of her corset, the sharp silhouette of the safety pin with which she held up her stockings. But the chest scan showed two alien objects: in front of the steel-toothed zip of the boiler suit, against Alma's bending ribs, were the shapes of a pin and a heart. When the brooch and the locket were laid against the transparency, their outlines corresponded exactly.

Fodor realised that this single image nullified everything that Alma had produced in the past ten weeks. Even if real supernatural events had taken place in Beverstone Road in February, they could have no value now.

Fodor had tried always to give Alma the benefit of the doubt, but the scan proved how cannily she had worked her tricks. He tried to piece together how her methods had developed. In the early days of the investigation, she must have brought small objects from home in her handbag and, when she used the ladies' room on arrival at Walton House, transferred them to accessible hiding places on her body: the corset, an armpit, the elastic around a knicker leg. Once Fodor instituted the strip searches, she had been forced to become more devious. She must have concealed the items in her vagina when she visited the ladies' room on arrival, so that the searchers could not see them when she undressed, retrieved them when she visited the cloakroom for a second time, during the tea break – however closely she was supervised in the lavatory, no one would stop her from putting a hand between her legs to dry herself – and swiftly transferred them to parts of her body that she could easily reach. She had to adjust her routine again when Fodor asked that she stop visiting the ladies' room in the tea break. She must instead have made the second switch in the library as she changed her clothes, by rummaging quickly in her knickers and lodging the apports elsewhere. In the seance room, she managed to tease the objects out of her clothing, using falls, faints and shudders to disguise her actions. Fodor had noticed that apports often appeared when she was turning or bending or the sitters were distracted – by a knock at the door, for instance, or the clatter of her teacup hitting the floor.

To confirm his theory, Fodor asked Miss Scott and the Countess whether they had seen Alma put a hand down her tights at any point after the strip search that afternoon. Miss Scott said that she had noticed Alma tuck her vest into the tights several times, while pulling at the suspender straps on her corset. The Countess, too, had seen Alma fiddle with the straps, so much so that she had suggested to her that she might be more comfortable in an elastic stretch corset, without suspender attachments. Alma, tetchily, had said that only her own corset gave her the necessary support – a curious claim, the Countess thought, since the corset was loose-fitting and all of its bone stiffeners had been removed.

Dr Wills informed Fodor that on the drive to Walton House that day, Alma had told him that George was in love with her. Les was 'relatively impotent', she said, and was jealous of George, who he wanted out of the house. This undermined even more of her claims. Fodor had guessed that Alma was drawn to George, but if her feelings were reciprocated it was all the more likely that he had colluded with her tricks. George or his sister-in-law Rose were the sole witnesses to the psychic shoplifting in Croydon, the magic mice in Alma's house, the burning necklace and the potato-wine incidents. The attraction between Alma and George might explain why Les, too, had for so long gone along with her tall tales. He was competing for Alma's attention with his lodger as well as the Institute.

Fodor wondered about Alma's other feats. Some, such as the snapping and flying objects, could be attributed to expert legerdemain. Others might have required only psychological manipulation. At the Institute, Alma was surrounded by people who believed that supernormal events could take place, who expected that, in her presence, they might, and who very much hoped that they would. Fodor knew that smells, touches and temperature changes could all be induced by expectation and suggestion, and the effects were contagious: when one person felt sick or dizzy or cold, others were more likely to feel the same. Perhaps Alma's cups and saucers seemed to fly spontaneously only because no one was looking at her hands as she flung them. Perhaps Fodor did not detect the terracotta lamp after the visit to the Victoria & Albert Museum because propriety prevented him from thoroughly checking Alma's chest. Perhaps Alma had secretly bought a ring in a Croydon branch of Woolie's before the trip to the seaside, pointed out an identical ring at the jewellery counter of the Bognor branch, and then slipped the original into Fodor's film canister.

Fodor was fiercely disappointed. He had staked more on Alma than on any psychic subject. He had filed reports of her wonders to the *Journal of the American Society for Psychical Research* and invited the grandees of the psychical world to see her at work. Only that morning, he and she had been acclaimed in print by Horace Leaf. He felt betrayed by her deceit, and fearful about how the news would be received. Her fraud would dismay the Institute's patrons, as the latest in a run of failed investigations, and it would make prospective subjects uneasy, queering the pitch for future experiments. It would enrage the psychic press, which took Fodor's exposures of mediums as attacks on spiritualism, and help *Psychic News* to defeat his libel suit. All of this would threaten the Institute and Fodor's role within it. His anger was tinged with self-disgust. He had facilitated the fraud by his longing, his need to believe.

The other investigators were shocked by Alma's duplicity. The Countess, Alfons, Helen Russell Scott, Florence Hall, Dr Wills, Wilfred Becker and Laurie Evans had shivered along with Alma, felt their bellies tremble in sympathy, their heads pound and their skin creep. Fake mediums, said the Countess, made capital 'out of the profoundest emotions of their fellow-humans – out of their love and their fear'. She had felt great tenderness towards Alma, being joined to her, in Fodor's words, by 'bonds of sympathy and of love'. And if Alma had not been genuine, she had instead been cynical, violent, crude, mendacious. This amiable woman had vandalised her home, thrown things at her family, scratched and burnt herself, stolen from Woolworth's, strapped a finch to her leg, sneaked stones and jewels in and out of her vagina, smashed the Walton House china, and lied to her friends at the Institute again and again.

Fodor was still baffled by Alma's motive. The most obvious explanation for the fraud was that she had been in it for the money. The Institute had paid her about £18 to date, which, even with apport and travel expenses of a few shillings a week, was a tidy sum. But the Fieldings were not hard up. And besides, Alma's psychic phenomena had started in destruction and expense – all the cracked crockery, the broken ornaments, the dented furniture hardly spoke of a woman trying to use her gifts for gain. Even her psychic shoplifting was more anarchic than avaricious: she acquired items only to give them away. There were emotional benefits to her trickery – the warmth and admiration she found at Walton House, the escape from domestic drudgery and marital tension – but they did not adequately explain why Alma subjected herself to so much risk, and inflicted harm on herself, her belongings, her family.

Fodor noticed that Alma had often undercut her cleverness with exhibitionism. She seemed to flirt with revelation, performing a dance of confession and concealment, a restless shuffle between exposing and hiding the truth. Her attempt to bamboozle the psychical researchers had been silly, childish, a lark, a wheeze; but also serious, compulsive, unstoppable. The possibility of being caught – the erotic thrill of the chase – may have been intrinsic to her motivation. Fodor's neighbour Dick Woodward had also seemed to dally with disclosure. 'I am afraid you will catch me in what I do,' he muttered to himself as he danced around Fodor's flat in a haze of whisky: 'I want to talk.' Perhaps Alma's hoaxing, like his, was an enactment of something else: a secret that wanted to be told.

Fodor asked the others to let him persist a little longer, not just to delay making his failure public but to get a clearer sense of Alma's method and motive. They agreed to continue as if nothing had happened. The investigators would pretend that the X-ray scans had not been developed. Everyone was dissembling now.

Part Three

THE GHOST

'The "uncanny" is that class of the terrifying
which leads back to something long known to
us, once very familiar'

Sigmund Freud, 'The Uncanny' (1919)

Alma (standing) with her grandmother, Jessie, her sister, Doris, and her mother, Alice, circa 1912; Alma's father and brother, Charles and Charlie, 1925; and (left) Les in uniform, circa 1916

FIFTEEN

Who is this little child?

On arrival at Walton House on Tuesday 17 May, Alma told Fodor that her belly had been ticking like a clock all morning. She and a friend were on a tram in Croydon when it started, she said. The friend searched Alma's bag and clothes but found nothing: the sound came from somewhere inside her, below the waist.

In the preliminary hypnosis session, Alma sank back in the armchair with her head against the cushion, her eyes shut and her face blank. She was wearing a pleated skirt and a thick cardigan over a striped shirt with huge triangular lapels. Seated around her were the Countess, Helen Russell Scott, Florence Hall, Dr Wills, Laurie Evans and Fodor. Laurie and the Countess held Alma's hands as she went into trance. Then a child came through.

'My mummy, my mummy!' cried Alma in the tiny, high-pitched voice of a ghost girl.

'Who are you?' asked the Countess.

'My mummy. Me Pam.'

'Who is your mummy? Is Mrs Fielding your mummy?'

'No.'

'Who are you coming to?'

'My mummy come to see me.'

Alma started to breathe very fast and to roll her head from side to side.

'Is Bremba there?' asked the Countess. 'Can you speak to us?'

'Good afternoon,' intoned Bremba.

'Who is this little child?' the Countess asked him.

'I don't know yet.'

'It is not Mrs Fielding's?'

'Oh no.'

When asked about the spirit tiger, Bremba assured them that it was very fond of Alma, and clawed her only in play. It sounded like an outsize version of a witch's familiar; or like the pet leopard in *Bringing Up Baby*, a screwball romantic comedy starring Katharine Hepburn and Cary Grant that had recently opened in London.

'I would rather like it to scratch me,' said the Countess. 'Do you think that would be possible?'

Dr Wills agreed: 'And I wouldn't mind being scratched either, in the interests of science!' The doctor was getting flippant, now that he knew about the fraud.

'All the time you say you do not mind,' said Bremba, reprovingly, 'there is a secret fear in your heart.'

'Is it still Jimmy that is concerned in the apports?' asked Fodor.

'Jimmy is just looking on,' said Bremba. 'Jimmy wishes to apologise for Sunday night.'

'We know nothing about it,' said Fodor. 'What happened?'

'Ask her.'

When Alma emerged from trance, Fodor asked what Jimmy had been up to. On Sunday, she said, she and her family went to see Dolores Smith give clairvoyance at Queen's Hall. Afterwards, at Rose's house in Haslemere Road, George and his brother William had been laughing about something that happened at the seance. Jimmy, as if in protest at their mockery, threw a cup and saucer across the room and smashed one of Rose's dinner plates.

Fodor noted the return of Jimmy's aggression: 'As a scapegoat, Jimmy was still very useful. The incident spoke eloquently of Mrs Fielding's instinct for retaliation which was, perhaps, the basic motive of all Poltergeist phenomena.' It was obvious to him that Alma had herself thrown the plate, the cup, the saucer. But it was strange that she was angry with George, her accomplice, for laughing at the supernormal. She seemed confused and defensive. Perhaps she sensed that she had been found out.

To prove where Alma stowed the apports as she was being searched, Fodor considered instructing the female investigators to feel for hidden objects under her labia while she was undressing, but he guessed that they would not go along with this. Instead, he asked them to make Alma's manoeuvres more difficult by holding her hands as they pulled on her tights in the library. She would then be obliged to massage the apports up from her underwear while she was in the seance room, with everyone watching. Fodor speculated about the 'quite unusual muscular agility' with which she must be manipulating the objects. His curiosity was acquiring a sexually inquisitive edge, edging further into voyeurism.

While naked in the library with the female searchers that afternoon, Alma swung a leg into the air – so high that she was almost doing the splits – and rested her outstretched limb on a chair so that Mrs Kelly, the Institute's treasurer, could see into the hollow at the top of her thigh. It was a defiant self-exposure, an angry answer to the investigators' suspicions. Mrs Kelly and the Countess dressed Alma, pulling a pair of tights on to her, tucking in her vest and adjusting her suspenders – it had been agreed that she must not be allowed to touch herself in any way. Dr Wills came in to the library to fasten the customary bandages.

In the large seance room at 4 p.m., Alma complained of discomfort. The tights were too small, she said, and were cutting into her. She tugged at them irritably as she sat down. She remarked that the atmosphere in the room was strange. 'She fairly well suggested that we are thinking of her vagina as a hiding place,' said Fodor. 'She said that she feels a pain down below. She rather seemed to suspect my mind.'

Alma paced the studio with different sitters. At one point, Laurie whispered to Fodor that she seemed to have pushed something up to her chest, and Fodor indicated to the Countess that she should search her. The Countess put her hand to Alma's chest, felt around the right breast and the hollow of the left, then continued to her ribs for a more thorough probing. This was an unusually direct and humiliating examination. Alma silently allowed it.

At 5.20 p.m. Alma remarked: 'I think we're going to be unlucky.' Fodor suggested that they bring the sitting to a close.

In the library with the female sitters after the seance, Alma said that she felt dreadful, very sick. Then she cried out that the tiger had scratched her, and when the searchers checked they found marks between her shoulder blades. As she lay down on the library sofa, she said that she was swelling. The other women noticed that her belly was bigger, the abdomen so large that her skirt would not close.

They measured her waist and found that it was thirty-two inches at its widest point. The flesh seemed to be moving. Dr Wills came in to the library and listened to Alma's stomach: he could sense a sort of muscular contraction. Alma said that she felt throbbing. The Countess heard pulsing inside. Fodor was called in.

Alma looked pregnant, and when Fodor touched her stomach he detected a light thudding in the flesh. He thought at first that it was her heartbeat, but when he touched the Countess's stomach, by way of comparison, the pulse was far fainter. Alma had once told Fodor that producing apports was like giving birth. Now, when he bent his ear to her bulging abdomen, he could hear a rhythmic tick like the beat of a foetal heart.

Alma's swelling seemed connected to the incubus visits, about which only Fodor knew. He was reminded of the case of Esther Cox of Nova Scotia, who had swollen up in bed one night in 1878, apparently impregnated by a demon. The evil presence went on to terrorise her and her family by lighting fires, throwing objects, scratching her skin with crosses. Esther's phenomena began after a shoemaker tried to rape her.

Alma undid her skirt to massage her stomach. She put a hand between her legs, then clasped both hands on her knees and complained of a sudden pain. 'Give me a drink,' she whispered. A glass of water was lifted to her lips. She opened her hand to reveal a small cut stone and an old coin. She was trembling all over. She said that the objects were burning her, and that her thigh was stinging. The Countess and Mrs Kelly felt Alma's leg, and detected a nut-shaped bulge beneath the fabric of her suit. She said that the back of her hip was swelling. Fodor felt above her buttocks, and confirmed that her flesh seemed to have expanded.

Since Alma's corset had been undone, the men left the room to let her finish dressing. As she stood up, a thick piece of linen, four inches square, fell to the floor. She straight away leant down, picked it up and smelt it. The cloth had no odour, she said. An artificial scarab beetle also fell from her: it was the size and shape of the protuberance on her thigh, which had now disappeared.

When Fodor came back, he was handed the square of linen. He sniffed the fabric, and made out a faint acrid tang that reminded him of vaginal discharge or urine. He guessed that Alma had wrapped the scarab, the stone and the coin in this piece of cloth and pushed them into her vaginal passage. Because she had been forced to wear tights, and was closely watched before and during the seance, she had been unable to retrieve the package until she inflated her stomach and massaged herself in the library. The linen had fallen because she had not afterwards managed to push it far enough back into its hiding place.

Fodor took Alma into the weighing room, where he handed Dr Wills the cloth. Fodor saw Alma's eyes widen with fear: 'It does not smell,' she repeated. Dr Wills said that he had a cold, so was unable to smell anything anyway. Fodor thought that Alma seemed very distracted: she paid no attention to the fact that her weight had fallen to 7 stone 3½ lbs.

Alma's abdomen had returned to its usual girth of twenty-nine inches by the time she left the Institute, and she was able to do up her skirt. On the journey to Victoria station in Dr Wills's car, Fodor sat next to her on the back seat. He felt around her hips, and confirmed that the flesh above her buttocks had subsided. Though Alma's methods of producing apports were becoming clearer to him, the swelling had been weird. She seemed that day to have played out a pregnancy and birth. She had arrived at Walton House with a ticking in her tummy. She had complained of an ache in her stomach, then throbbed and ballooned before bringing forth objects. Perhaps Alma had symbolic as well as practical reasons for choosing her vagina as a hiding place.

In Fodor's log of the Thornton Heath case, a narrow strip of paper is glued in to the entry of 17 May, the day that Alma's stomach swelled and the cloth fell. 'Mrs Fielding's baby girl was 3 months old when she died,' reads the typed insert. 'She was not christened but her name was to have been June. There was another baby boy aged 15 months. He was called Lawrence Peter. He also died.' It is unclear exactly when, or why, Alma gave this information. Fodor's analysis of the afternoon's events continues on the next page, without reference to the children.

Laurie took the square of cloth for analysis at John Bell & Croyden, a renowned pharmacist in Marylebone. The examination revealed cells, bacteria and microscopic traces of blood that the chemist deemed 'very likely caused by Vaginal discharge'. The apports must have been wrapped in this linen as Fodor had guessed. This explained how Alma had managed to conceal and quickly release sharp objects. By tugging a corner of the cloth package, she could pull several items out of herself at once.

On Thursday 19 May, reports reached London that German troops were gathering near the Czech border and Hitler was threatening to annexe the Sudetenland, a western region of Czechoslovakia populated chiefly by ethnic Germans. The British warned that they would intervene if he invaded. After several weeks of stasis, war seemed imminent again.

Fodor spoke to Alma over the telephone that morning. She was barely audible. She told him that she could not keep coming to the Institute. 'I am going crackers.'

'Is it domestic trouble?' he asked. He was struggling to remain sympathetic.

No, Alma said: she kept falling over, and her stomach kept swelling up. It had inflated four times on Wednesday. And last night she had a ghastly experience that she dared not disclose to Les.

Alma's voice was low, cracked and halting. Fodor relented a little, and asked her about her experience.

She had woken, she said, to the touch of something hard and cold. She felt sheer horror and was unable to move. After a few seconds the 'thing' left her and she heard the flapping of wings. In the morning she woke limp and wan, with two blood-clotted punctures on her neck. Alma said she was afraid that she was going mad.

Fodor told her that if she came to the Institute for a private sitting on Friday, he and his colleagues would help her to find an explanation. In the meantime, she should keep her bedroom light on at night.

Fodor decided to visit Alma at home without warning that same afternoon. Dr Wills agreed to drive him and Laurie down to Thornton Heath. If they took Alma by surprise, Fodor reasoned, they would be able to see if she had any marks on her neck.

George opened the door to the researchers. He had 'an ugly look' in his eye, Fodor observed, and hesitated before letting them in. He then turned away without a word. Les and Don were out at work, and Alma was in the kitchen. She called to her guests that she was washing herself, and hurried upstairs to dress. She took a long time but came down eventually, said Fodor, 'trim and nice '.

The usually agreeable George was in a belligerent mood. He told Fodor that Alma was 'queer' all of yesterday and again today. He did not want her to carry on visiting the Institute. In three months' time, he predicted, he would have to buy a wreath for her funeral.

Alma pulled her hair aside for Fodor and Dr Wills to examine her neck. Below her ear they found two punctures, an eighth of an inch apart. The skin was swollen and red, with faint, straight scratches by each incision. The wounds were healing – they had not been made within the last few hours, said Dr Wills, and might well have been inflicted at midnight as Alma claimed. She seemed to have been telling the truth about that at least. Laurie took a photograph.

Since George seemed so hostile, Fodor suggested that they go elsewhere to discuss the night's events. Alma took Fodor, Laurie and Dr Wills to the house of her friend Mabel, who was at work in the Welcome Café.

Alma spoke into Fodor's voice recorder as she told her story. Her account of the midnight attack was stripped back, plain and horrible.

She had gone up to her room at 10.15 p.m., she said. As she approached the bed, she heard a fluttering noise and felt a vibration in the air. She fell asleep but at about midnight woke with the sensation that there was something on her left-hand side, 'something like a body'. She could not move or speak, and she sensed blood draining from her. 'I felt something hard and round pressed into my neck. I felt no pain but pins and needles all along my neck. The thing itself was quite still. It was the size of a man's head.' Something seemed to be biting her, she said. 'I thought that whatever was pinching my neck and pressing on the muscles was causing me to be paralysed. You want to pull away and you cannot. Did you ever have a dream of trying to run away from something but not being able to move?'

'There was no noise?'

'No. This thing was quite still. The body pressing against me was a dead weight. It felt cold, nasty and there was a smell. The same smell we had before, passing across the bed like bad meat.' Alma said that she had smelt something similar as a child. 'A neighbour's husband died. He had a growth in his head. It had burst after he died. The coffin was not screwed down. Mrs Anderson, the widow, did not want to go in and asked my mother to go. I hung on to her skirt and got as far as the door. The smell wafted out. It was horrible.'

In *Psychic Self-Defence*, a manual published in 1930, the occultist author Dion Fortune warned that a feeling of weight on the chest at night, 'as if someone were kneeling on the sleeper', was a sign of attack by an elemental being: 'the weight is due to the concentration of etheric substance or ectoplasm'. Fortune identified other markers of psychic assault, including several that Alma had reported: nervous fatigue, flying objects, an odour of decomposition.

The 'thing' left suddenly, Alma said. 'I heard the same flapping noise, a sudden swish through the air with a regular beat. It went towards the window.' Alma had left the top of the window ajar when she went to bed. She had also left the curtains open, so that the room was dimly lit by the street lamp outside, but she saw not even a shadow of her attacker as it departed. Exhausted, she fell asleep.

When Alma woke in the morning, her neck felt sore. 'I put my hand up and felt two little lumps. Then I looked into the glass. I had to stretch my neck to see it. The thought crossed my mind that I scratched myself. But I don't think I could scratch myself like that.' She could taste blood: 'that peculiar tang which one gets when a tooth is bleeding'.

Alma was very cold, she said. 'My hands were dead, white and bloodless, my face awful. I felt as after an operation when I lost an enormous lot of blood and had the feeling that I was gradually sinking.' Les had felt the same way when shrapnel hit him in the thigh during the war, she said: 'He was bleeding to death. He had then the sensation of gradually sinking.'

Recently, Alma said, Les had been experiencing these sensations again, and he had heard a fluttering in the bedroom. 'He has been complaining of feeling terrible every morning. For some time he has been dreaming that someone cut his throat. I put it down to the war. He had this dream before the trouble in our house started. He has it once a month. He says he is fighting. He is in the war in his dream.'

Alma added: 'I will tell you of a strange dream. Sometimes I feel that I am not here, that I am not really alive. I feel that I died on the operating table. I always felt that way since a certain kidney operation that it was not me at all. It seems to me as if another person took possession of my body.'

'I often dream that I am in a hall of coffins,' she continued. 'There are some steps leading up from it. I am not sure how many coffins are there. Lots of coffins. I seem to come out of one of them. But I am not in the coffin. I am standing and watching.' She said that she tried to wake out of the dream but could not. 'It feels that I am dead and want to get back to my body. I feel that whatever comes out of that coffin, I am trying to get back into my body when I try to wake up, but I cannot get back. When I wake up my heart is beating terribly. I cannot breathe.'

'You must get it out of your head that you are not yourself,' Fodor told her.

'Nothing can get it out of my head,' said Alma. After her operation, she said, she had told Les, 'I am not really here. I am dead. You don't know it. You cannot really hear me.' When she touched Les or George, she claimed, they did not feel her. Nor did they hear her steps. 'Since that operation I don't feel as if I were walking. I never have the feeling of walking but a sensation of floating.' Alma was describing a radical dissociation, in which her spirit had divided from her body, and she had herself become a ghost, her foothold in the world shadowy, insubstantial.

'Who is then the present Mrs Fielding?' Fodor asked.

'You know that I am always kind to animals,' said Alma. 'I always have been. Yet I have the awful feeling that I want to hurt them. My cat's back toe is cut off right at the joint. It is sliced off clean. I have a horrible feeling that I did it, but I did not intend to do it.'

In Patrick Hamilton's *Gas Light*, first staged in 1938, a man tries to persuade his wife that she is insane, that she commits 'fantastic, meaningless mischiefs' such as removing pictures from walls and hiding tiny items. He accuses her of injuring the paw of the family's dog. Alma, as if guilt or suspicion had possessed her, was accusing herself of a similar attack. Having flirted with the occult, and lied to those who were trying to help her, she feared now that a hostile force had invaded her, and was sending her into fugue states so that it could act out its violence. Alma said that, like Les, she sometimes woke screaming at night. She screamed when Les touched her.

There was a peculiar parallel between Les and Alma's night experiences. Both felt drained of blood, paralysed, prey to terrifying visions. They had both been similarly helpless when the poltergeist first struck. Les had been lying in bed with bloody, toothless gums, while Alma's pelvis had burnt and pulsed. Perhaps the poltergeist's violence drew on Les's memories as well as Alma's.

According to Fodor's friend Hereward Carrington, the 'trench dreams' experienced by shell-shocked soldiers were symptoms of repressed fear. They were products of the 'long periods of tension, of waiting… expecting an attack, never knowing at what moment, and how, the enemy is going to strike.' Les's nightmares may have been revived by the threat of another war, in which his only son would be required to serve. The horrible images that woke him at night were not only flashbacks but also premonitions.

In J. B. Priestley's play *I Have Been Here Before*, serialised in the *Daily Mail* in April 1938, a married couple meet a German professor in a Yorkshire inn. The husband tells the professor that he has been 'half-dotty' since serving in the war, while his young wife is fixated by fortune telling and horoscopes, 'always longing for marvels and miracles, not even wanting to be sane'. He is caught in the pain of the past while she flees into fantasies of the future. The professor tells them that they are experiencing the same phenomenon: 'We each live a fairy tale created by ourselves. We move along a spiral track. What has happened before – many times perhaps – will probably happen again.' Priestley based his play on the theory of eternal recurrence advanced by the Russian esotericist P. D. Ouspensky. For Fodor, this kind of time travel was a psychological rather than a metaphysical event: as Freud argued, there were those so snared by the past that they could do nothing but repeat it.

Fodor cancelled the sittings with Alma on Tuesdays and Fridays, which had been advertised in *Light*. 'The public sittings with Mrs Fielding will have to be stopped for an uncertain period,' he told C. V. C. Herbert of the SPR. 'She is suffering from the strain and we have decided to keep her in private sittings for some time to come.'

Alma seemed more disturbed than ever. To find the origin of her phenomena, Fodor realised, he would have to take her dreams and inventions as seriously as if they had been real.

SIXTEEN

The cunning of ten thousand little kittens

Fodor invited Eileen Garrett to Walton House in the afternoon of Friday 20 May, in the hope that she might relieve Alma of her frightening new phenomena. Alma wore a silver crucifix. A lit stick of incense was placed on a round table at the centre of the circle, and the sitters – Alma, Eileen, the Countess, Dr Wills, Fodor and Laurie – recited the Lord's Prayer. Mrs Hall, as usual, made notes.

When Bremba's voice emerged from Alma, Fodor asked for his explanation of the bites on her neck. Bremba said that while Alma was undergoing a kidney operation a year earlier, her body had been taken over by the soul of an Indian girl, and that Alma's own soul, in the form of the blood-sucking bird, was now returning for sustenance. Bremba said that the researchers must kill the bird in order to release Alma's spirit and enable it to return to her body and oust the Indian girl.

Dr Wills asked: 'Is it your wish that her own soul should come back completely into her own body?'

'Yes,' said Bremba. 'When this is done she will be healthy and the flesh firm on her bones.'

'What shall we do?' asked Fodor.

'There is only one thing to do,' Bremba replied. 'To wait for it.' He advised the researchers to stake out the bird while Alma and Les were in bed. They should leave the bedroom light on and the windows open, he said, and not make a move until the bird had settled on Alma.

'What then?' asked Fodor.

'Shoot it?' asked Laurie.

'In any way you please,' said Bremba.

'How shall we know it is the right bird?' asked Laurie.

'It has an animal's body. I think you call them bats.'

'A large bat?' asked Fodor.

'Take her to the Zoological Gardens. Do not rouse her suspicions, but point out the vampire bats there and watch her reactions.'

Laurie interjected. 'It is a purely practical question, but what is her husband going to say if we arrive with traps and rifles? Is he going to consent to it?'

'I will see to that,' Bremba assured him.

'Then we will do the rest,' said Laurie.

Bremba was vague about when the bat would next appear ('I cannot tell you that. I am not allowed in the Middle Sphere') but he had thoughts on how to destroy it. He recommended that the researchers catch it in a net and wring its neck.

Fodor guessed that Alma was familiar with the Dracula story. Bram Stoker's gothic novel of 1897 had inspired two recent movies starring the

Hungarian-American actor Bela Lugosi, whom Fodor had known in New York. In Stoker's version of the myth, Dracula's victims become vampires too. They sleep in coffins by day, and rise by night to seek fresh blood. The hall of coffins in Alma's dream was an image straight out of a vampire movie.

Fodor told Bremba that they had a powerful medium in the circle that day who might be able to help restore Alma's soul. He asked Bremba if he would like Eileen Garrett's spirit guide to come through.

'That would be very good,' said Bremba. He bade the sitters farewell. Alma sat in silence, her eyes still closed.

Eileen Garrett changed places with the Countess and took Alma's right hand. Alma trembled as Eileen went into trance.

'I Uvani,' came a voice from Eileen's body. 'I give you greeting, friends. Peace be with you in your life, in your work and in your household.' The spirit guide addressed Fodor: 'I am indebted to the honour to speak with you, my estimable doctor.'

Fodor explained Alma's difficulties to the guide: 'The position is this, Uvani. You have on your left a young medium whose control has just told us that during an operation twelve months ago her soul was cast out and an alien spirit – an Indian girl – has taken possession of her ever since. Her soul is trying to come back and two nights ago she had a visitation – a vampire sucking her blood. Until her own soul returns to her body she cannot be well.'

Uvani told the investigators to treat Alma with trust and kindness, regardless of whether the vampire story was wholly true. 'I think you are dealing with an obsession,' explained Uvani. 'Therefore it can be difficult or dangerous, for you know an obsession becomes a reality. You have seen it happen in a man who has, for instance, shell shock. In certain phases of mind he has a dissociation, he moves away from the mechanics of the body, gets into contact with someone who may be looking for a stimulation of this nature, and so you have a change of personality.'

The theory – as explained in Fodor's *Encyclopaedia* – was that a psychologically damaged individual was prey to occupation by an earthbound spirit. It was similar to the Jewish myth of the dybbuk, in which a tormented or vengeful soul could possess the body of a living person. In Shlomo Ansky's play *The Dybbuk*, widely performed in eastern Europe and the United States in the 1920s, a young woman is taken over by the angry spirit of her dead suitor. Uvani's description made it clear that obsession was a psychological state, which only sometimes developed into supernatural possession.

'Well, what do you want us to do?' asked Fodor.

'Make a circle in her own home,' said Uvani.

'Would you come with us,' asked Fodor, 'and see what could be done?'

Uvani agreed to visit the Fieldings' house, and in the meantime left a message for Alma. 'I would ask her soul to know that there is nothing in this that could hurt her unless she so opens the door and makes it possible.'

When Alma and Eileen both came out of trance, Fodor informed them of the advice that Uvani had given. In the conservatory, he asked Alma again about the night-time visits. She told him that Les had been scornful of the researchers' theories. 'Do they think a bird can come in the window and bite you in the neck?' he had scoffed. 'That is a lot of rot!' And yet Les was frightened, Fodor observed: he had dreamt of his throat being slashed in a trench, heard the fluttering in the bedroom. Alma said that he had changed sides of the bed with her several weeks earlier because he too had felt a cold presence lying next to him – 'like a dead thing', he said – and he refused to swap back.

Fodor thought that, after the original poltergeist attack, Alma might have staged the production of apports and the self-projections as a way of mastering her scary experiences. She had tried to cast herself as the orchestrator of the investigation instead of its object. But by parodying the supernatural, she had let in something that she could not control.

In Norman Collins's novel *London Belongs to Me*, the bogus medium Mr Squales exploits lonely widows by claiming to channel the spirits of their dead husbands, and is punished for his cynicism when the ghost of a murdered woman comes to haunt him. In E. F. Benson's short story 'Spinach', a pair of stage clairvoyants discover that their holiday cottage is haunted by a murderer. They, too, are being taught a brutal lesson.

Ronnie Cockersell, who had submitted to many of Fodor's experiments, underwent a similar awakening. He confessed that he had resorted to fraud in the seance room, faking the voices of the dead and secretly manipulating the spirit trumpets. 'Success as a physical medium is like a drug,' he said. 'In my queer mental state, I wanted more and more. Having once taken the step of cheating, it became easier and easier to do it again.' Ronnie felt both glee and self-loathing. 'The state of mind produced by these fluctuations between exultation and remorse can well be imagined. I was sick mentally.' The spirit guides that he had invented 'began to take possession of me. I began to hear their voices in my head and to believe in their reality.'

Fodor had noticed something similar when his neighbour Dick Woodward fooled him into believing that he could levitate flowers. One night Fodor found the American in his apartment, almost delirious, his eyes full of fear, complaining of a fierce headache and horrible visions. He screamed when Fodor touched his leg. 'It seemed to me possible,' wrote Fodor, 'that he attracted something to him, having opened the psychic door, and the thing would not leave him.'

Those who knew Alma were becoming frightened. George as well as Les now wanted her to stop visiting the Institute. The medium Mrs Sharplin, who had predicted the arrival of Bremba, got in touch with Helen Russell Scott on Saturday to tell her that Alma had been on her mind. She had a strong feeling that there was something seriously wrong, she said. Alma was very vulnerable to forces around her, and seemed to have drifted into the 'lower astral', a primitive dimension inhabited by elementals such as poltergeists and demons. These forces would cause trouble in her home, she told Miss Scott, and make Alma prone to deceit. 'She will get into the grip of a vampire, unless you take great care.' A vampire, she warned, sucked the essence from its victims' blood, leaving them ill or insane. Mrs Sharplin said that she would no longer take part in Alma's sittings, because they made her unwell: she had never felt so heavily 'drawn on' by anyone before.

Many spiritualists and occultists believed in vampires. In *We Do Not Die*, Fodor's colleague Shaw Desmond characterised poltergeists, vampires and incubi as one 'darkened, twisting, writhing form and elemental shape, moving in a certain dark viscosity, emergent, threatening'. Such creatures were usually taken for dreams and hallucinations, he said, but 'the rats and snakes of delirium are real and not imagined. They feast vampire-like upon the soul.' Dion Fortune, in the guide to black magic that she published in 1930, described two recent cases of vampirism. She knew of a soldier who returned from the Western Front as a vampire after having sex with corpses in the trenches, and of a young woman who had lost her fiancé in the war and now became paralysed as she slept, trapped in dreams from which her dead lover refused to release her. In Fortune's examples, as in Alma's night terrors, sex had merged with violence. The living assaulted the dead and the dead the living.

Fodor feared that Alma's situation was spiralling out of control. He decided to accept Uvani's advice: rather than turn up at the Fieldings' house with guns and nets, as Bremba had suggested, the researchers would take Eileen Garrett to Thornton Heath to conduct a therapeutic seance.

Irene wanted to come too – she could see that the case was starting to alarm her husband. On Sunday 22 May, she and Fodor, Mrs Garrett and Laurie Evans joined Les, George and Alma at Beverstone Road. Don again stayed away.

Eileen Garrett asked Les whether he thought that Alma was psychic.

'Yes,' he said.

Alma remarked, 'He often thinks that it is not me at all who is talking to him.'

Eileen told Alma that she must develop her gifts: 'You have to become a medium.' When her own husband had insisted that she stop her psychic experiments, she said, she was tormented by nightmares and delusions. 'There were times when I used to scream, when I used to plot how to kill him to get away from him.' She became briefly insane, and saved herself and him by ending the marriage.

Alma turned to Les. 'I threatened to leave you in a storm of temper.'

'Which I say was not you talking to me,' said Les.

Eileen explained to Les and Alma that mental absences were typical of mediums. For two years she had herself suffered from amnesic episodes that could last for several hours. During an air raid in the war she had been tending to wounded soldiers in Euston when she became worried about her daughter, Babs, the only one of her four children to have survived infancy. All at once she found herself in Hampstead with the child. 'How I got there I don't know. I could not remember what happened.' Eileen said that Alma's psychic episodes were a form of escape. Without them, she warned Les, the marriage would come under even greater strain.

'You may part with her in the morning,' she said. 'She is as you want her to be. In the evening she may be a hellcat – suspicious, tearful, difficult. It all goes with it. These are the symptoms. She may be melancholy and tearful or terribly high-spirited. The personality is torn this way and that way, until you begin to say, "This is nobody I know."'

Alma agreed. 'The first time was after my operation,' she said. 'I had a fit of real temper. I sobbed on the stairs in the middle of dinner. I wanted to throw everything about in the bedroom. That was the beginning of it.' Alma was at last identifying herself with the poltergeist violence.

'It is the gradual dissociation of personality,' explained Eileen. 'Something is pushing and pushing through. It is like an eruption. If you push it down here it will come up there.'

Eileen Garrett had identified psychic women in haunted homes before, among them Katherine Kelly, the morphine addict at Ash Manor. She suspected that

Mrs Kelly, more than her homosexual husband, was the source of the supernormal energy in the house. 'There is a suppression of artistic qualities in her which leads to confusion,' Eileen told Fodor. 'She is really the dynamo.' When Eileen declared a woman psychic she gave her a chance at freedom. A medium could escape a lonely marriage, a tortured inner life, a deadening routine. Even the tricks of the seance room might be a necessary subterfuge for those deprived of love or denied power.

Les asked: 'Can you carry on being a medium and keeping a home?'

'I don't see why being a successful medium would not make a successful wife,' said Eileen.

She turned to George. 'How do you feel about it, with your own strong intuition?'

'I am not interested,' said George. 'I don't believe in it at all.'

'How can you account for the things which have happened?' Laurie asked him.

'I cannot account for them. I saw an unseen force at work. As regards spirits or ghosts, you can talk to me until Christmas.'

'I like a good honest sceptic,' said Eileen Garrett. 'I am myself not sure where I am.'

Fodor asked Eileen if they could consult Uvani.

Mrs Garrett leant back in her chair, yawned, shook and quivered until finally the voice of Uvani emerged from her. Fodor explained the domestic situation to him.

'I am an Oriental,' said Uvani grandly, 'and must bring an Oriental consciousness to bear on the problem.'

'Do not let anybody believe you are a weak character,' Uvani told Alma. 'Don't you any of you believe that you are dealing with a very weak, quiet little lady who is going to be put here or there. Stronger than Madame Fielding there is a subconscious point of view that will take her willy-nilly, that will not let her be happy unless she does follow it.'

Uvani told Les, 'You are dealing unfortunately with a very strong submerged personality. There are times when Madame can be quite vicious and cruel.' He asked: 'Do you feel your wife loves you?'

'Yes.'

'Madame, do *you* feel sure?'

'Yes.'

'Above all else?'

'Yes,' Alma repeated and then, more equivocally: 'I have always respected my husband.'

Uvani assured Les that Alma's psychic development need not threaten his authority. 'She must not feel that she is an important and extraordinary person, too good to be her husband's wife,' the spirit guide recommended. 'She is a wife, a companion, and a helpmate.' Just that week in the divorce courts, the judge who dissolved the marriage of the clairvoyant Estelle Roberts observed that her husband had been jealous of her career. As a celebrated medium, Estelle had been lifted into a social sphere in which he had no part. Uvani was advising Les and Alma how to avoid such a fate.

He reminded Les that much of his power was illusory. 'If you do not give her love, sympathy, I tell you she will take it. I do not tell you something you don't know. You will find her using the cunning of ten thousand little kittens and you will find yourself deceived. What she will have done she will have completely forgotten.'

'You are an agreeable man, my son,' Uvani told Les, 'generous, kind, you are a man with a very big heart. Why should she not love, respect and admire you, and want to do exactly what you want done?'

'Madame,' Uvani added, 'what you do not know is that the things you have been hinting at can be really true. That is where the laugh is a little at you. This is a very serious moment.' Uvani warned Alma that she might think that she was using 'mischief' to imper-sonate the supernatural, while in fact she had opened herself to a genuine possession. 'What you do not know is that things are more serious than you think. You actu-ally have a control.'

Uvani blessed the household and withdrew from Eileen's body.

Eileen's spirit guide had pulled off a spectacular act of negotiation, himself showing considerable cunning in his bid to hold together the Institute's experiments and the Fieldings' marriage. Uvani had warned Alma of the dangers of fraudulence while reassuring her that she was talented and powerful. He had tried to win over Les by appealing to his kindness and assuring him – man to man – that his authority could survive her adoption of a career.

Fodor was harsher with Alma when they were alone in the kitchen. He asked if she understood what Uvani had meant when he referred to her 'mischief'. Alma said, 'Not quite.' Fodor told her that she ought to know – during the past week the researchers could have asked her some very embarrassing questions. There were punishments as well as rewards for following a psychic path, he said, and her ghastly night experiences were probably brought about by what she had done. If she didn't keep away from mischief, he told Alma, there was no telling what would happen. She might think that she was riding the Devil, but it was possible that the Devil was riding her.

Alma was silent, and then said that she understood.

George, meanwhile, confided to Eileen that he was sleeping in Alma and Les's room, at the foot of their bed. Les was so scared of being alone with Alma that he had overcome his jealousy and asked George to join them at night.

The Welsh psychoanalyst Ernest Jones, a member of Freud's inner circle, argued that the vampires, incubi and succubi of nightmares were projections of incestuous wishes. Dreams of vampires in particular, said Jones, indicated a longing to copulate with or consume the dead, a necrophiliac impulse often accompanied by the smell of rotting flesh. The dreamer, by attributing lust to rapacious spirits, was disavowing his or her own desires. By this theory, Alma's night-time attacks revealed her suppressed feelings for someone in her past.

'Dreams are disguised desires,' explained Jones in *On the Nightmare*. 'But when the distortion of the wish-fulfilment is insufficient to disguise from consciousness the nature of the repressed desire, then the sleep is broken and the subject wakes to his danger. Conflict of this fierce intensity never arises except over matters of sexuality. The panic-stricken terror stems from the dimly realised possibility that the forbidden desire is overmastering the rest of the self.' In nightmares of this type, said Jones, the dreamer had just the experiences that Alma described: a sense of overwhelming dread, a feeling of weight on the chest, and helpless paralysis.

In 'The Face', one of E. F. Benson's *Spook Stories*, a married woman dreams of a leering young stranger. 'I shall soon come for you now,' he warns. She tries to run from him and to scream for help, but finds herself paralysed and mute, with 'the breath of that terrible mouth upon her'. She wakes screaming. On a visit to an art gallery soon afterwards she sees a seventeenth-century portrait of her assailant. She wonders whether she saw this painting when she was a child, and retained the image in 'the mysterious unconsciousness, which flows eternally, like some dark underground river, beneath the surface of human life'. Early impressions could 'fester or poison the mind like some hidden abscess', she observes. 'That might account for this dread of one, nameless no longer, who waited for her.' She stops short of suggesting that the memory of a real assailant might have lodged in her mind.

Two days later, in the morning of Tuesday 24 May, Alma phoned Fodor to tell him that they had received an anonymous call. George had answered the telephone to a woman who informed him that Alma was a fraud, though probably an unconscious one. Alma said that it was terrible that George had taken the call: he was upset and angry.

She said to Fodor: 'I feel there was something on the X-ray plate, wasn't there?'

'Yes,' said Fodor. 'When you come in we'll talk about it.'

Fodor did not know who had telephoned the Fieldings' house. Perhaps it was the Countess, who was about to travel to the Continent and would not return to the Institute until late June. She had objected in the past to Fodor's attempts to hoodwink Alma, and might have wanted to warn her about his discoveries.

At Walton House, Fodor told Alma what they had found on the X-ray and on the dropped piece of cloth. She protested – weakly – that internally she was so small that it would be impossible for her to hide anything and that she never used linen as a 'stopper' except during her period. She asked what the caller had meant by 'unconscious fraud'. Fodor explained that a second self, or alternate personality, could perpetrate a hoax without the knowledge of the conscious self.

Fodor said he hoped Alma would continue to visit Walton House, but under the circumstances the Institute could not pay her for the sittings. The contract was for psychic experiments, not for the 'curative treatment' that was now required. Fodor was telling Alma that she was not wonderful in the eyes of the researchers any more, but sick. He had continued to pay her after the X-ray, so that she did not realise that she had been caught, but he could no longer justify spending the Institute's funds on her.

Alma left in a state of anxiety and distress.

The next morning Alma called Fodor to say that Les would not let her return to the Institute. He considered 'a contract a contract', she claimed, and refused to allow her visits if she were not paid. But Fodor was having none of it. He said that it was up to her, of course, but the situation was serious. If she broke off now, she would be left to her own devices, and he took no responsibility for what might happen to her. It would look very bad, he added, for her to call a halt to the sittings: everyone would assume that she had been found out as a cheat. So far, he said, no one else knew about the X-rays. This was a tacit threat: if Alma did not comply with his wishes, Fodor could make the evidence public.

Alma said that she would come to Walton House on Friday without Les's knowledge.

Just as the incubus in Alma's bed had been replaced with a vampire, so the investigation had changed character. At first, Fodor had been as enchanted as a lover, feeding Alma with ideas and suggestions, rewarding her for her daring and invention, coaxing and grooming her. Now he was probing and aggressive, unpicking her with X-rays of her chest and pelvis, sniffs at her apports, visits sprung on her at home, threats of exposure. The more worried he became about Alma's mental state, the more roughly he treated her. In his anger and frustration, he had even imagined that the searchers might grab her genitals in search of secret objects – in effect, he had considered staging a sexual assault. It was little wonder that Alma's body no longer felt her own.

René Magritte was photographed at the London Gallery in Mayfair that spring with a cigarette dangling from his mouth and his arm draped round *L'Évidence éternelle*, five framed oil paintings mounted one above another on a Plexiglass stand. Each painting showed a segment of a woman's naked body, cropped almost as tightly as Fodor's X-rays of Alma's torso: the head, the breasts, the pelvis, the knees, the feet. Magritte had scrutinised, dismantled and reassembled his nude, and in doing so created a cut-up woman, somewhere between image and object, possessed but also broken.

The High Court wrote to Fodor that week asking him to submit evidence for his suit against *Psychic News*. He and the defendants had two weeks to supply documents, the court informed him, and the trial would be held a few weeks later. Fodor feared the worst. Everything about his investigation of Alma – his use of X-rays, her fraud, her distress – would give his enemies more ammunition.

When Alma visited the Institute for a therapeutic session on Friday 27 May, she had put on two pounds in weight. Fodor hypnotised her ('Your eyelids are getting heavier and heavier… They are heavy as lead and you are going to sleep... sleep... sleep...') and when she was in trance he encouraged her to gain even more ('Repeat after me... I will add two more pounds to my weight'). While she was having tea in the conservatory after the seance, her belly began to swell again, as if in enthusiastic response to his instructions. Her skirt had to be undone and her waist when measured was found to be thirty-four inches round, even bigger than last time. Her stomach was hard. She wished there were an X-ray machine handy to scan her abdomen, she said, in case there was a 'psychic baby' inside.

Alma offered no explanation for the damning shapes on the scan that had been made of her chest. Instead, she told Fodor a ghost story from her childhood. When she was seven, she said, she lived in a big old house in Bensham Manor Road, Thornton Heath, in which the windows and mirrors used to mysteriously clean themselves at night. Alma's mother suggested one day that they smear the panes with ashes. The family came down the next morning to find the glass clear and shining again.

The following Tuesday, the researchers discovered that Alma had lost half a pound. As she lay on the buttoned leather couch beneath the window in the small seance room, Fodor took her hands and talked her into a trance. Then he reprimanded her.

'Mrs Fielding, you have not carried out, regarding your weight, my suggestion. You have not added two pounds to your weight. Can you account for this dis-obedience? Why have you not increased your weight?

Will you answer me? Speak! Can you hear me speaking? Speak! Speak! Speak! Can you hear me? Can you hear my voice? Can you hear me speaking, Mrs Fielding? Answer me! Answer me! You must answer me! Can you hear me speaking to you? I give you two minutes to answer. In two minutes' time you must speak. You must speak in two minutes.'

His voice became louder and sterner with each command but Alma remained silent. Her brow was knitted and her head moved from side to side.

'Will you speak?' asked Fodor. 'Do you prefer to write?'

A pencil and paper had been placed on a box at the side of the sofa. Fodor put the pencil in Alma's right hand.

She moved the pencil across the paper. 'Be warned,' her hand wrote.

'Of what, Mrs Fielding?' said Fodor. 'Will you speak to me? You cannot possibly disobey. Will you answer me? Can you hear my voice? Answer me. Can you hear me?' Fodor was losing his composure, and in the absence of the Countess, now on holiday on the Continent, there was no one to protect Alma.

Afterwards, Alma said that she had felt 'buried alive' while in trance, as if she were down a deep well, and when she tried to shout could not be heard. She felt herself being pushed, but could not tell by what or whom.

Fodor was coming to feel trapped in this investigation himself, unable to let Alma go until he had rid her of the disturbing manifestations that he might himself have induced.

Fodor hypnotised Alma again that afternoon.

'Good afternoon,' said Alma, her forehead furrowed and her face flushed.

'Who are you?' asked Fodor.

'I am Bremba.'

Bremba admonished Fodor for the way that he had treated Alma: 'You found the medium could not answer, so you shouted and shouted. That is wrong. You should let her rest.'

Fodor asked Bremba about the incriminating square of linen. Bremba replied with the observation that there was 'more than one lady in the room' when the linen was found: 'I leave you to draw your own conclusions.' Fodor was shocked by the insinuation that one of the other sitters had dropped the cloth.

Bremba was behaving like 'a cornered criminal', wrote Fodor, 'whose last defence is to claim a frame-up'. Alma should have shown better sense. 'The accusation was not only a complete give-away but it also alienated the sympathies of the ladies who so far were the medium's best friends and were ready to make any allowance for her.'

Alma was drinking a cup of tea during the break when Laurie heard something fall; behind her chair he found an eighteen-carat gold ring inset with a cluster of seed pearls and a ruby. This was an unusually valuable apport, worth £3 or more. Even now Alma was trying to appease the investigators with gifts.

Alma cried out that she had been scratched. Fodor and Laurie took her to the small seance room, where she pulled off her sweater to reveal three six-inch streaks from her clavicle all the way round to the small of her back. Laurie pressed his thumb into her flesh and watched the skin redden.

At Alma's request, Fodor fetched the X-ray scans from the library and showed them to her. The apports were black against her pale ribs. They looked more solid than the bones in her body.

SEVENTEEN

All dreams are true

'Les is cross with you,' Alma told Fodor the next Thursday, 2 June. 'He says you have been giving me the suggestion that I bite him.'

Fodor expressed astonishment: 'Why should I suggest such a thing?'

'Oh, I'm only teasing. But every time he comes near me I want to bite his neck. The other night I was sitting on his knee and Jean was on his other knee and I could hardly stop myself from biting him. I can't think why.' Jean, George's niece and Rose's daughter, was now fifteen.

Alma said that, as she was preparing for bed, a coat hanger had flown out of the wardrobe and just missed Les's head.

Fodor took Alma's warnings seriously. In his notes he observed: 'A woman who can deliberately burn her neck can deliberately bite her husband's neck at night and suck his blood. I predict that this will, eventually, come to pass.' He was afraid that the vampire fantasy might even be a prelude to murder.

At Walton House a few days later Alma told Fodor that she often stayed awake at night, waiting for the bat or the incubus. One afternoon she had been overcome by a sudden longing, and had been unable to resist biting George's neck. She seemed to be turning vampiric: hostile, sexualised, thirsty for blood. She showed Fodor her arms. There were tiny red points on the skin, in groups of three.

The poltergeist action in Beverstone Road picked up again. A jug hopped off a pedestal in the hall, a wine decanter smashed in the dining room, a cup and saucer leapt from Alma's hand. While lying in the bath one Sunday morning, Les heard a deep voice calling him – 'Les!' – from outside the door.

Alma's eyesight had started to fail, she informed Fodor as she arrived at the Institute on Friday 10 June, squinting. She could hardly see him or his colleagues. Everything was going dark.

While Alma was under hypnosis on the sofa, Fodor told her that her loss of sight was a repetition of her last episode of blindness, in 1929. She hated the sight of somebody or something, and because she couldn't expel this person or thing from her life she made herself blind so as not to see it. If she would only admit the cause to herself, her eyes would begin to improve. He urged her to remember on waking what had happened nine years ago to trigger her loss of sight. Fodor was drawing on Freud's argument that a disowned memory could return as a physical symptom: if the memory was put into words, the symptom might disappear.

When Alma came round, he asked her whether her vision was any better.

'Worse,' she replied.

He asked if anything significant had happened before she last went blind. All Alma could think of, she said, was the death of her baby. But that was twelve years ago. On Sunday she visited his grave, she added; it made her very sad. She had started to visit the cemetery in secret. 'I never tell my husband when I go to graveyards,' Alma said. 'I don't know why I conceal the fact. He only said the other day: you never go now to baby's grave. I did not tell him that I always go up there.'

Fodor asked her what was going on at home. Alma said that she and Les had argued about money. The man who was subletting the café that she used to run in Thornton Heath had failed to pay the rent, and the landlord was claiming the arrears from the Fieldings. Les was angry.

Fodor told her that she hated the sight of her husband and as she could not blot him out, she blotted out her own vision. Alma went pale. She protested that she loved Les.

Over the phone on Saturday, Fodor told Alma, 'You would be better off by hating a little more and loving a little less.' He explained: 'By repressing hatred, we bottle it up. Instead of being spent in a burst of temper, it causes an inward pressure.'

The next time that she visited Walton House, Alma had recovered her sight. Fodor was relieved that at least one of his interventions had worked. He wrote to Eileen Garrett, who was on holiday in the south of France, to tell her of his success: 'I think I have saved her from getting a renewed outbreak of the hysterical blindness which she had 9 years ago.' Eileen, who had donated money to the Institute to research Alma's case, replied: 'I am glad you are taking care of her.'

Fodor solved some of the mysteries of Alma's other phenomena. He learnt that the magically rising marks on her arms and back were characteristic of dermatographic urticaria, a disorder in which light scrapes on the skin produced temporary weals. The scratches sometimes rose and reddened after a delay of a few seconds or minutes, creating the illusion that they appeared spontaneously. As for her inflating belly, a Hungarian friend – a professor of medicine at Harvard University – told Fodor that Alma might, consciously or unconsciously, be swallowing air and using muscular contractions to push up her diaphragm, a condition known as aerophagia.

The immediate crisis in Europe had passed by June – it emerged that there was no significant build-up of German troops on the Czech border – but anti-Semitic feeling continued to spread across the continent. In Budapest the government imposed stringent racial classifications, barring Jews from the civil service and restricting their economic rights. In Berlin, civilians attacked Jews in the streets. In London, fighting broke out when fascists paraded through a Jewish neighbourhood in the East End.

On 11 June the former foreign secretary Anthony Eden repeated his warnings to the prime minister.

'Retreat is not always the path to peace,' he told Chamberlain. 'The world is saying we're yellow. There must always be a point at which we must make a stand.'

Fodor realised that Alma was still in a fragile state, perhaps on the edge of a breakdown. Since the Countess was on holiday, he let Helen Russell Scott take the lead in the next seances. Miss Scott was so suggestible, or sensitive, that even after the revelations of the X-ray she saw spirits around Alma.

'Come along,' said Miss Scott, discerning a female figure next to Alma at the seance of 14 June, 'take better hold of her. Can you talk to us?'

Alma tried to speak but Fodor and Miss Scott could hear only a low murmur.

'Come along, friend. Try again,' said Miss Scott. She put her fingers to Alma's pulse.

'Greeting, my brother,' said Alma.

'Greeting,' said Fodor. 'Who is it?'

'Mevanwe. I cannot get near my brother.'

It was the Indian girl whom Bremba had described. She told the sitters that she had died five years earlier, aged sixteen. She said that she was frightened.

'Why have you been attracted to the medium?' asked Fodor.

'Because her soul is dead.'

'What do you mean by that?'

'She cast her own soul out.'

Miss Scott felt the girl fade. Alma's face and body relaxed. Miss Scott sensed another presence. 'Something else here,' she said. 'I don't know what it is.' She stared at Alma. 'Yes, come along. You are with friends. You are all right.'

A thin, high voice came from Alma: 'Mummy.'

'You want your mummy,' said Miss Scott. 'You are all right. Don't be frightened.'

'My mummy,' repeated the voice, beseechingly.

'Can you tell us your mummy's name?'

'She is not come?' said the child. 'She said she will come.'

Alma gulped and her head fell forward. Then she spoke in her normal voice.

'I have not been anywhere,' she said. 'I have an empty feeling.'

During Alma's seance of Friday 17 June, everyone smelt violets: waves of scent, coming and going, in the seance room and the hall, near Alma and far from her.

Fodor noticed a scar on Alma's upper lip, and asked how she had acquired it. She said that when she was seven years old a man – the older brother of a friend of her sister – had picked her up, thrown her into the air and kissed her as he caught her. It was a very hot day. The man's dog, seized with jealous rage, flew at Alma's face and bit her lip. The dog then foamed at the mouth, ran into the street and was killed by a passing car. The man took Alma to a hospital. 'I always remember the needle ready to cauterise the wound,' she said. 'I was scared. I got out of the man's arm and ran, the doctor running after me. Blood was everywhere.'

There was something heightened, hysterical, condensed about Alma's story, a peculiar symmetry: the dog and then the girl in flight, their mouths spurting blood and spittle; the man who came at the girl with a kiss and the man who came at her with a needle. Maybe Fodor was both men to Alma, the seducer and the sadist, an admirer who put her in danger, a doctor who attacked her.

Fodor discussed Alma's case with the American psychoanalyst Elizabeth Severn, with whom he had started to undergo a course of analysis himself.

Elizabeth Severn believed that psychic breakdown was often caused by a traumatic event. She had herself suffered a breakdown as a young woman in the American Midwest, and in the 1920s had travelled to Budapest to be treated by Sándor Ferenczi, a member of Freud's circle. In their sessions, she and Ferenczi uncovered a horrific series of events in her past, so hideous as to be barely believable. It seemed that her father had sexually assaulted her, pimped her out to other men, drugged her, and forced her to shoot a man dead. Ferenczi speculated that the girl had survived these horrors by splitting herself into separate personalities: a hurt child self, a caretaker self, and a soulless, mechanical body.

As a medic in the Great War, Ferenczi had seen the effects of violent shock on soldiers. As a psychoanalyst in Hungary, he found very similar symptoms in patients who had been sexually assaulted as children. 'Sexual trauma as the pathogenic factor cannot be valued highly enough,' he wrote in 1932. 'Even children of very respectable, sincerely puritanical families, fall victim to real violence or rape much more often than one had dared to suppose. The immediate explanation – that these are only sexual phantasies of the child, a kind of hysterical lying – is unfortunately made invalid by the number of such confessions, e.g. of assaults upon children, committed by patients actually in analysis.'

Ferenczi died in 1933, his pioneering work on trauma and sexual abuse unpublished in English. Elizabeth Severn had by then moved to London, where she outlined his findings in her book *The Discovery of Self*. 'The importance of *trauma* as a specific and almost universal cause of Neurosis,' she wrote, 'was first impressed on me by Ferenczi, who, probing deeply, had found it present in nearly all his cases. He thus resurrected and gave new value to an idea which had once, much earlier, been entertained by Freud, but which was discarded by him in favour of "phantasy", as the explanation of the strange tales or manifestations given by his patients.' Freud held that the psyche was shaped by childhood sexual fantasies, which should not be mistaken for facts.

In her book, Severn explained the theory of trauma that Ferenczi had formulated in his sessions with her. After a severe emotional shock, she said, 'The psyche *breaks*, is fragmented into bits too small for any one of them to retain anything more than its own tiny portion of the total catastrophe. There is no *memory* of the event because the shock is too great.' Ferenczi speculated that those patients who had experienced the 'little death' of trauma acquired a kind of psychic sensitivity, as if they had become revenants from another sphere. Severn adopted this idea, arguing that the splintering of the self created the gaps and elisions that made it possible to move between planes. She explained to Fodor that Alma's reported losses of memory, vision, mobility – the ambulatory amnesias, the blindness, the paralyses, the sense that her soul had left her body – might reflect a blank in her psyche, an erasure caused by shock.

'All dreams are true,' said Mrs Severn, 'and but the ghosts of our pasts.'

'Was your childhood happy?' Fodor asked Alma on Tuesday afternoon.

'Yes,' she replied, 'except that I was blamed for everything. My mother blamed me, but my father used to stick up for me. Doris, my sister, who is three years older, was preferred by my mother. Her suggestions were always taken in place of mine. If I bought any-thing for Mother for her birthday and my sister also did, she would turn to me to say, "Isn't Doris a good girl – look what she bought for me." She would not say to my sister, "Look what Alma bought for me." It hurt me very much.' Alma had this in common with the Countess: a mother and older sister so close that they shut her out.

Alma gave Fodor three sketches that she had made over the weekend. She had drawn them while in trance, she said. One depicted a church south of Croydon, near a pub that she had visited on Sunday. Another showed a woman holding a child. The third was of a dark, bearded man in a hat, with closed eyes, whose leering face she said that she had seen in a vision while sitting with Rose by the church.

Fodor asked Alma about her dreams. In one recurrent dream, she told him, she had to enter a cave alone. She would scrape the sand from the cave mouth and inside find a message in a foreign language on a piece of crumbling yellow parchment. 'I must find someone to understand this,' she would think. The air in the cave was thick with the smell of fungus.

Fodor asked about her sexual experiences. She told him that she had cried hysterically and fainted when Les first tried to have intercourse with her. She said that she had often longed to be a nun: when she was a young child; then at the age of fifteen or sixteen; and again when she was twenty-three, when her son died. 'I just wanted to get away from everything.' She told him that though George was in love with her, and very jealous of other men, he had always been a 'gentleman' – in other words, they had not slept together. Alma, Les and George were effectively frozen in their love triangle, each of them separate and alone.

Only four sitters convened for that day's seance: Fodor, Mrs Kelly (the Institute's treasurer), Mrs Taylor (the librarian) and the Countess, who had just returned to London from Florence.

Soon after four o'clock, Alma spoke in the voice of Bremba. 'I would like to tell you,' he said, 'that the vision she saw on Sunday was a gentleman belonging to the church she was near on that day. He was hung for interfering with small children. She was probably sitting on the spot where one of the outrages took place. Tell her he will not harm her.'

Alma's head drooped, lifting as she returned to consciousness.

'Do you remember anything?' asked Fodor.

Alma struggled to speak, eventually managing to whisper: 'I have a sensation of somebody very big and hard, my flesh hard, a tightening around the throat as though pulling up like that, as though I was swelling. But I don't remember the words. It is more a sensation than a remembrance.'

Alma fell silent, then said that she felt the tightening at her throat again. 'I feel being pulled up.'

As she spoke, all four sitters noticed two red rings on her neck, as if it was being squeezed by invisible hands. They were overlapping bands, each a quarter of an inch thick. Fodor felt sure that she had not touched her neck during the seance. He was struck by Bremba's reference to sexual assault. This was the first time that the subject had arisen in the seance room.

As Alma was walking up the stairs at Walton House before the next session, on Friday 24 June, Fodor saw her pluck something from her handbag and throw it behind her. He heard a clatter below, and turned to see a polished green stone at the foot of the stairs – malachite, he thought. He said nothing about having seen Alma's movement just before the stone hit the ground.

Upstairs, Fodor asked Alma about the death of her infant son. In the span of twelve months, she told him, she had also lost her father (Charles Smith), both of her maternal grandparents (Jimmy and Jessie Bannister), her father's mother (Mary Smith) and an uncle. 'A black year, indeed,' said Fodor.

Alma reported that the red rings had remained for forty minutes after Tuesday's seance. 'I had a terrible throat since the last sitting,' she said. 'Very tight and sore. I thought it was ulcers. It is now better. I had difficulty in swallowing. I could hardly speak.' At a local club on Tuesday night, she told Fodor, the waitress who served her a glass of stout noticed a mark appearing on her neck: 'Look what is coming up on your throat,' said the waitress. 'Big red rings.'

'Will you tell me all the words which you can associate with poltergeist?' asked Fodor.

'Devilment. Destruction. Torment. Willpower. Something persistent. Something with purpose behind it. Something pushing you on and on, and you cannot get back. Curiosity.'

'Any names?'

'Grandfather.'

The afternoon's seance was again preceded by a recital of the Lord's Prayer. Mrs Taylor, Mrs Kelly, Laurie and Fodor sat in silence as Alma's face stiffened and her eyes widened. Her eyelids rose and fell until, at 3.50 p.m., they dropped shut. Her hands were in her lap, the fingertips touching.

The Indian girl spoke through her, almost in a whisper. 'Greeting. Mevanwe. No more afraid. White brother always been friend.'

Mevanwe asked the sitters, 'Why does the medium visit... I do not know the name of places where the dead rest? She visits them so often.'

'Do you object to that?' asked Fodor.

'No, but it worries me.'

'Can't you keep her away?'

'Not always. She has great willpower. It makes me cold. I do not like death.'

'Why does your medium like it?'

'My medium likes to go to dark places.'

At 4.25 p.m. Alma's head sagged. She looked sleepy as she came round, and flinched at the light.

Fodor asked her whether she often visited graveyards. Alma said that she frequently went to the Mitcham Road cemetery in south Croydon to visit her son's and her father's graves. She liked going there.

After tea Fodor took her to be weighed.

'You were very naughty, you know,' he said. 'You threw that stone. I saw you take it out of your bag.'

Alma was startled. She denied having thrown the stone, insisting that she had never seen it before.

'Why should I do such a thing?' she asked. 'If you think that of me, it is better that I stop coming. I would not for a moment consider coming if I thought that you didn't believe me. I want to find out things.'

Fodor suggested to Alma that she might have thrown the stone to test him, but she repeated that she had not thrown it. He retracted his accusation.

'I will tell you frankly, I did not see it. I only thought I saw it from the corner of my eye. I did accuse you because I wanted to see your reaction. It is one of the many psychological tests which we have to employ.'

Fodor told Alma that she knew much more about herself, inside, than they did, and it was only with her help that they could discover things. He gave her an interpretation of her cave dream – the cave represented the womb, and the fungus smell recalled her guilt about a foetus that she had lost. She responded, 'I tell you, birth and death mean the same thing to me... they are identical.'

He told her that she might harbour a second self. She said: 'There are several Mrs Fieldings. I always felt it. I had to do things which I could not understand.'

Before Laurie left Walton House, Fodor asked him to compose a memorandum about his first impressions of Alma's poltergeist. He wrote:

On looking through my notes on the Thornton Heath case made on my first visit to the house (Feb 23) I experience afresh the feeling I had at that time; that is to say an utter belief in the genuineness of the phenomena and also of the good faith of Mrs Fielding. In view of what we now know this is important. Moreover, I find that having deprived her of the benefit of every doubt in regard to the phenomena there still remain a number of incidents which defy a normal explanation…

I am more than ever convinced that her reactions to the various breakages etc were entirely genuine. Her absolute terror in the initial stages was quite unmistakeable. I also find reference in my notes to the behaviour and reactions of George Saunders and I feel now as I felt then that whatever the position may have been in later days he had no part in anything that took place in the house and was as much 'in the dark' as anyone.

Fodor, too, still believed that a supernatural disturbance had occurred in the Fieldings' home. He thought that it had been caused by a 'landslide' in Alma's unconscious mind, a repressed, violent hatred that launched destruction on herself and others. When the attacks abated – as poltergeist outbreaks usually did in days or weeks – Alma had invented phenomena to hold the researchers' interest, to keep an escape route from her world to theirs and from her unconscious to her conscious life. Many of her actions in this phase were deliberate, Fodor accepted, but some so impulsive as to slip the leash of choice or intention.

Fodor believed that Alma's apports and elaborations had stemmed from a feverish wish for change, escape, self-expression, but they had also ushered in unbidden experiences, such as the visits of the incubus and vampire, that were rooted in her past. These had the *unheimlich*, or uncanny, charge that Freud identified: a sense of something obscurely understood, at once recognised and strange. The night-time visits intensified when Alma realised that she was under suspicion. 'Her false miracles were accompanied by strange secondary phenomena,' wrote Fodor. 'Her unconscious was signalling, economically, that trouble was rife below.'

EIGHTEEN

We are body

Alma telephoned Fodor on Saturday to tell him that she had woken in the night to find that she could not move. 'There was the weight of a man on my side, on the left as before, and something fastened on my neck.' She heard a fluttering sound, experienced a feeling of sinking. 'This morning I feel terribly weak.' She had left her hair loose to hide the marks on her neck from Les.

'Have you heard of vampires?' asked Fodor. Until now, he had referred to vampires only when she was in trance.

'I have read ghost stories,' said Alma, 'but I don't remember any vampire stories.' Les had seen a film called *The Vampire*, she recalled, but told her not to watch it. 'He said it was rubbish and it would give me nightmares.' This was probably *The Mark of the Vampire* (1935), a notoriously disturbing picture, which – like *Dracula* in 1931 – starred Bela Lugosi.

Fodor noticed that the latest vampire visit had taken place the night after he saw Alma throw a stone down the stairs. Perhaps her second self had speared her neck with a hairpin to punish her for her clumsiness, having done the same after she dropped the square of linen in May. Alma had a strong masochistic drive, Fodor observed: she played a double role, as aggressor and victim. But then he, too, had taken a double role, as Alma's champion and her inquisitor. In the course of the investigation, their relationship had acquired a sadomasochistic shape, admiration and desire becoming entangled with secrecy, deceit and control. Just as the poltergeist had turned her into a shoplifter, Fodor had drawn her into imposture. Perhaps he was the genie she had summoned, the imp who had led her astray, and her feelings of persecution were expressing themselves as marks on her skin.

It struck Fodor that Alma could have modelled her night visitor on him. She might well associate him with vampire mythology. Like Count Dracula, he was an educated and cosmopolitan foreigner – in fact, the Count's homeland, Transylvania, had been a Hungarian territory before it was granted to Romania in 1920. He was a friend of Lugosi, the most famous vampire actor in the world. And he was Jewish. From Bram Stoker's novel onwards, the characterisation of Dracula as a ruthless, rapacious parasite drew directly on anti-Semitic tropes. To Alma, Fodor realised, '*I was the vampire*, not sexually, but by exposing her fraudulent phenomena.' She had unconsciously cast him as her persecutor. The origins of this fantasy, he guessed, lay deep in her past.

In the morning of Tuesday 28 June, he briefed Elizabeth Severn on the developments in Alma's case.

Mrs Severn said that she felt sure that Alma had been assaulted as a girl. She believed that Alma's vision of the man with an evil face was a memory, fused with her wish to see her assailant hanged for his crime. 'In cases of violent dissociation,' she said, 'there is almost always a sexual trauma in the background.' She supposed that Alma had been abused by her father, but Alma's attacker might have been another man in her circle, such as her grandfather Jimmy, or her mother's brother George, whose face she had drawn after the incubus incident and who had trained her as an acrobat when she was a girl.

It was natural that Alma did not remember the assault, Mrs Severn told Fodor. The incident would have been blanked from her consciousness even as it happened. Instead, she repeatedly relived it in her body: in weals, burns, bites and scratches, in the press of cold flesh against her as she lay in bed. Alma had told Fodor that when the red rings appeared on her neck she felt a swelling and tightening of her throat, as if she were being possessed by 'somebody very big and hard'.

Alma's fear that the incubus had made her pregnant, said Mrs Severn, was the unconscious fear that followed rape even in small children. The whole poltergeist outbreak, she said, was an expression of 'desire, fear, horror and anger'. She agreed with Fodor that Alma's tricks communicated her experience as effectively as her kinetic projections. 'The child part in her is just as interested in doing it by fraud as by psychic force. It can have the same satisfaction from both.' Elizabeth Severn explained that a traumatised child became amoral, expressing her own breakage by breaking all sorts of rules. 'She says in fact: the impossible has happened to me. To show that something impossible can happen, I shall do this and that.'

Mrs Severn suggested that the bicycle accident to which Alma sometimes referred, which took place when she was on holiday with her father, was a cover memory for the original attack. 'It reopened an old wound. She uses it as a pretext to say that an accident had occurred to her. There have been many similar cases with shell-shocked soldiers during the war. The shock of the battle reopened an old wound and shook the psychic structure into dissociation. They managed the first shock, but the second was too much.'

Fodor recalled the crumpled note that the ghost from the cupboard left by Alma's bed – 'Scrawls and smuts on a scrap of clean paper!' – which seemed to communicate both a feeling of being dirtied and a wish that the experience be known. According to Alma, her mother had burnt the note, as if to destroy the trace of what had happened to her. Fodor thought that Alma's physical phenomena were further attempts at disclosure, 'dumb and confused complaints and appeals for help on the part of the forgotten child'. Even now, she was rendered almost mute as soon as she spoke of the evil man who interfered with children, her throat growing so sore that she could barely speak. Freud argued that a person who had experienced a traumatic event reproduced it as an action instead of a memory: 'He repeats it, without knowing, of course, that he is repeating it... and in the end, we understand that this is his way of remembering.'

It was possible, Fodor realised, that other women's supernatural experiences had a similar origin. Perhaps the powers of many psychic women and poltergeist girls were derived from experiences of violation. The Countess had childhood nightmares of men bearing down on her as she lay in bed; Eileen Garrett had learnt to separate her mind from her body after she was roughly petted by a group of huntsmen; the Romanian peasant girl Eleonore Zugun was persecuted by her father in the shape of 'Dracu'. Fodor wondered if even the story of Gef the talking mongoose expressed something awry in the relationship between James Irving and his daughter Voirrey.

When Fodor first met Alma, she had described supernatural forces as 'things which we are not meant to know', as if weird activity stemmed from the suppression of knowledge, a necessary forgetting. A childhood assault was an experience so terrible that it insisted on expression; and also so terrible that it was unspeakable – it could take only unconscious, indirect, otherworldly form.

A ghost was the sign of an unacknowledged horror. It indicated a gap opened by trauma, an event that because it had not been assimilated must be perpetually relived. There were no words, so there was a haunting.

On Tuesday afternoon, Alma entered the small seance room with Fodor, Florence Hall and Mr

Swift, a psychologist who had agreed to conduct a word-association test.

Alma sat in an armchair while Fodor read out the 101 words on the list that he and the psychologist had compiled, pausing between each for Alma to reply with the first word that occurred to her. Mr Swift timed her responses and Mrs Hall noted them.

Word-association tests were designed to tap in to a subject's unconscious by revealing unusual connections or blocks. Alma replied easily and conventionally to many of the apparently potent words on Mr Swift's list, such as 'rape' ('bad', she said), 'father' ('kindness'), 'coffin' ('death'), 'roses' ('sweet'). She took more than three seconds to respond to 'hanging' (with 'ghastly'), 'lodger' ('room') and 'parliament' ('mixed-up', a reference to the political turmoil of the time). Motorcar, fender, Japan, pancake and calendar also slowed her down, and she froze on 'bicycle', to which it took her twenty-two seconds to respond – with 'pleasure'.

The Countess joined the group after the session, when Fodor resumed his enquiries about Alma's childhood.

'You remember the ghost you saw coming out of the cupboard for years,' he said. 'Can you tell me whether the face reminded you of anyone?'

'I never saw it clearly. I could not see the actual nose and eyes or the features. I never actually saw the face at all.'

'Has anyone else seen that cupboard ghost or only you?'

'I don't know.'

'What about Doris or your brother?'

'As far as I know they never did. They used to say I was ridiculous.'

'Tell me,' said Fodor, 'what does the word "cupboard" suggest?'

'Odds and ends, spiders, mice, damp smell, mildew, fishing rods, books, dreams.'

When Fodor pressed her for other memories, Alma described for the first time an episode that had taken place seven years earlier, in 1931. She was twenty-seven, and pregnant. While washing clothes in a tub, she was shocked to see a dead rat bob to the water's surface, the top of its body burnt away. That night she went into labour, she said, and the next day she gave birth to two dead babies: a boy and a girl. Alma's story offered a clue to what she was reliving when she pushed inanimate objects from her body in Walton House. The miscarried boy was 'perfect', Alma said. The girl was deformed, like the rat, the top of her body incomplete. Alma believed that the shock of seeing the headless rat had damaged the foetuses in her womb. In pregnancy, as in the seance room, the border between one being and another was permeable.

Alma suddenly exclaimed that she felt something touching her right arm. She rolled up the sleeve of her cardigan to reveal four long scratches running down from the right shoulder blade.

Fodor invited Alma to lie on the conservatory sofa, where he returned to some of the key words of the association test. 'Rape,' he said. Almost immediately she answered, very agitated: 'Horror. Doubt. Death. Trees. Darkness. Damp. Horrible face. A pair of big glasses. Something very cold. A slithering movement, something with scales on. Flesh is hard. A church. Terrific lot of people.'

Fodor gently explained to her that he had prompted her with the word 'rape' because there were indications that she had been sexually assaulted as a child and that this was the chief cause of her trouble. Alma seemed very affected by this suggestion, and on the verge of tears. Fodor told her that she had every reason to feel hurt and to hate the man who had hurt her.

She became more upset. When she read newspaper reports about the rape of children, she said, she always wondered about the effects on the victims, about whether they remembered and what their mothers told them.

Alma recalled once having an erotic dream about a little man with scales like an alligator. 'I will tell you what he looks like,' she said. 'Have you been in the garden and found a brown, hard chrysalis, all scales, one on top of another?' She associated this man with the slithering movement that she had described.

Alma confessed to sometimes wishing that she was dead. 'Since childhood I was always haunted by ideas of suicide.' These thoughts had returned four or five months ago, she said, at about the time that the supernatural disturbances began. 'When a train comes into the station I have to keep a tight grip on myself. I have to retreat to the wall of the waiting room until the train goes by. I feel as if I would be pushed forward to kill myself.'

She told Fodor that she liked cemeteries so much that she used to steal broken pieces of tombstones as a child.

Alma had not been able to recall a sexual attack, exactly, but Fodor's suggestion had unleashed a rush of fearful associations.

In Algernon Blackwood's short story 'Chemical', published in 1935, a young man in a Bloomsbury boarding house becomes curious about a fellow lodger whom he rarely sees. As the weeks pass, the landlady occasionally checks with her new guest that all is well, that he has not been 'interfered with' in any way. He assures her that he is fine. Very late one night, he hears a noise outside his room and opens the door to see his elusive fellow lodger dragging a bulging sack across the landing. He notices that the lodger has a thin red line of contused blood around his neck, and that tears stain his cheeks. He feels a horrible sympathy for him, a recognition. He watches him open a door on the landing and stuff his heavy load into it, upright. The lodger disappears.

The landlady finds the young man collapsed on the landing, next to the empty cupboard. 'May God forgive me,' she says.

When the man recovers, he learns that twenty years ago his landlady's son was hanged for killing his father. Only the words 'interfered with' hint at the motive for the murder. The hiding of the body in the cupboard mimics the concealment of another secret. Blackwood's story, like the landlady, does not name it.

Alma called at Walton House at five o'clock the next day, Wednesday 29 June, with a picture, which she claimed to have made in trance, of a mother and child. She hadn't slept the previous night, she said. She felt as if she had pulled herself into a shell and wanted to shut everything out. Fodor explained that this was the effect of a childhood in which she had been badly hurt. Alma replied with a curious non sequitur, saying that she hated Les for his refusal to comfort her after the death of their second son. She had cried night after night, she said, but Les would not put his arms around her. It was this that inspired her to attack him with a carving knife in the autumn of 1926. 'I swore that I would never cry again if I was hurt,' she said. 'I have never done so.'

The Countess, since her return from Italy, had become alarmed by the turn that Alma's sessions had taken. She was especially disturbed when Fodor informed her of his conclusions on the case: that the poltergeist activity stemmed from Alma's psychic disintegration, which in turn was rooted in a trauma that she had suffered in childhood. To the Countess this seemed far-fetched and dangerous. The sexual abuse of children, especially within a family, was an abhorrent subject, and Fodor had already risked the Institute's reputation with his exposures of mediums and his psychosexual theories about the supernormal – the lawsuit with *Psychic News*, which had forced the Institute's chairman to resign, was still pending. In effect, Fodor's psychical research had transmuted into a study of abnormal psychology; he was suggesting that supernatural power was a function of mental breakdown.

The Countess hated to think what the membership would make of Fodor's latest findings. She feared that the Fielding case might destroy the cash-strapped Institute altogether. She also worried for Alma. The more the researchers pressed her, the more her guilt and fear manifested themselves. The investigation, like an abusive relationship, had moved from enticement to coercion, from flattery to threat. To save his career, Fodor might now even be planting thoughts in Alma's mind, mesmerising her like the Jewish enchanter Svengali in George du Maurier's *Trilby*.

Both the Countess and Fodor were present when Alma went into trance on Friday 1 July. She repeatedly swallowed, flexing the muscles in her throat. Then she shrieked, threw up her hands to cover her face and flung herself over the arm of the chair. Fodor took her hands in his, telling her not to be afraid. Alma settled, and greeted the investigators in the voice of Bremba.

'Why this blood-curdling scream?' asked the Countess.

'Maybe she is frightened to know something,' said Bremba. 'Some vague memory must hold her.'

Fodor tried to impress on Bremba how important it was for Alma to retrieve her memories.

The Countess ignored this. 'What I really want to know is, are you only there when you are talking to us?'

she asked Bremba. 'What happens when the medium wakes? Where are you then?'

'I pass beyond,' said Bremba.

'Where to? To sleep?'

Bremba did not reply. The Countess tried another tack: 'Tell me, are you a spirit?'

'You call us spirits,' said Bremba.

'But what do you call yourselves?'

'We are body.'

Bremba brought the session to an end. 'I am going,' he said, and then, 'I think the medium remembers...' Alma screamed again, first covering her face with her hands and then, screaming still, flinging herself across the chair.

On coming round, Alma said that she remembered nothing at all.

In the library afterwards Alma mentioned that she had asked her mother whether anything bad had happened to her in childhood. Her mother had replied that Alma twice came home late from school, at 8 p.m., saying that a man had given her sweets. Perhaps Alma's mother was pointing away from the house with this story, admitting to the possibility of an attack while denying any responsibility for it.

It had been Bremba who introduced the idea of a childhood assault, with his account of the hanged man, and Alma had gestured towards confirming it with her screams and half-memories, the swelling in her throat. But Fodor could not be sure. Hoping to obtain proof that his theory was accurate, he asked Alma if she would agree to an injection of scopolamine, a drug used as a truth serum. Alma said that she would have to discuss it with Les.

At home that night, she said, she woke up screaming.

The Countess had had enough: of Fodor's theories and of Alma's suffering. Appalled by the proposal that they inject Alma with a serum, she told Fodor that he must suspend the seances. The Countess was stepping in to shield her friend as well as the Institute, calling a halt to a dangerous game.

Fodor reluctantly conceded that Alma could do with a rest. He needed one too. At Walton House on Tuesday 5 July he suggested to Alma that she take a break until September, reminding her that the Institute would in any case be closed in August. She became very anxious. Fodor noticed a 'slight wildness' in her behaviour, and she told him that she had a swelling under her arm that might be cancer. She let him feel it. Fodor, afraid that her feelings might be manifesting as a tumour, urged her to visit the hospital.

At 6 p.m., half an hour after she left, Alma called Fodor from a public telephone box in great distress. She said that she had 'mentally' listened to him and the Countess talking about her. She had heard him say that just because one phenomenon was genuine, it did not follow that they all were. She said that he had spoken of an incident in which he held her hands, and that she had heard them discussing the Institute's money problems. Why had Fodor not told her, she asked, that he thought it was all a fake? And why hadn't he told her about the financial difficulties? She would willingly have kept coming for free.

Fodor was unsettled by the accuracy of Alma's account. After she left the building (or after he believed that she had left the building), he and his colleagues had sat in the office talking about the Institute's hardship and Alma's phenomena, much as she described.

Fodor told her that she had imagined the conversation because she was upset about the enforced holiday. Alma replied that she had plainly heard the discussion in her mind.

Fodor rang Alma the next day, telling her that she could come to the Institute to talk any time. She had had an awful evening, she said. All the dirty crockery piled on the kitchen table smashed itself to pieces. She went to watch Les play in a darts match, but people kept getting up and moving away from her, saying that someone had pinched them. Glasses kept smashing. She did not dare stay.

At the Institute the following week, the council convened without Fodor to discuss Alma Fielding's case. The Countess spoke out against Fodor, criticising his bizarre theories, his desire to inject Alma with drugs, and his unregulated use of psychoanalytic techniques. She said that he had even wanted the investigators to take Alma to the Tower of London and encourage her psychically to steal the Crown Jewels. The council, which included Wilfred Becker, Gerald Wills, Helen

Russell Scott, Eric Cuddon and Shaw Desmond, decided to terminate the investigation.

When Fodor was informed of the decision, he was furious. He blamed the council's fear of the 'prim, elderly' lady members, who found his psychoanalytic approach 'indecent'. Defiantly, he began writing up a report of the Fielding case, aware that the other investigators would not approve of his conclusions. 'Findings such as these were highly distasteful to my colleagues and superiors in the II,' he said, 'as they would weaken the spiritist hypothesis and also brought in elements that offended the high moral tone of the members of the board.'

Fodor wrote to Eileen Garrett, who was on holiday on the Côte d'Azur, telling her that the Fielding case was closed and offering to return the money that she had donated. He was bullish about his findings. 'I have now written nearly 5,000 words of the Fielding report,' he told Eileen. 'It is the most fascinating investigation of our days.' He said that he wished that he and his family could join her in Juan-les-Pins, as she had suggested, but they could not afford to travel so far south.

Fodor's libel suit would not be heard now before October, as the courts were soon to break for the summer. At the end of July he left London with Irene and Andrea for a holiday in Brittany, on the northern coast of France.

Fodor's theory rested on his belief that Alma had been sexually assaulted as a child. It was possible, he knew, that she had not suffered such an assault at all. She may simply have played along with him, responding to his need for a psychoanalytic solution to her story as nimbly as she had responded to his need for supernatural adventures. Alma was reactive, metamorphic, wildly adaptive; throughout the investigation she had become whatever others suggested or required. And yet this very fluidity might point to the truth of Fodor's hypothesis.

Sándor Ferenczi, after his analysis of Elizabeth Severn, had concluded that the victims of childhood assault were unusually compliant. An early sexual trauma created a fractured personality with no centre, unmoored and suggestible. When a child was abused, explained Ferenczi in 1932, 'he feels enormously confused, in fact, split – innocent and culpable at the same time – and his confidence in the testimony of his own senses is broken.' Such children were compelled 'to subordinate themselves like automata to the will of the aggressor, to divine each one of his desires and to gratify these'. In later life they responded to figures of authority in a similar way. They developed a hypersensitive, porous, almost clairvoyant capacity to anticipate, interpret and fulfil the desires of others. They had a remarkable power to assess their environment and calculate the best way to survive. Even their memories were malleable.

By this theory, Alma's capacity to manipulate herself and others was a product of the same history that left her susceptible to liminal experience. Her vigilance, developed because she had lived in circumstances of danger, made her an expert deceiver. Her compulsive lies were symptoms of her assault, and the confusion of her memories its curse. All the apparent obstacles to believing her were, in Ferenczi's formulation, recast as marks of abuse.

Fodor had noticed that supernatural events were unusually able to communicate the splintering and contradiction of a traumatic experience. Ghosts conjured the uneasy sense that something both was and was not real, that an event recurred as if it were outside time, undead. The mediums and poltergeist girls and shell-shocked soldiers of the 1920s and 1930s expressed in life what modernist authors and surrealist painters expressed in art: jarring dislocations, the return of buried experiences, a fragmented consciousness interrupted by dream and nightmare. During a seance the past was allowed to occupy the present, alternate selves found voices, the impossible was made real. Ferenczi's theory of trauma was formulated in the field hospitals of Europe and performed in its seance rooms.

But Fodor's interpretation of Alma's experience remained a conjecture, no more provable or disprovable than a haunting by disembodied beings. He knew that he might be wrong. As Elizabeth Severn said after unearthing the lurid story of her own shattered childhood: 'And still I don't know if the whole thing is true.'

NINETEEN

Boo!

Poltergeists continued to trouble Britain that summer. In August the residents of a boarding house in Golders Green, north London, reported raps, scratches, knocks, bangs, footsteps, cracks, creaks and sighs. One lodger left without giving a reason. 'I knew what it was,' said his landlady. 'He had seen the ghost.' A worker at Blackpool Pleasure Beach said that he, his wife and their lodger had noticed objects moving around the house. 'When we told a policeman of our experiences, he laughed,' said the husband, 'but while he was actually taking notes, a clothes brush suddenly flew off the piano and a brass fire-iron stand in the fireplace turned upside down.' Poltergeists, said the *Manchester Guardian*, were symptoms of a disordered age, in which 'once-established things break loose from their moorings and bang around our bewildered heads'. The *Observer* ran a piece on the 'poltergeist weather' besieging the country: 'The severity of the thundery downpours is remarkable enough,' the paper noted, 'but more extra-ordinary is their caprice.' During the storms, said *Two Worlds*, a ghost horse was seen galloping along the sea-front at Deal in Kent. The more powerless people felt, the more liable they were to find significance in ordinary events, to attribute magical meaning to a mislaid utensil, a startled animal or a burst of rain.

The psychical researcher Harry Price was chasing down a poltergeist in the Midlands, another in the Lake District and two in Scotland. 'I have never had such a time,' he told the *Yorkshire Evening Post*. Price was also writing a book about the spectres at Borley Rectory in Essex, which he had rented for an extended ghost hunt from May 1937 to May 1938. The Borley haunting had been at its most intense in the early 1930s, when the Reverend Lionel Foyster and his much younger wife Marianne lived in the rectory with their adopted daughter Adelaide and a lodger called Frank Pearless, also known as François d'Arles. The poltergeist threw stones and bottles, rang bells and broke windows. A ghostly nun, said to have been walled up alive, wrote messages on the walls: 'Marianne please help get.' The five-year-old Adelaide reported seeing 'something horrible' by the curtain in her bedroom.

Daphne du Maurier published her gothic psychological thriller *Rebecca* in August. The novel's nameless narrator, riven by envy and self-doubt, fears that her husband is still obsessed with his first wife. The memory of the dead woman is laid only when her house is razed by fire. 'I looked upon a desolate shell,' says the narrator as she surveys the ruin of Manderley, 'soulless at last, unhaunted, with no whisper of the past about its staring walls.' The exposed interior of the house looks back blankly, scoured of history. The *Daily Herald* praised du Maurier's 'wonderful ability of catching a moment of time like a pinned butterfly, and extorting from it all its beauty or its dread'.

In New York City, DC Comics retired its trench-coated 'ghost detective' Dr Occult, and replaced him with Superman.

Fodor returned to London from northern France at the end of the month to learn that he had been fired from the International Institute for Psychical Research. Though he had almost single-handedly run the organisation for the past four years, its council had cast him out. When he went to Walton House to collect his belongings, he discovered that his report on the Fielding case, which he had left in a locked drawer in his office, had been confiscated. Nor did he have access to the transcripts, notes and images that he had gathered since February.

On 2 September Fodor wrote to the leading psychical journals to express his fury at his dismissal, at the seizure of his manuscript, and at the Institute's suggestion that it had sacked him to save money. 'The finances of the Institute have always been bad,' he said, in a letter published by *Light* and *Occult Review*. 'Yet I always succeeded in securing the necessary support. I informed a member of the Council some time before they decided to dispense with my services that I would not draw my salary from September on until funds would become available.'

'I have been one of the founders of the IIPR,' he declared. 'I have directed its research for 4 years with considerable sacrifice. I have built the Institute with my sweat and blood. It belonged to me more than to any member of the Council.' He called on the Institute's members to defend him. 'I am positive they will not approve of the manner with which the Council have treated me. I am entitled to satisfaction. I mean to get it.'

Even Eileen Garrett was trying to distance herself from Fodor and the poltergeist case. 'I find myself being unfairly quoted as upholding the "Fielding Mediumship",' she wrote to him. 'Let me hasten to explain that I have no interest in this mediumship, and had not been favourably impressed by the phenomena I witnessed, or by Mrs Fielding herself. I tried as tactfully as possible to allow you to be aware of this fact.' Uvani, she said, had been particularly diplomatic during the sitting at the Fieldings' house. 'You will be good enough, therefore, to refrain from quoting Uvani or myself on the subject of Mrs F if you should make a report of your findings.'

With Hitler openly threatening to invade Czechoslovakia, it seemed certain that there would be a war with Germany. Air-raid shelters were dug in Hyde Park, minutes from the Fodors' apartment in the Edgware Road, and the first evacuees left London. Fodor, feeling more unwelcome than ever in England, applied for visas for his family to emigrate to the United States.

On 30 September – two days after the Fodors' visas were issued – Chamberlain signed an agreement in Munich that allowed Germany to annexe the Sudeten region of Czechoslovakia in return for a promise to make no further territorial claims. The prime minister declared that he had secured 'peace for our time'. *Psychic News* triumphantly reprinted an article in which Estelle Roberts's Red Cloud, among other spirit guides, had promised that there would be no war. Under the Munich agreement, Czechoslovakia returned most of Transcarpathia, including Fodor's home town, to Hungary, whose government immediately launched a campaign against the Jews of the region.

In an International Institute newsletter in October, Fodor received an apology of sorts from the council, or at least an acknowledgement of his efforts: 'The Council and the members of the Institute are sincerely grateful for the energy and initiative which Dr Fodor put into the work during his term of office, and desire to take this opportunity of expressing their appreciation of his services, which have made the Institute widely known.' The council returned Fodor's manuscript to him, along with a copy of the 'poltergeist diary' that he had compiled, while retaining the rest of the evidence in the Fielding case. Laurie had become the new research officer, a role in which he was to be helped by his girlfriend, Barbara, and by the Countess. Laurie let it be known that the Institute would adopt a more sympathetic attitude to spiritualism and to mediums.

The investigation of ghosts was 'basically a psychological inquiry', Fodor declared in his column for the *Journal of the American Society for Psychical Research*, 'concerned with motives and emotions, and not with facts'. He wrote to Alma, offering to complete the inquiry into her poltergeist with a course of psycho-analysis, but she did not reply.

Fodor was still waiting for his libel suit against *Psychic News* to be heard – it had been postponed to November – and he was worried about the outcome. The collapse of the Fielding investigation seemed to show that the journal had been right to describe him as ruthless towards mediums, scornful of spiritualism, fixated on sex. It would be very difficult for him to prove libel. Nonetheless, he accepted a commission from the weekly news magazine *The Leader* that was likely to give his enemies further evidence of his scepticism. He needed the money.

The Leader advertised Fodor's series on the super-normal as 'the greatest show-up of spirit "miracles" ever printed', though it disguised the identities of the mediums that he exposed. The first of his seven articles, on 1 October, featured 'the Tiger Lady', as he referred to Alma. The second piece – 'I Unmask the Muslin and Cheese-cloth Ghosts' – told of how he caught a 'foreign Wonder' (Lára Agústsdóttir of Iceland) emitting 'knickerplasm', and 'a little frightened man in the North' (Mr Stewart of Dundee) cavorting in a white sheet. In 'I Hunt the Table-Rapping Ghosts', on 29 October, Fodor recalled a chaotic sitting in Tottenham, north London, during which a wardrobe was rocked and tipped by the spirit of a Roman slave called Hedger. Fodor had to step forward to catch the cupboard as it pitched forward onto the seance circle, and by the end of the session was fending off a drunken medium with an empty beer bottle.

In New York City on Sunday 30 October, the American actor Orson Welles broadcast a dramatisation of H. G. Wells's novel *The War of the Worlds* in the guise of a live news bulletin. Some of those who heard the show believed that Martians really had invaded New Jersey. At the end of the broadcast Welles assured his audience that it had been a Halloween prank. It was as harmless, he said, as 'dressing up in a sheet, jumping out of a bush and saying, "Boo!"' In an era of such uncertainty, it was almost irresistible to stage fantasy as documentary, to dance on the line between fact and fiction.

Yet the same uncertainty left many people unable to tolerate ambiguity. To an extent, the International Institute had broken with Fodor because its council could not accept that Alma might be both a liar and a victim, and he both sceptical and sincere. The desire to demonise could have vicious consequences. Freud's protegé Ernest Jones gave a talk in north London that autumn in which he argued that the Germans had made the Jewish people a repository for their self-loathing. In the Nazi attacks of 9 to 10 November later known as *Kristallnacht*, or the Night of Broken Glass, thousands of Jewish homes, schools, businesses, hospitals and synagogues were destroyed; tens of thousands of Jewish men were arrested and imprisoned; hundreds were killed.

Sigmund Freud had moved to London in June, three months after the German occupation of Vienna. At eighty-one, he had been suffering from cancer of the mouth and jaw for fifteen years, and he knew that his latest lesions were inoperable. Freud spoke warmly of the country that gave him asylum – 'lovely, free magnanimous England' – while observing that most Londoners were neurotics, trapped by their memories. 'They cannot escape from the past,' he wrote, 'and neglect present reality in its favour.'

When Irene Fodor learnt that Freud was in the city, she urged her husband to solicit the great man's views on the Fielding case. Fodor was reluctant. He was still shaken by his expulsion from the Institute, and he doubted that Freud would have any interest in his ideas. Besides, he knew that Freud was very ill. But Irene was determined. As her daughter Andrea said, she 'had the nerve for anything'.

Freud was wary of supernatural belief. To imagine that thoughts could control objects or that the dead could return was, he argued, a regression to the animistic fantasies of childhood. 'The whole thing is so patently infantile,' he said. Before the war he had fallen out with Sándor Ferenczi and Carl Jung over their supernormal sympathies. But his attitude had softened. In 1921 he admitted to Fodor's friend Hereward Carrington, 'If I were at the beginning rather than at the end of a scientific career, as I am today, I might possibly choose just this field of research.' Psychical scientists believed that there might be secret forces at work in the world around them, Freud observed, while psychoanalysts were convinced that the hidden energies lay within people themselves. There was some overlap between these positions: Freud had come to accept that unconscious thoughts might be telepathically transferred. For the most part, though, he avoided discussing psychical research, fearing that psychoanalysis would be tainted by association with another suspect science.

On a damp, gloomy autumn day, Irene made her way to Freud's new home in Hampstead, north-west London, a modern red-brick house in the Queen Anne style. Fodor accompanied her, but hung back when she approached the door of 20 Maresfield Gardens and rang the bell. There she stood in the quiet street: a small, pretty, self-assured Jewish-Hungarian emigré with a huge bunch of orange tiger lilies.

Fodor saw the door open and his wife disappear inside. He waited on the wet pavement in an agony of suspense.

Irene introduced herself to the housekeeper by saying that she wished to pay tribute to Professor Freud on behalf of all the women of England. She waited in a spacious hallway from which she could see a recreation of Freud's Viennese study and consulting room, with his green tub chair, his couch and his collection of antique carvings and figurines – Egyptian, Greek, Roman. He had once compared these statuettes to the treasures of the unconscious: they were objects that had been so deeply buried that they had been preserved intact, as if frozen in time.

Freud was in bed that afternoon, but he agreed to receive Irene. She was led up a wide, turning staircase to his room, where she presented him with the tiger lilies. He invited her to join him for a cup of tea. She sat at Freud's bedside and told him about her husband's plight.

After forty-five minutes, Irene emerged from the house triumphant, her cheeks flushed and her eyes shining. She told Fodor that Freud had agreed to read his study of Alma Fielding.

Back in their apartment, Fodor packaged up his typescript and – 'in fear and trepidation', he said – posted it to Maresfield Gardens. His report described the investigation of Alma's phenomena over the past few months, the discovery of fraud and the inquiries that followed. It concluded that the cause of the poltergeist outbreak and the subsequent tricks was a sexual assault in Alma's childhood.

On 22 November, Fodor received a reply, written by hand in German.

Freud said that he had found the early parts hard going. For a sceptic like himself, he admitted, some of the evidential detail was tiresome. But by reading to the end, he said, 'I have found myself richly rewarded. Your attempt to turn the interest from the question of whether the observed phenomena were genuine or fraudulent, your efforts to study the medium psychologically and to uncover her previous history seem to me to be the right steps… It is very regrettable that the IIPR would not follow you. I also hold it very probable that your conclusions regarding this case are correct. Naturally, it would be desirable to confirm them by a real analysis of the party. This apparently cannot be done.' He invited Fodor to collect the report from Maresfield Gardens.

Fodor was overjoyed: 'The sun shone out and life became wonderful again.' He rushed to Freud's house to retrieve the manuscript.

Freud welcomed Fodor and returned his report to him. Fodor asked for permission to quote his letter if the manuscript were published. Freud agreed. 'He was kind and gracious, encouraging me to stick to my guns and fight for the truth as I saw it.'

In Fodor's account, both Alma's eerie experiences and her fraud were explained by the damage done to her in childhood. His theory made haunting consistent with psychoanalysis: not a counter-argument that suggested that some gifted individuals could make contact with another world or with their subliminal selves, but a proof of the uncanny power of repression.

Fodor made a copy of Freud's letter and sent it to the Institute without comment.

'This letter,' he said, 'was my vindication.'

As 1938 drew to a close, the spiritualist journal *Two Worlds* reflected on twelve months of alarm and unrest, of economic hardship at home, bloodshed and persecution abroad. But it had been a wonderful year for spiritualism: 'Never have meetings been so large,' the journal reported, 'never has there been so great a call for good mediumship, never has the public Press nor public opinion manifested so keen an interest.'

Since Fodor's court case was again delayed, this time to the new year, he accepted a freelance ghost-hunting assignment in December. His client was a film editor, a single woman of about forty whose cottage in Chelsea was haunted. Fodor learnt that eighteen years ago she had suffered a stillbirth. More recently, in the summer of 1938, she had been jilted by a man she loved. This rejection, he guessed, had revived the shock of her child's death. She had 'made herself into a living dead person', he said, 'a kind of Zombie, a ghost'. Buoyed by his encounter with Freud, Fodor told the film editor that the poltergeist's knocks and raps were attempts by her unconscious self to call attention to her buried trauma. His interpretation seemed to do the trick: the ghost left the cottage.

In February, Fodor sent the Fieldings a copy of his report on the Thornton Heath poltergeist, explaining that he hoped to publish it as a book. Alma and Les went to the Institute to protest. The organisation was still based at Walton House, although, to cut costs, it had amalgamated in December with the British College of Psychic Science to become the International Institute for Psychic Investigation. The Fieldings spoke to Wilfred Becker, who wrote to Fodor to warn him that they might make trouble. The couple, said Becker, were horrified by the report. Fodor's references to Alma 'were painful to them both' and 'would seriously damage her reputation in the eyes of her friends and neighbours'. He appealed to Fodor's good sense and his compassion.

If Eileen Garrett's supernormal marriage counsel-
ling had helped to bring Les and Alma together, their
opposition to Fodor's book united them further. By
reading about Alma's deception and her disturbance,
Les gained a new perspective on his wife, as well as a
fear of what the book might do to their family.

Fodor's suit against *Psychic News* was heard before a
special jury in the King's Bench Division of the High
Court of Justice in the Strand on 1 March 1939. He was
represented by Kew Edwin Shelley, KC, a copyright
lawyer of Indian descent who sat on the International
Institute's council, while Wilfred Becker, also a council
member, had agreed to appear as a witness for him. Les
and Alma were in the courtroom, she having received
a summons to give evidence against Fodor for the
defence.

Shelley told the court that *Psychic News* had libelled
his client by suggesting that he was unfit to be a psychical researcher. The defence replied that the journal
had been justified in its reports: Fodor had insulted
the great spirit guides, persecuted mediums, and
published revolting theories about the sexual aspects of
mediumship.

'I am not persecuting mediums,' began Fodor, 'and
I have never done so.'

'Who are the great spirit guides?' asked Justice
Singleton.

'They are a sort of managers from the great beyond,'
said Fodor, 'who take charge of mediums.'

'Are they capable of being insulted?' asked the judge, to laughter in the court.

In response to questions from the defence barrister, Fodor said that he had uncovered about twenty mediums practising fraud, and on occasion had passed the details to *Psychic News*. The journal had declined to publicise them.

When the defence mentioned the Thornton Heath case, Fodor interrupted with a request to the judge. 'May I ask your lordship to instruct the press not to reveal the lady's name,' he said, 'as that would endanger her family's happiness and her own health? The revelations that are to follow would have disastrous consequences on the lady, whom I regard as being a psychopathic subject rather than a fraudulent medium.' The judge said that he was sure that the press would accede to this request. Alma was referred to in the papers as 'Mrs F'.

Was it true, the defence lawyer asked, that Fodor had suggested that Mrs Fielding and her investigators visit the Tower of London to see if she could 'apport' the Crown Jewels?

Fodor confirmed that he had proposed such an excursion. 'It would unquestionably establish whether the so-called poltergeist is able to get something through a glass case, which is secured with burglar alarms. My suggestion, however, was not kindly received by Countess Wydenbruck, a member of the council of the IIPR. She said, "Suppose the medium does apport the Crown Jewels. We shall all land in gaol." I was willing to risk gaol, but they would not allow me.'

He also agreed that he had wanted to administer a truth serum. 'Scopolamine might have brought out deeply buried psychic injuries from her mind.'

'Was Mrs Fielding a sick woman?' asked the defence lawyer.

'She was a sick woman before we started the investigation,' said Fodor, 'but throughout the period of the investigation she began to improve, until some very strange and disturbing psychic phenomena occurred, which made me fear that she might lose her mental balance unless treatment could be given so successfully that she would calm down.'

The case continued over three days. Maurice Barbanell, the editor of *Psychic News* since its foundation in 1932, gave evidence in defence of his journal. On being questioned by the judge, Barbanell agreed that he was himself a medium 'to a little extent', with a spirit guide who went by the name Big Jump.

Also speaking on behalf of *Psychic News* were its owner and co-founder, Arthur Findlay, who had resigned as chairman of the International Institute when Fodor brought his libel suit, and the journalists who had written the articles to which Fodor objected. Two mediums, both friends of Barbanell, testified that their calling had nothing to do with sex. One was the clairvoyant Estelle Roberts, who with her spirit guide Red Cloud could command audiences of 6,000 at the Albert Hall, and the other was Louisa Bolt, at whose home Fodor and Laurie had tested the 'psychic telegraph'.

Shaw Desmond, of the Institute's council, took the stand to say that he had never known a prominent medium caught in fraud, and was aware of no relationship between psychic power and sex, except perhaps in poltergeist cases. Under cross-examination, he agreed that Fodor always treated mediums with scrupulous fairness.

Wilfred Becker attested to Fodor's integrity, as did C. V. C. Herbert of the Society for Psychical Research. Fodor chose not to submit the approving letter from Freud to the court because he did not want to drag him into the controversy. The endorsement might not have helped Fodor anyway: to win this case, he needed to prove his respect for spiritualists and mediums rather than the validity of his psychosexual theories.

In the summing up, on 3 March, Justice Singleton questioned whether Fodor had much reputation to lose. He could understand that the *Psychic News* articles might have 'narked' him, he said, but the jury should remember that it was dealing with a man who had gone to the Isle of Man to meet a talking mongoose.

After deliberating for fifty minutes, the special jury nonetheless found for Fodor on two of the four libel charges, and awarded him a total of a hundred guineas (£104) in damages.

Alma had not been called to give evidence, but she spoke to Fodor in the courtroom. 'You will never publish that book,' she told him. It was the last time that they met.

Chamberlain's appeasement policy had done nothing to curb Hitler's persecution of Jews and other minorities, nor his hunger for more territory. In January, the Führer had warned that the coming war would eliminate all Jews in Europe. On 15 March, he invaded Czechoslovakia, breaking the promise that he had made in Munich.

Two days after that, on 17 March 1939, Fodor sailed for New York with his wife and daughter.

Fodor had found a radical way of explaining Alma's fraudulent phenomena, as the products of damage rather than conscious deceit. Alma was sick, he insisted, and many of her actions involuntary. His argument was generous, in that it relieved Alma of blame and allowed that her violence and lies might be the fruits of abuse, but it was also partial. By casting Alma as a victim of her past, Fodor minimised the danger in which his investigation had put her, and he belittled her creative achievement.

Alma's haunting had, at least in part, been a deliberate, inventive and outrageous hoax. She had enacted a wild, months-long magic-realist extravaganza at the International Institute for Psychical Research, a piece of performance art in which she was both the lady-sawn-in-half and the magician who cuts a slice through her. In a stream of phenomena rich in symbolism and silliness, she had scripted a drama that revealed as much about her audience as herself. She used her investigators' beliefs – mystical and psychological – to give shape to her chaotic inner life. She depicted suffering in the scratches, punctures, cuts and burns on her skin; sexual craving and dread in the incubus and vampire visits. She laid claim to a crazy fertility, in which her belly could instantly swell, and her hands and feet could give birth to living creatures, ancient relics and Woolworth's merchandise. Through the episodes of projection and possession, she acted out her sense that she did not exist securely on one plane, in one self, in one moment. Through Jimmy the poltergeist, she unleashed aggression, mischief and spite. Through Bremba, she demanded respect. Through Mevanwe and the spirit child, she voiced helplessness and fear.

The reporter from the *Croydon Advertiser* bumped into Alma in Thornton Heath in May. She looked well, Jack said: plumper, less worn. She told him that the poltergeist was still with her. Jimmy threw crockery around from time to time, but he also brought her brooches, old coins and lumps of gold quartz. Alma said that she hesitated to wear the jewellery outside the house, in case it was recognised – after all, she didn't know where it came from.

TWENTY

A lane to the land of the dead

When Britain finally declared war on Germany in September 1939, the Fieldings decided to leave Croydon and set up home on the coast.

Les leased a flat piece of land halfway down the cliff at Branscombe, east Devon, a spot that the family had visited for a camping holiday that summer. He bought a self-assembly bungalow in London, and arranged for the sections to be delivered to the clifftop by train and lorry, then lowered to the plot on ropes. He and Don laid the foundations in the spring of 1940. The building had casement windows, a panelled front door and a pitched roof, which was camouflaged with paint as protection against enemy bombers. George helped the family to move in.

The village of Branscombe ran along a lane in the valley behind the cliff: a few dozen houses, a meeting hall, a general store, a post office, a bakery, a forge, a cobbler, a butcher, a school, three pubs, a Methodist chapel and an Anglican church. The blacksmith acted as postman, delivering letters and parcels to the 500 or so residents, including those in the scattered cliff dwellings. A coastguard station and searchlight sat on the red mudstone above the bungalow, a clutch of holiday chalets and a tea room on the shingle beach below.

Les and Don joined the Home Guard; though Don was eligible for conscription, having turned eighteen in September, he had not yet been called up. Les took charge of the nightly patrol along the clifftop and of the machine-gun emplacement above the beach. He and Don were issued with rifles. Don bought a Lewis gun, which he kept under his bed, and a second-hand New Imperial motorcycle, which he rode to work. Both men did twelve-hour shifts at a secret munitions works in the back of a hair-lotion factory in the village square. The BBC's radio programme *Music While You Work* was piped into the workshop each day to offset the grunt and bang of the lathes. All the machines were quickly turned off one night when a German pilot was shot down nearby – if the enemy learnt that shells and torpedo parts were being made in Branscombe, the village might have become a target for bombers.

Alma volunteered as a nurse with the St John Ambulance brigade, tending convalescent soldiers in the nearby town of Sidmouth. Don enlisted with the army in 1943, when he was twenty-one, and served as a dispatch rider in France and Norway. Les became a constable with the Royal Marine Police.

Croydon was bombed heavily from August 1940 onwards, in part because its aerodrome had been adopted as a Royal Air Force fighter base. Five thousand residents of the borough were killed, and 60,000 buildings damaged. Alma's mother Alice suffered a fatal

heart attack at 42 Haslemere Road in 1942; she left all
her belongings to her favourite daughter, Doris, who
moved in to the property. On 1 July 1944 the street was
hit by a V-1 'doodlebug', which destroyed ten houses
and killed three people. The flying bomb blew out all
the windows of Dorrie's house and hurled the front
door halfway up the stairs.

London was strewn with such scenes. A bed sat in the
street. A double-decker bus reared out of a crater. Store
mannequins lay broken on the pavement. Papered bedroom walls stood open to the rain. The photographer
Lee Miller took pictures of these fractured, once-
familiar objects. They were surrogates for the mangled
bodies that could not be shown and metaphors for the
dislocation of the people left behind. The bombing had
transformed the imaginary mash-ups of the surrealists
into real urban landscapes.

The ghost stories that the Anglo-Irish novelist
Elizabeth Bowen wrote in London in the war years
came to her like 'huge and inchoate particles', she
said. 'I do not feel I "invented" anything. Sometimes
I hardly knew where I stopped and somebody else
began.' Even in her pre-war stories, Bowen had
ascribed life to objects, as if they had become vehicles
for human feelings. Now, she observed, 'People whose
houses had been blown up went to infinite lengths to
assemble themselves – broken ornaments, odd shoes,
torn scraps of the curtains that had hung in a room –
from the wreckage.' The domestic items left by a
bombing, like the items thrown around Alma's home,

seemed scattered parts of the self. Bowen barely felt that she was writing fiction at all any more, she said, but simply channelling the spirits of the living. 'It seems to me that during the war the overcharged sub-consciousness of everybody overflowed and merged. We all lived in a state of lucid abnormality.' The ghosts of the last war haunted the new conflict. In Bowen's 'The Demon Lover', a married woman catches a taxi from a shut-up London square, and realises that her driver is her first fiancé, who was killed on the Western Front. She screams in terror when she sees his face, and is screaming still as she is driven away, beating her gloved hands at the closed windows of the black cab.

The ghost hunter Harry Price published two books about Borley Rectory in the 1940s, as well as an anthology – *Poltergeist Over England* – in which he likened the Blitz to a supernatural attack. A *Manchester Guardian* article of 1941 described both poltergeists and Nazis as products of 'a subconscious uprush of desire for power'; 'both suck, like vampires, the energies of adolescents; both issue in noise, destruction and terror'. Another *Manchester Guardian* piece observed that the bombs were outdoing the ghosts of the 1930s. 'Those of us who survive this war,' predicted the paper, 'are not going to be greatly alarmed by a waltzing wardrobe.' The mediums of the last decade had been discredited by their false promises of peace. Perhaps the spiritualist spell cast by the First World War would be broken by the unparalleled horrors of the Second.

In 1941, the navy launched an inquiry into the Scottish medium Helen Duncan – who had once refused Fodor's request to film her by infrared light – after reports that she had psychically intercepted a state secret about the sinking of a warship. The investigation uncovered deceit rather than ethereal espionage, and in 1944 Duncan became one of the last people to be convicted of fraud under the Witchcraft Act.

The International Institute for Psychic Investigation pressed on, with a reduced programme. In 1945 it renamed itself for a second time, becoming the Institute for Experimental Metaphysics, and in 1947 it stopped operating altogether.

Countess Nora Wydenbruck and Alfons Purtscher saw out the war in Holland Park. As Civil Defence volunteers, they patrolled the streets of west London by night, putting out fires with hand-held water pumps. They twice had to extinguish blazes set off by incendiary bombs on the roof of their own house. After the war the Countess made friends with the poet T. S. Eliot, and became the German translator of his *Four Quartets* and *The Cocktail Party*. In the first of these, Eliot listed some of the supernatural and psychological fashions that had flourished in the previous decade, from horoscopes to clairvoyance to dream analysis, describing them as 'pastimes and drugs' that always became popular 'When there is distress of nations and perplexity/Whether on the shores of Asia, or in the Edgware Road.'

The Countess published several further books – novels, biographies, translations and memoirs – before her death in London in 1959. Alfons died four years later. Gerald and Hilda Wills remained in Putney, where the doctor died in 1969.

Sigmund Freud died in Maresfield Gardens on 23 September 1939, three weeks after the outbreak of war. Elizabeth Severn moved that year to New York, where she worked as a psychoanalyst. Sándor Ferenczi's paper on the effects of sexual abuse on children was published in English in 1949, and thirty-five years later the publication of his clinical diaries revealed how his theory of trauma had emerged from his psychoanalysis of 'RN'. Elizabeth Severn's identity as RN was uncovered in 1993, twenty-four years after her death.

Eileen Garrett moved to New York in 1940 and set up a parapsychological institute and a publishing company. She became a *grande dame* of psychical research, giving employment to Fodor and many others. She died in 1970, leaving her daughter and granddaughter to run her small empire.

Ronnie Cockersell pursued a career as a psychic, but in 1958 was caught burgling a house in London and sentenced to two years in prison. He was found dead in his flat in Fulham in 1968, having taken an overdose of barbiturates. He left a note explaining that he was 'tired of this planet'.

Voirrey Irving moved from the Isle of Man to the mainland after the war; when interviewed in 1970, she insisted on the truth of the tale of the talking mongoose.

'Gef even kept me from getting married,' she told the reporter. 'How could I ever tell a man's family about what happened?'

Hylda Lewis, the flower medium, left London after being exposed as a fraud. In Old Southcote Lodge in Berkshire, she befriended Florence Hodgkin, an Irishwoman whose grandson Howard later became a well-known abstract artist. Florence wrote to *Light* in 1940 to describe how a psychic friend – probably Hylda – had noticed a group of fairies and a gnome entering the lodge. 'The Fairies are still with me,' said Mrs Hodgkin.

> They are seen in railway carriages – an astonished passenger once described the antics of my Gnome, who was climbing out of the window, running along the foot-board to the engine and back over the roof. In a London drawing-room an unknown woman made her way to me to say she had been watching my Fairies. I asked what she had seen. 'There are six in your lap at this moment and one sitting on your shoulder.' The correct number: there are six and a Queen.

Laurie Evans and Barbara Waring married in 1939 and had a son. During the war Laurie's friend Laurence Olivier – whom he had met at Twickenham Studios in 1930 – hired him as production manager on the film *Henry V*, and then as general manager at the Old Vic theatre. Laurie and Barbara subsequently divorced, and in 1960 he married for a fourth time. By then he was the most influential theatrical agent of his generation, representing Olivier and many other actors, among them Ingrid Bergman, Albert Finney, Alec Guinness, Rex Harrison, Wendy Hiller, John Mills, Celia Johnson, James Mason, Maggie Smith, Ronald Reagan and Vivien Leigh. Laurie was a well-loved figure in the theatre world: clever, inquisitive, witty and rich. He turned up to first nights in a chauffeur-driven Rolls-Royce. At his grand house in Surrey he introduced visitors to his white cockatoo Max, a birthday present from John Gielgud.

After the war Alma's sister Dorrie and her brother Charlie both moved out to Branscombe. Alma sometimes went back to Croydon to stay with friends. For months at a time in the late 1940s and early 1950s she lived with Frank Martin, a car salesman, above a junk shop just south of Thornton Heath. George was living about five minutes' walk away with his new wife, Kathleen, and still working as a cobbler. By alternating between Devon and Croydon, Alma was able to escape her marriage without breaking it altogether. Les, as Uvani had advised, let her go her own way.

Frank Martin and his brother Dick had lived round the corner from the Fieldings in the 1930s, in a house stuffed with curious old objects. Perhaps the Martin brothers had been a source for some of Alma's more outlandish apports. And perhaps her brother Charlie had provided others – one of his many sidelines in the 1930s was to breed mice to feed the snakes at London Zoo.

When Don was demobilised he moved to his grand-mother and aunt's old home in Haslemere Road. He married a farmer's daughter named Rigmor, whom he had met while serving in Norway, and found a job as a plumber. Rigmor gave birth to two sons, Barry and Leslie, in 1946 and 1954. She became unhappy. Having been brought up in wild, open country on the edge of a fjord, she hated the narrow terraced streets of Thornton Heath. When Don was at work her older son, Barry, would hear her throwing pans and smashing crockery in the kitchen, like Alma's poltergeist. Rigmor began to sew and sell blouses to fund a trip to her homeland. By 1972 she had raised enough money to travel to Norway with her younger son. She never returned to England, and Barry did not see his mother for thirty-two years.

Apart from her long visits to Croydon, Alma stayed with Les on the cliff in Devon. Les described these as the happiest years of his life. He and Alma lived simply, with no telephone, plumbing or electricity. They used a hand pump to draw water from a spring. Les some-times worked on local farms and Alma occasionally made flowers from crêpe paper and wire, which she sent by train to a shop in south London. The bills were low – rent and rates were less than £5 a year – and the housework minimal.

A farmer grew potatoes and anemones at the far end of the Fieldings' cliff plateau. His donkeys brought seaweed up from the beach to fertilise the crops, and then carried the harvest through the steep passes to the village. Les planted peach and apple trees on the rich green turf in front of the bungalow, and a vine at the entrance. He caught fish in the sea, raised rabbits and ducks, grew vegetables. For fuel, he bought Calor gas cylinders in the village and carted them through the cliff pass in a wheelbarrow purchased with John Player's cigarette coupons. On winter nights the gas hissed softly in the mantle, and pork roasted in a miniature cast-iron oven. Les and Alma invited villagers over to parties at which they would drink home-made wine. From the front door they could see the dark sheet of the sea.

Alma occasionally held seances in their bungalow and in village houses. At one sitting, the table thumped excitedly and knives and forks leapt in the air. At another, pennies rained down from the ceiling. At a third, the son of one of the cliff farmers heard jingling and spirit voices, and felt a great heaviness in his legs and upon his shoulders. Afterwards he saw a small bell tumble out of Alma's sleeve, its Woolworth's label still attached. Despite the evidence of trickery, he was unsettled by the experience: his physical sensations had been real.

The daughter of another farmer remembered that there was 'something funny' about the Fieldings. Several villagers wondered what they were doing there, tucked away on the far side of the cliff. Were they on the run? Were they hiding from something? Were they spies? There was an air of mystery about them. Alma could still make others feel her disturbance and unease.

When Les suffered a heart attack in the 1960s, he and Alma moved to a tiny, rose-covered white cottage opposite the thirteenth-century church in the middle of Branscombe. Alma became ill, with inflammations and infections of her bowel, and after being diagnosed with diverticulitis had part of her intestine removed.

Don had remained close to both his parents, and after Les's death in 1973 he invited Alma to live with him and his son Barry in Thornton Heath. Barry was working as a telephone engineer on the Croydon exchange. 'I'm moving in with you, ducks,' Alma told him. Barry was made uncomfortable by his grandmother – her smell, her colostomy bag, her sloppy cooking habits. She reminded him, he said, of Irene Handl, a comic actress known for playing forthright and sometimes crafty Cockney chars. Alma told unsavoury stories, some of which suggested an abiding anger. There was a man she used to know in London, she said, who when drunk would walk the streets with a cow's udder pinned to his trousers so that it seemed that his 'willy' was hanging out of his flies; he would then ostentatiously produce a knife, slice off the appendage and fling it aside. This was a practical joke designed to shock, a sadistic jape, in which a teat was butchered in place of a penis. Barry had also heard tales of Alma's spooky past, and he was frightened about what might happen when she was in the house.

Barry's brother Leslie returned from Norway to England to go to university, and sometimes stayed at Haslemere Road. His grandmother Alma was 'creative', he recalled: he was never quite sure which of her stories were invented and which real. For years he didn't believe a word of the poltergeist tale, but one day his father, who had never expressed a view on the supernatural, mentioned matter-of-factly that he had witnessed the poltergeist's mischief. In the spring of 1938, Don claimed, a back-scrubbing brush from the bathroom in Beverstone Road had twice floated downstairs behind him.

Alma moved back to Devon in 1974. She died two years later, and was buried next to Les in Branscombe churchyard.

I met Barry Fielding in the house in Devon that he and his father had shared until Don's death in 2003. Barry told me that Don, as a boy of five, had been frightened one day by the sound of Alma weeping in the front room of their house in Croydon. Afterwards, Don learnt that she had been sitting with the body of his baby brother, Laurie. I realised that this was one of the children that Alma had told Fodor about on 17 May 1938, the day that her belly ballooned. She had spoken of an unchristened girl, June, who died at three months, and a boy, Laurence.

Barry told me that he had not heard of the girl, who would have been his aunt, but he showed me a family photograph album that contained three pictures of the boy. The photos of Laurie Fielding seemed to have been taken on the same summer's day in 1926. In two of them he is perched on a grass bank with Don and another child. In a third, he is in his mother's lap, a dark-eyed one-year-old with flushed cheeks and soft black hair. Alma leans back on the grass, smiling. The baby, dressed in a white smock, frowns with concentration at something in his hands.

Back in London, I looked up the records of births and deaths in Croydon in the 1920s and 1930s, but could find no trace of a female Fielding baby. The yet-to-be-christened girl may have died before even her existence was registered, though this would be unusual if she lived as long as three months. Perhaps Fodor misunderstood, and Alma miscarried a female baby, or June was one of the stillborn twins that she delivered after seeing the dead rat. Perhaps, like other stories that Alma told, the fleeting existence of June was a mingling of the imagined and the real. But the birth and death of Laurence Peter were just as she reported. According to the public records, he was born on 7 June 1925. He would have turned thirteen on the day in 1938 that Alma's eyes apparently began to fail.

Fodor's notes show that after 17 May Alma returned several times to the subject of her lost son: she spoke of her compulsive, secret visits to Laurie's grave; she identified the baby's death as the event that might have caused her to attack Les in 1926 and to go blind in 1929. But in his account of Alma's case, Fodor mentioned her second son only in passing. 'At eighteen she had her first baby,' he wrote; 'at twenty-one, the next ... At twenty-two her second baby died of tubercular meningitis.' He did not seem to have considered that the boy's death might be a source of enduring pain to Alma, or that Les's reaction to it might have laid the charge for the poltergeist attack.

Fodor had noticed that many mediums were bereaved mothers, and that the convulsions of trance could resemble a woman's labour throes. Lizzie Bullock, the transfiguration medium, took up clairvoyance after the deaths of two babies, and during her spirit possessions she behaved, said Fodor, 'as if she actually were to give "birth" to the phantoms'. Fodor attributed her grimaces to orgasms, but she might also have been undergoing the spasms of labour, or of grief. Lizzie said that she had converted to spiritualism when she felt the weight of a spirit child in her arms. Eileen Garrett, too, became a medium after the deaths of her sons, and at her first seance with Fodor moaned and shook so much, he said, that he feared that she would deliver a baby. It was she who saw the aura of a baby around Alma, and suggested that she had lost a child.

Alma was twenty-two when Laurie contracted tubercular meningitis. He probably seemed merely tired and cranky in the early summer of 1926, as the bacteria in his lungs spread to the membranes around his brain and spinal cord. But in August he suddenly fell down. He collapsed into a stupor, then a coma. He died on 2 September 1926 in the Thornton Heath workhouse infirmary.

Laurie's body was returned to the family home in Maplethorpe Road, where it lay for three days in a lined white coffin in the front room. It was then that Don heard his mother sobbing by the boy's corpse.

On 6 September the coffin was taken for burial at the Mitcham Road cemetery, and lowered into a hole in front of Alma's father's grave. Charles Smith's body had been taken to the burial ground that June in a hearse pulled by two horses, at a cost of £21. Laurie's interment was a simpler affair, costing just under £9. Both graves were at the back of the cemetery, almost against the wall. Afterwards, Laurie was rarely mentioned by the family. In October, Alma's aunt Nell – her father's sister – referred in a letter to Les and Alma's 'little trouble'.

The autumn of Laurie's death was the same autumn that Alma was poisoned by anthrax, tried to stab her husband, and broke out of the house in her night-clothes, screaming 'Fire!' and 'Murder!' She tore along the street, her mouth black with disease, like the bolting, frothing dog that she said had once attacked her. She seemed crazed beyond ordinary grief or sickness. Alma told Fodor that she had been beside herself with anger at Les for failing to comfort her. Perhaps she was also terrified that she had exposed her son to the illness that killed him. Her father had returned from the Croydon tuberculosis sanatorium to die at home in Maplethorpe Road at the end of May 1926, and Laurie succumbed to tubercular disease in the same house three months later. Alma may have blamed herself for her boy's suffering and his death.

Sándor Ferenczi believed that a traumatising event was always a repetition of a previous crisis. The shell-shocked soldiers he encountered, he said, were men in whom the horrors of war had cracked open already fractured psyches. If Alma had been assaulted as a child, as Fodor and Mrs Severn believed, the loss of her baby may have awakened intolerable feelings from her early life. 'Traumatic aloneness,' said Ferenczi, 'is what really renders the attack traumatic, that is, causing the psyche to crack.' The lasting effects of trauma, he argued, resulted from the absence of a kind, understanding environment. Laurie's death, terrible in itself, was made catastrophic for Alma by Les's seeming indifference. In failing to comfort her, Les may have unwittingly repeated the silence with which her mother betrayed her when she was a child. Twice, those who should have protected and consoled Alma – her mother, her husband – refused even to acknowledge her suffering. When Laurie died, Alma's pain was all the sharper because she had failed to protect her own child too.

'My mummy, my mummy!' cried the spirit child who spoke through Alma on 17 May 1938. A month later the voice emerged again, still pleading: 'Mummy. My mummy. She is not come? She said she will come.'

In New York City in the 1940s, Fodor trained as a psychoanalyst. He lived in an apartment on the Upper East Side of Manhattan with Irene and Andrea, and rented a consulting room nearby. When the Germans invaded Hungary in 1944, Irene's parents and Fodor's brother Lajos, a leader of the resistance, were among the 400,000 Hungarian Jews killed by the Nazis.

After the war Andrea Fodor became a prima ballerina with the Metropolitan Opera Ballet. She married Ervin Litkei, a Jewish-Hungarian musician who had survived the German invasion of his country, and they had a daughter.

With the help of Freud's letter, which he framed and hung on his wall, Fodor built up a successful psychoanalytic practice. In 1945 he gave a paper to the Association for the Advancement of Psychotherapy in which he outlined what he had learnt from Alma's story. 'The Poltergeist is not a spirit,' he said, 'it has no identity, it brings no messages from the dead; it is a bundle of projected repressions bent on destruction and mischief because it is born out of rage and frustration.' In his book *Haunted People*, published in 1951, he elaborated the theory of 'poltergeist psychosis': a person could suffer a kind of 'psychic lobotomy', he said, in which a devastating mental shock loosened an infantile, repressed part of the psyche, a vengeful poltergeist personality. He cited a sequence in the 1945 British horror film *Dead of Night* in which a ventriloquist's dummy comes to life and murders its master.

Fodor believed that Alma's fraud, like her supernatural experience, was rooted in pain. He thought that the objects that leapt into life around her in February 1938 were animated by feelings that she could not own: her sexual desire; her obscure sense of fear, violation and abandonment; her wish for power; her rage. The poltergeist was her surrogate. It was a force of insurrection, a protest, a scream.

As a psychoanalyst, Fodor sometimes treated haunted patients: a married woman whose incubus brought her a 'mad, happy darkness'; a teenage boy who eventually vanquished his poltergeist by becoming a science-fiction writer. 'Find the frustrated creative gift,' advised Fodor, 'lift up a crushed ego, give love and confidence and the Poltergeist will cease to be.' He regretted the probing techniques that he had adopted as a psychical researcher in England. His attitude had undergone 'a tremendous change', he told *Psychic Observer* in 1943. He took 'no more joy in tying up mediums and exalting instrumental findings', he said. 'I see now psychical research has tried to be too scientific for years and has gone bankrupt as a result. Mediums do not function well if they are used as guinea-pigs. They are human beings with the same virtues and vices as the researchers themselves.' He was sorry for the harshness with which he had treated Alma, and saw that his methods had expressed his own frustration and fear. But he had also helped to lift her up, as he had the science-fiction boy, by treating her as precious and astonishing.

Fodor learnt in 1943 that the medium through whom his father had seemed to speak in 1927 had concealed the fact that he was himself fluent in Hungarian. As for the Hebrew words that the seven-year-old Nandor had heard at his grandfather's burial, perhaps those had been spoken by the rabbi giving a blessing over the grave. But Fodor already knew that the voices of his forebears had not issued from their spirit selves.

In several books about his psychic adventures of the 1930s, Fodor returned to the case of Alma and her poltergeist. He also tackled new psychological territory. In *The Search for the Beloved* (1949), he examined birth from the point of view of the baby. The baby's expulsion from its mother's body, he argued, was the original traumatic experience, and the womb was the model for every paradise, from the Garden of Eden to Aladdin's Cave to the Never-Never Land to Shangri-La. He cited Alma's cave dream as an instance of the longing for this place, speculating that his own search for the supernatural, too, had been a search for the floating bliss of pre-natal existence. 'We all have lived in another world,' he said, 'before we were born.' The woozy, enveloping atmosphere of the seance room was one such haven. Fodor signed a copy of his book for his old friend Laurie Evans.

Harry Price died in 1948. Eight years later an SPR investigation concluded that the Borley Rectory haunting of the 1930s had been a hoax, perpetrated by Price at some points and by the rector's wife Marianne Foyster at others. Marianne seemed to have faked some of the phenomena in order to conceal a liaison with her lodger. Price joined in because he hoped that the story of 'the most haunted house in Britain', as he proclaimed it, would bring him fame and riches. Fodor defended Price. 'He was intensely selfish, jealous and intent on his own glory at all cost,' he said, 'but these weaknesses of his character do not detract from his reputation as an honest investigator and ruthless exposer of frauds.' Fodor's faith said more about his own integrity than that of his adversary.

Alma was wrong to predict that Fodor's study of her would not be published. *On the Trail of the Poltergeist* was printed in New York in 1958 by the Citadel Press. Fodor omitted any mention of Elizabeth Severn or Eileen Garrett, and he disguised the identities of the Fielding and Saunders families, but the book otherwise gave a scrupulous and vivid rendition of the four months in 1938 in which he investigated Alma's poltergeist. Fodor argued both that emotions could cause weird phenomena and that hoaxes could be as interesting as real supernormal events. Lies and tricks and jokes, like ghosts, could be expressions of suffering.

A review in the *Journal of the Society for Psychical Research* speculated on how 'Mrs Forbes', as Fodor referred to Alma, might have achieved some of her effects. She could have hidden a flat steel spring in her corset, suggested the reviewer, secretly pulling it up to fire an apport across the room, and pushing it down again when her audience was distracted by the crash of the object's landing. To capsize the armchair in the Institute library, she might have looped a black thread over a knob on the chairback, yanked the thread as she sat down in another seat, and quickly ravelled it up as she walked over to inspect the fallen chair. Perhaps she used similar techniques to generate poltergeist activity in Beverstone Road.

Some of Fodor's psychoanalytic colleagues commented on his study. Gustav Bychowski agreed that Alma was severely dissociated but thought that her narcissism and exhibitionism had been dangerously encouraged by the researchers. Paul Federn thought it likely that Alma had indeed suffered trauma of some sort as a child, but wondered if the rape was a fantasy. Joseph Wilder observed that the prostitutes of ancient Rome had produced the smell of violets by drinking a tablespoon of turpentine oil and urinating afterwards.

In the years after the publication of Fodor's book, psychologists identified other natural explanations for apparently supernatural experiences. Alma's visits from the incubus and the vampire might have been episodes of sleep paralysis, which render people unable to move or speak when they wake. These neurological events are characterised by an intense pressure on the chest and sometimes a tingling of the nerves, like the feeling of pins and needles that Alma described. Some of those who undergo a sleep paralysis become sexually aroused. Some have visions of intruders: witches, vampires, incubi, succubi, alien abductors. A few feel the press or penetration of a cold penis. To experience such sensations while perpetrating a supernatural fraud – or reliving a traumatic event – might feel terrifying: like a satanic punishment.

Since the 1980s, researchers in the psychology of supernatural belief have found a correlation between childhood trauma and adult experiences of paranormality. People who have been sexually abused as children are unusually likely to report supernatural events. Psychologists speculate that damaged children learn to use fantasy as a form of escape, while their desperate wish for control generates delusions of psychic power. Fodor believed that the desperation sometimes produced real supernatural force.

By the time that Fodor's book about the Thornton Heath poltergeist was published, psychical research had become an esoteric subject, no longer taken seriously by most scientific thinkers. Yet his ideas about poltergeist psychosis found expression in fiction. In *The Haunting of Hill House*, a novel of 1959, Shirley Jackson explores the possibility that a disturbed individual can trigger supernormal events. She describes a ghost hunt conducted under the aegis of the psychical researcher Dr John Montague, in which weird incidents seem to emanate from a young woman called Eleanor Vance. When Fodor was invited to serve as a consultant on the film adaptation of the novel, in 1963, he asked Shirley Jackson if she had read his work, and she confirmed that she had.

The filmmakers proposed to Jackson that they present the events in her novel as the hallucinations of a woman in a mental asylum, but she discouraged this approach: the story was about real supernatural happenings, she said. Like Fodor, she chose not to explain away psychic experiences as madness or lies. Fodor wrote an article about *The Haunting of Hill House* shortly before his death in 1964, in which he observed that Jackson had adopted 'the modern approach' to the supernormal: 'The creaks and groans of furniture, the imbalance of a spiral staircase and the abnormally cold spots are objectifications of the mental anguish and chill of Eleanor's soul, the violent slamming of doors are explosive manifestations of inner conflicts.'

This strand of psychological gothic emerges again in Stephen King's novels *Carrie*, in which a humiliated teenager's suppressed feelings erupt in supernatural violence, and *The Shining*, in which ghosts are awakened by the obsessions of the living. It runs through books and films such as Barbara Comyns's *The Vet's Daughter*, Daphne du Maurier's *Don't Look Now*, Toni Morrison's *Beloved*, Hilary Mantel's *Beyond Black*, Sarah Waters's *The Little Stranger*, Jennifer Kent's *The Babadook*. To the question of whether a haunting was real or fantasised, psychological or supernatural, the answer given by such stories was: both. A ghost could be imagined into being, from a feeling repressed so forcefully that it acquired uncanny power. 'Our irrational, darker selves,' wrote Elizabeth Bowen, 'demand familiars.'

Fodor's ideas about trauma took years to be accepted. Only towards the end of the century did it become commonplace to think that a profoundly shocking event might be erased from consciousness, as Sándor Ferenczi and Elizabeth Severn had described, creating a fragmented, dissociated identity, flashbacks, recurring dreams. The key to cure was the recovery of the memory. But when a traumatic memory seemed to surface, as in Alma's story, there could be doubt about whether it had been salvaged or invented. This uncertainty continues to haunt the subject. Some events are so dark that to find them is an act of imagination as much as memory. They lie between history and fiction. Perhaps there are still feelings for which only a ghost will do.

Epilogue

In December 2017 I returned to the SPR archive in Cambridge. I again queued briefly at the taxi rank, climbed into a cab and asked for the university library. As the taxi pulled away from the station, the driver asked me what I was researching. He turned slightly in his seat, and I saw that he was the same dark-haired man who had picked me up at the railway station in January. I was unnerved by the coincidence, and reminded for a moment of the malevolent cab driver in Elizabeth Bowen's 'The Demon Lover'.

I told the driver that I thought we had met when I was last in Cambridge, eleven months ago. He remembered. I asked him to tell me more about his psychic experiences.

The cab driver told me that he had vampires attached to his spirit. He had summoned them, he said, on the recommendation of his spirit guide. 'Go for vampires,' the guide advised. 'Stay away from fluffy bunnies and fairies. You're more suited to the darker side.' Two psychics had told him that he had vampires in his bloodline.

'Not that I do anything dark and horrible,' he assured me. The vampires, like the two-headed snake that had dangled from his neck in January, came to relieve him of suffering. 'Most of my spirits specialise in healing,' said the cab driver. 'In fact, the vampires are fantastic healers.'

He said that he summoned the spirits with his mind and that they sustained themselves by sucking energy from other people, on his instructions.

'Really? You can tell them to do that?'

Yes, he said. The practice did no harm. People sucked of their vitality might just feel a bit tired.

Had he had any bad experiences?

'For some reason,' said my driver, 'I keep attracting demons. I did have a demon stuck to the side of my face. I could feel it clawing constantly and it took me about three months to get rid of it.' I thought of the claws on Alma's back, the jabs in her pelvis, the teeth in her neck.

The taxi driver lifted his right hand from the wheel and pressed it hard against his cheek.

Les and Alma's sons Peter (left) and Don (right) with another child in the summer of 1926

LIST OF ILLUSTRATIONS

NOTE ON SOURCES

The main sources for this book are 'The Fielding (Forbes) Poltergeist Diary', in the Eileen J. Garrett Library at the Parapsychology Foundation, New York; the Mediums and Research files in the archive of the Society for Psychical Research at Cambridge University Library; and Nandor Fodor's publications, especially *On the Trail of the Poltergeist*. These sources are detailed below, along with the other books, journals, newspapers and manuscripts I have used. I have also drawn on conversations with Andrea Fodor Litkei, Barry Fielding and Leslie Fielding, as well as papers and photographs in their private collections.

BIBLIOGRAPHY

MANUSCRIPTS

Society for Psychical Research Archive, Department of Manuscripts and University Archives, Cambridge University Library

MS SPR/19 [papers relating to Eileen Garrett]

MS SPR/31 [papers relating to the International Institute for Psychical Research]

MS SPR/Mediums: Abbott, Mr & Mrs

MS SPR/Mediums: Agustsdotter, Fru Lara [Lára Agústsdóttir]

MS SPR/Mediums: Brown, Harry

MS SPR/Mediums: Bullock, Mrs

MS SPR/Mediums: Cockersell, R.

MS SPR/Mediums: Dickson, Mrs J.

MS SPR/Mediums: Fielding, Mr A. [Alma Fielding]

MS SPR/Mediums: Garrett, Mrs Eileen

MS SPR/Mediums: Harrison, Mrs

MS SPR/Mediums: Kolb, Theodore

MS SPR/Mediums: Leaf, Horace

MS SPR/Mediums: Lewis, Miss Hylda

MS SPR/Mediums: Pap, Lajos

MS SPR/Mediums: Richardson, Mr & Mrs

MS SPR/Mediums: Rasmussen, A.

MS SPR/Mediums: Roberts, Estelle

MS SPR/Mediums: Schermann, Raphael

MS SPR/Mediums: Singleton, Mr [Louisa Bolt, aka Mrs Singleton]

MS SPR/Mediums: Woodward, D. A. [Richard Woodward]

MS SPR/Mediums: Zugun, Mme [Eleonore Zugun]

MS SPR/Research/ Cloud Chamber Experiments
MS SPR/Research/ H66 [Bethnal Green & Barkingside hauntings]
MS SPR/Research/ H149 [Ash Manor haunting]
MS SPR/Research/ H276 [Aldborough Manor haunting]
MS SPR/Research/ P15 [Thornton Heath poltergeist]
MS SPR/Research/ Psychic Photography

Eileen J. Garrett Library, Parapsychology Foundation,
New York, NY

'The Fielding (Forbes) Poltergeist Diary'

National Archives, Kew, Richmond, Surrey

J54/2351 [documents from Fodor's libel suit at the High Court of
Justice, March 1939]

Hoover Institution, Stanford, California

Nandor Fodor papers, 1921-1945, 80031

Firestone Library, Princeton University, Princeton, New Jersey

Hereward Carrington papers C1159, Box 1, Folder 46

College of Psychic Studies, London

IIPR members' advice cards, seasonal programmes, income and
expenditure accounts, and correspondence between Fodor and
Mercy Phillimore

British Institute of Psychoanalysis, London

CFD/F12/01 [letter from Fodor to Ernest Jones, 23 Oct 1953]

Harry Price archive, Senate House Library, University of London

HPC/4B/295 [Nandor Fodor, 1936-1938]
HPC/7/19 [International Institute for Psychical Research Ltd
1934-38]

HPC/7/22 [Press cuttings concerning the International Institute for Psychical Research]

Eric John Dingwall papers, Senate House Library, University of London

MS912/1/244 [letters from Fodor]
MS912/1/22 [scrapbook including correspondence with Fodor]
MS912/1/10 [scrapbook including letters from Fodor]

General Records Office

Death certificates of James Stephen Bannister, Jessie Bannister (née Richardson), Alma Daisy Fielding (née Smith), Donald Richard Fielding, Laurence Peter Fielding, Leslie Edward Fielding, George Joseph Saunders, Alice Maud Smith (née Bannister), Charles Smith, Doris Smith, Arthur Gerald Wills

Private papers

Private papers of Barry Fielding, Axminster, Devon
Private papers of Andrea Fodor Litkei, New York, NY

BOOKS & ARTICLES

Addison, Adrian, *Mail Men: The Unauthorised Story of the Daily Mail* (London, 2017)
Angoff, Allan, *Eileen Garrett and the World Beyond the Senses* (New York, 2009)
Asquith, Cynthia, ed., *The Ghost Book* (London, 1926)
—*The Second Ghost Book*, with an introduction by Elizabeth Bowen (London, 1952)
—*Shudders: A Collection of New Nightmare Tales* (London, 1929)
Auden, W. H., *Another Time* (London & New York, 1940)
Bennett, Ernest, *Apparitions and Haunted Houses: A Survey of Evidence* (London, 1939)
Benson, E. F., *Spook Stories* (London, 1928)
Blackwood, Algernon, *Shocks* (London, 1935)

Blum, Deborah, *Ghost Hunters: William James and the Scientific Search for Life After Death* (New York, 2006)

Bowen, Elizabeth, *The Cat Jumps and Other Stories* (London, 1934)

—*The Demon Lover and Other Stories* (London, 1945)

Brandon, Ruth, *The Spiritualists: The Passion for the Occult in the Nineteenth and Twentieth Centuries* (New York, 1983)

Briggs, Julia, *Night Visitors: The Rise and Fall of the English Ghost Story* (London, 1977)

Buse, Peter, and Stott, Andrew, ed., *Ghosts: Deconstruction, Psychoanalysis, History* (London, 1999)

Carrington, Hereward, *Haunted People: The Story of the Poltergeist Down the Centuries*, with Nandor Fodor (London, 1953)

—*Historic Poltergeists and the Saragossa Ghost: International Institute for Psychical Research Bulletin I*, with Nandor Fodor (London, 1935)

—*Modern Psychical Phenomena* (New York, 1919)

—*A Primer of Psychical Research* (New York, 1932)

—*Psychical Phenomena & the War* (New York, 1918)

Carter, Angela, *The Bloody Chamber and Other Stories* (London, 1979)

Christie, Agatha, *The Hound of Death and Other Stories* (London, 1933)

Cohen, David, *The Escape of Sigmund Freud* (London, 2009)

Collins, Norman, *London Belongs to Me* (London, 1945)

Comyns, Barbara, *Our Spoons Came From Woolworths* (London, 1950)

—*The Vet's Daughter* (London, 1959)

Conan Doyle, Arthur, *The Land of Mist* (New York & London, 1926)

—*The New Revelation* (New York & London, 1918)

Coward, Noel, *Blithe Spirit: An Improbable Farce in Three Acts* (New York & London, 1941)

Crowe, Catherine, *The Night-Side of Nature; or, Ghosts and Ghost-Seers* (London, 1848)

Desmond, Shaw, *We Do Not Die* (London, 1934)

Devereux, George, ed., *Psycho-Analysis and the Occult* (New York, 1953)

Dingwall, Eric J., Goldney, Kathleen M., & Hall, Trevor H., *The Haunting of Borley Rectory: A Critical Survey of the Evidence* (London, 1956)

Dreiszeiger, Nandor, *Church and Society in Hungary and in the Hungarian Diaspora* (Toronto, 2016)

du Maurier, Daphne, *After Midnight and Other Stories* (London, 1971)

—*The Apple Tree: A Short Novel and Several Long Stories* (London, 1952)

—*Rebecca* (London, 1938)

du Maurier, George, *Trilby* (London, 1895)

Dunne, J. W., *An Experiment with Time* (London, 1927)

Dymond, Sue, *Branscombe's War 1939-1945* (Bridport, 2013)

Edwin, Ronald [Ronald Cockersell], *Clock Without Hands* (London, 1955)

Eliot, T. S., *Four Quartets* (London, 1943)

Ellenberger, Henri F., *The Discovery of the Unconscious: The History and Evolution of Dynamic Psychiatry* (New York, 1970)

Farquharson, Barbara, & Dymond, Sue, *Cliff and Beach at Branscombe: A Working Landscape* (Bridport, 2014)

Ferenczi, Sándor, *The Clinical Diary of Sándor Ferenczi*, ed. Judith Dupont, trans. Michael Balint & Nicola Zarday Jackson (Harvard, 1988)

—'Confusion of the Tongues Between the Adults and the Child', *International Journal of Psychoanalysis* 30 (1949)

Ferguson, Rachel, *The Brontës went to Woolworths* (London, 1931)

Flournoy, Théodore, *From India to the Planet Mars* (New York & London, 1900)

Fodor, Nandor, *Between Two Worlds* (New York, 1964)

—*Encyclopaedia of Psychic Science* (London, 1934)

—'Freud and the Poltergeist', *Psychoanalysis: Journal of Psychoanalytic Psychology* 4 (1955–56)

—*Freud, Jung and Occultism* (New York, 1971)

—*The Haunted Mind: A Psychoanalyst Looks at the Supernatural* (New York, 1959)

—'I Psychoanalyze Ghosts', *Mechanix Illustrated*, September 1949

—*The Lajos Pap Experiments: International Institute of Psychical Research Bulletin II* (London, 1936)

—'A Letter from England', monthly bulletins in the *Journal for the American Society for Psychical Research*, 1936 to 1939

—'The Lure of the Supernatural', *Psychiatric Quarterly* 20 (1945)

—*On the Trail of the Poltergeist* (New York, 1958)

—'The Poltergeist Psychoanalysed', *Psychiatric Quarterly* 22 (1948)

—'The Psychological Approach to the Problems of Occultism', *Journal of Clinical Psychopathology and Psychotherapy*, July 1945

—*The Search for the Beloved: A Clinical Investigation of the Trauma of Birth And Prenatal Conditioning* (New York, 1949)

—*These Mysterious People* (London, 1935)

—*The Unaccountable* (New York, 1968)

—'Was Harry Price a Fraud?' *Tomorrow* 4 (1956)

Fort, Charles, *Wild Talents* (New York, 1932)

Fortune, Christopher, 'The Case of "R. N.": Sándor Ferenczi's Radical Experiment in Psychoanalysis', in *The Legacy of Sándor Ferenczi*, ed. Lewis Aron & Adrienne Harris (Abingdon, 1993)

Fortune, Dion, *The Demon Lover* (London, 1927)

—*Psychic Self-Defence* (London, 1930)

Frankel, Jay B., 'Ferenczi's Theory of Trauma', *American Journal of Psychoanalysis* 58 (1998)

Franklin, Ruth, *Shirley Jackson: A Rather Haunted Life* (New York, 2016)

French, C. C., & Kerman, M. K., 'Childhood Trauma, Fantasy Proneness and Belief in the Paranormal', paper presented to the 1996 London Conference of the British Psychological Society, Institute of Education, University of London, abstract published in *Proceedings of the British Psychological Society* 5 (1996)

Freud, Sigmund, *New Introductory Lectures on Psycho-analysis*, trans. W. J. H. Sprott (New York, 1933)

—*The Psychopathology of Everyday Life*, trans. Abraham Brill (New York, 1914)

—*Totem and Taboo: Resemblances Between the Mental Lives of Savages and Neurotics*, trans. Abraham Brill (New York, 1919)

—'The Uncanny', trans. Alix Strachey, in *Collected Papers, Vol. 4* (London, 1925)

Frosh, Stephen, *Hauntings: Psychoanalysis and Ghostly Transmissions* (London, 1988)

Garrett, Eileen, *Adventures in the Supernormal* (New York, 1949)

—*My Life as a Search for the Meaning of Mediumship* (New York, 1975)

Gardiner, Juliet, *The Thirties: An Intimate History* (London, 2010)

Gaskill, Malcolm, *Hellish Nell: Last of Britain's Witches* (London, 2001)

Gauld, A., & Cornell, A. D., *Poltergeists* (London, 1979)

Goldin, Horace, *It's Fun to be Fooled* (London, 1937)

Goldston, Will, *Will Goldston's Card System of Exclusive Magical Secrets* (London, 1920)

—*More Exclusive Magical Secrets* (London, 1921)

—*Further Exclusive Magical Secrets* (London, 1927)

Goodheart, William B., 'C. G. Jung's First "Patient": on the Seminal Emergence of Jung's Thought', *Journal of Analytical Psychology* 29 (1984)

Greene, Graham, *Brighton Rock* (London, 1938)

Gryn, Hugo (with Naomi Gryn), *Chasing Shadows* (London, 2000)

Gurney, Edmund, Myers, Frederic W. H. & Podmore, Frank, *Phantasms of the Living*, Vols 1 & 2 (London, 1886)

Hamilton, Patrick, *Gas Light: A Victorian Thriller in Three Acts* (London, 1939)

—*Hangover Square* (London, 1939)

Hankey, Muriel, *James Hewat McKenzie, Pioneer of Psychical Research* (London, 1963)

Harvey, Karen, 'What Mary Toft Felt: Women's Voices, Pain, Power and the Body', *History Workshop Journal* 80 (2015)

Hayward, Rhodri, *Resisting History: Religious Transcendence and the Invention of the Unconscious* (Manchester, 2007)

Hazelgrove, Jenny, *Spiritualism and British Society between the Wars* (Manchester, 2000)

Hole, Christina, *Haunted England: A Survey of English Ghost-lore* (London, 1940)

Hopper, B. J., *Enquiry into the Cloud-Chamber Method of Studying the 'Intra-Atomic Quantity': International Institute for Psychical Research Bulletin III* (London, 1936)

Houran, James, & Lange, Renée, *Hauntings and Poltergeists: Multidisciplinary Perspectives* (Jefferson, North Carolina, 2008)

Hufford, David, *The Terror that Comes in the Night: An Experience-Centred Study of Supernatural Assault Traditions* (Philadelphia, 2016)

Inglis, Brian, *Science and Parascience: A History of the Paranormal 1914-39* (London, 1984)

Irwin, Harvey J., *The Psychology of Paranormal Belief: A Researcher's Handbook* (Hatfield, Herts, 2009)

Jackson, Shirley, *The Haunting of Hill House* (New York, 1959)

Jaher, David, *The Witch of Lime Street: Seance, Seduction and Houdini in the Spirit World* (New York, 2015)

Jennings, Humphrey, 'In Magritte's Paintings', *London Gallery Bulletin* 1, April 1938

Jones, Ernest, *On the Nightmare* (London, 1931)

Josiffe, Christopher, *Gef! The Strange Tale of an Extra Special Talking Mongoose* (London, 2016)

Jung, Carl, 'The Psychological Foundations of Belief in Spirits', *Contributions to Analytical Psychology* (London & New York, 1928)

King, Stephen, *Carrie* (New York, 1974)

—*The Shining* (New York, 1977)

van der Kolk, Bessel, *The Body Keeps the Score: Brain, Mind, and Body in the Healing of Trauma* (New York, 2014)

Langdon-Davies, John, *Air Raid; The Technique of Silent Approach, High Explosive Panic* (London, 1938)

Laursen, Christopher, 'Reimagining the Poltergeist in Twentieth-Century America and Britain', PhD thesis, University of British Columbia (2016)

Layard, John, 'Psi Phenomena and Poltergeists', *Proceedings of the Society for Psychical Research* 47 (1942-45)

Light, Alison, *Forever England: Femininity, Literature and Conservatism Between the Wars* (London, 1991)

Linehan, Thomas, *British Fascism, 1918-39: Parties, Ideology and Culture* (Manchester, 2000)

Link, Kelly, *Get in Trouble: Stories* (New York, 2016)

Lodge, Oliver J., *Raymond; or, Life and Death* (London & New York, 1916)

—*The Survival of Man: A Study in Unrecognised Human Faculty* (London, 1909)

Loftus, Elizabeth & Ketcham, Katherine, *The Myth of Repressed Memory: False Memories and Allegations of Sexual Abuse* (New York, 1994)

Luckhurst, Roger, *The Invention of Telepathy, 1870-1901* (Oxford, 2001)

—*The Trauma Question* (London & New York, 2008)

Machado, Carmen Maria, *Her Body and Other Parties* (Minneapolis, 2017)

Machen, Arthur, 'Opening the Door' in *When Churchyards Yawn*, ed. Cynthia Asquith (London, 1931)

Mantel, Hilary, *Beyond Black* (London, 2005)

—*Every Day is Mother's Day* (London, 1985)

—*Giving up the Ghost: A Memoir* (London, 2003)

—*Vacant Possession* (London, 1986)

McCorristine, Shane, *Spectres of the Self: Thinking about Ghosts and Ghost-Seeing in England, 1750-1920* (Cambridge, 2010)

Mitchell, T. W., 'The Contribution of Psychical Research to Psychotherapeutics', *Proceedings of the Society for Psychical Research* 45 (1939)

Morris, Richard, *Harry Price: The Psychic Detective* (Stroud, 2006)

Morrison, Toni, *Beloved* (New York, 1987)

Mott, Francis J., *Consciousness Creative: An Outline of the Science, Religion and Philosophy of Universal Integration* (Boston, 1937)

Mulholland, John, *Beware Familiar Spirits: An Investigation into the Occult and Psychic Phenomena* (London & New York, 1938)

Mullen, Lisa, *Mid-century Gothic: The Uncanny Objects of Modernity in British Literature and Culture After the Second World War* (Manchester, 2019)

Nash, Paul, 'The Life of the Inanimate Object', *Country Life*, 1 May 1937

Oppenheim, Janet, *The Other World: Spiritualism and Psychical Research in England, 1850-1914* (Cambridge, 1985)

Orwell, George, *Coming Up for Air* (London, 1939)

—*Keep the Aspidistra Flying* (London, 1936)

O'Sullivan, Suzanne, *It's All in Your Head: True Stories of Imaginary Illness* (London, 2015)

Overy, Richard, *The Morbid Age: Britain Between the Wars* (London, 2009)

Owen, A. R. G., *Can We Explain the Poltergeist?* (New York, 1964)

Owen, Alex, *The Darkened Room: Women, Power and Spiritualism in Late Victorian England* (Chicago, 1989)

—*The Place of Enchantment: British Occultism and the Culture of the Modern* (Chicago, 2004)

Perkins S. L., & Allen R., 'Childhood Physical Abuse and Differential Development of Paranormal Belief Systems', *Journal of Nervous and Mental Disease* 194 (2006)

Pfefferle, Justin, 'Surrealism and Documentary in Britain during the Second World War', PhD, McGill University (2015)

Phillimore, Mercy, 'Obituary: Nandor Fodor', *Light* (1964)

Pickford, R. W., 'An Hysterical "Medium"', *British Journal of Medical Psychology* 19 (1943)

Price, Harry, *Confessions of a Ghost-hunter* (London, 1936)

—*The End of Borley Rectory* (London, 1946)

—*Fifty Years of Psychical Research: A Critical Survey* (London, 1939)

—*The Haunting of Cashen's Gap*, with R. S. Lambert (London, 1936)

—*Leaves from a Psychist's Casebook* (London, 1933)

—*The Most Haunted House in England: Ten Years' Investigation at Borley Rectory* (London, 1940)

—*Poltergeist Over England: Three Centuries of Mischievous Ghosts* (London, 1945)

—*Revelations of a Spirit Medium*, ed. with Eric Dingwall (London & New York, 1922)

Priestley, J. B., *English Journey* (London, 1933)

—*Three Time Plays: Dangerous Corner; Time and the Conways; I Have Been Here Before* (London, 1947)

Prince, Morton, *The Dissociation of a Personality: A Biographical Study in Abnormal Psychology* (New York, 1906)

Pugh, Martin, *We Danced All Night: A Social History of Britain between the Wars* (London, 2008)

Purkiss, Diane, 'Losing Babies, Losing Stories: Attending to Women's Confessions in Scottish Witch-Trials' in *Culture and Change: Attending to Early Modern Women,* ed. Margaret Mikesell & Adele Seeff (Delaware, 2003)

Puskás, Julianna, *Ties that Bind, Ties that Divide: 100 Years of Hungarian Experience in the United States*, trans. Zora Ludwig (New York, 2000)

Rachman, Arnold W., *Elizabeth Severn: The Evil Genius of Psychoanalysis* (New York & Abingdon, 2019)

Raeyron, Thomas, and Loose, Tianna, 'Anomalous Experiences, Trauma, and Symbolization Processes at the Frontiers between Psychoanalysis and Cognitive Neurosciences', *Frontiers in Psychology* 6 (2015)

Rogers, Paul and Lowrie, Emma Louise, 'Varieties of Childhood Maltreatment as Predictors of Adult Paranormality and New Age Orientation', *Personality and Individual Differences* 92 (2016)

Rogo, D. Scott, 'Psychotherapy and the Poltergeist', *Journal of the Society for Psychical Research* 47 (1973-74)

Roper, Lyndal, *Oedipus and the Devil: Witchcraft, Sexuality and Religion in Early Modern Europe* (London & New York, 1994)

Rosenbaum, Ruth, 'Exploring the Other Dark Continent: Parallels between Psi Phenomena and the Psychotherapeutic Process', *Psychoanalytic Review* 98 (2011)

Saint-Amour, Paul K., 'Air War Prophecy and Interwar Modernism', *Comparative Literature Studies* 42 (2005)

Sayers, Dorothy L., *Strong Poison* (London, 1930)

Schweblin, Samanta, *Mouthful of Birds*, trans. Megan McDowell (New York, 2019)

Scott, Laurence, *Picnic Comma Lightning: In Search of a New Reality* (London, 2018)

Severn, Elizabeth, *The Discovery of the Self: A Study in Psychological Cure* (London, 1933)

Shephard, Ben, *A War of Nerves: Soldiers and Psychiatrists, 1914-1994* (London, 2000)

Sinclair, May, *The Intercessor and Other Stories* (London, 1932)

Spark, Muriel, *The Bachelors* (London, 1960)

Stekel, Wilhelm, 'The Sexual Root of Kleptomania,' *Journal of Criminal Law and Criminology* 2 (1911)

Sword, Helen, *Ghostwriting Modernism* (New York & London, 2002)

Tabori, Cornelius, *My Occult Diary* (London, 1951)

Taylor, Eugene, *William James on Exceptional Mental States: The 1896 Lowell Lectures* (New York, 1983)

Thurston, Luke, *Literary Ghosts from the Victorians to Modernism: The Haunting Interval* (Abingdon, 2012)

Timms, Joanna, 'Ghost-Hunters and Psychical Research in Interwar England', *History Workshop Journal* 74 (2012)

—'Phantasm of Freud: Nandor Fodor and the Psychoanalytic Approach to the Supernatural in Interwar Britain', *Psychoanalysis and History* 14 (2012)

Townsend Warner, Sylvia, *Lolly Willowes* (London, 1926)

Townshend of Raynham, Marchioness, and ffoulkes, Maude M. C., *True Ghost Stories*, with an introduction by Nandor Fodor (London, 1936)

Valentine, Elizabeth, 'Spooks and Spoofs: Relations between Psychical Research and Academic Psychology in Britain in the Inter-war Period', *History of the Human Sciences* 25 (2012)

Warner, Marina, *Phantasmagoria: Spirit Visions, Metaphors, and Media into the Twenty-First Century* (London, 2006)

Wassilko-Serecki, Zoe, 'Observations on Eleonore Zugun', *Journal of the American Society for Psychical Research* 20 (1926)

Waters, Sarah, *Affinity* (London, 1999)

—*The Little Stranger* (London, 2009)

Watmough, David, *Myself Through Others: Memoirs* (Toronto, 2008)

West, D. J., 'The 'Haunted' Dance Hall', *Journal of the Society for Psychical Research* 34 (1954)

West, Rebecca, *The Fountain Overflows* (London, 1957)

Whitfield, Sarah, *Magritte* (London, 1992)

Williams, Mary, 'The Poltergeist Man', *Journal of Analytical Psychology* 8 (1963)

Winter, Jay, *Sites of Memory, Sites of Mourning: The Great War in European Cultural History* (Cambridge, 1995)

Wiseman, Richard, *Paranormality: The Science of the Supernatural* (London, 2011)

Wolffram, Heather, *The Stepchildren of Science: Psychical Research and Parapsychology in Germany, c 1870-1939* (Amsterdam, 2009)

—'Trick, Manipulation and Farce: Albert Moll's Critique of Occultism', *Medical History* 56 (2012)

Woolf, Virginia, 'Henry James's Ghost Stories' & 'The Supernatural in Fiction', *Collected Essays*, Vol 1 (London, 1924)

Wydenbruck, Nora, *My Two Worlds: An Autobiography* (London, 1956)

—*The Para-Normal: Personal Experiences and Deductions* (London, 1939)

—*Woman Astride* (London & New York, 1934)

Young, Kevin, *Bunk: The Rise of Hoaxes, Humbug, Plagiarists, Phonies, Post-Facts, and Fake News* (Minneapolis, 2017)

NEWSPAPERS & JOURNALS

Croydon Advertiser
Croydon Times
Daily Express
Daily Herald
Daily Mail
Daily Mirror
Daily Sketch
Daily Telegraph
Empire News
Evening News
Evening Standard
Journal of the American Society for Psychical Research
Journal of the Society for Psychical Research
The Leader
Light
The Listener
Manchester Guardian
The Observer

Psychic News
Psychic Science
Psypioneer
Reynolds News
Spiritualist News
Sunday Graphic
Sunday Pictorial
Two Worlds

WEBSITES

ancestry.com: for records of birth, marriage and death, census returns, post office and city directories, passenger lists, naturalisation certificates, probate calendar.
branscombeproject.org.uk: history of Branscombe, east Devon
briansmithonline.com/memoirs: Thornton Heath between the wars
britishnewspaperarchive.co.uk: digital archive of selected British newspapers
iapsop.com: digital archive of spiritualist and occultist periodicals
psi-encyclopedia.spr.ac.uk: encyclopedia of psychical research
woolworthsmuseum.co.uk: history of Woolworth's in Britain

ACKNOWLEDGEMENTS

Huge thanks to Andrea Fodor Litkei, Nandor Fodor's daughter, for talking to me about her father and for giving me permission to quote from his writing. Thank you also to Lizette Coly, Eileen Garrett's granddaughter, for her generosity and support, and to Anastasia Damalas, Eileen Garrett's great-granddaughter, Eniko Puspok and Jeff Greene. I am very grateful to Barry Fielding, Les and Alma's grandson, for talking to me about his family and for giving me permission to reproduce photographs from his family albums, and to his brother Leslie for speaking to me from Norway.

Many thanks to Sian Collins, archivist at Cambridge University Library's Department of Archives and Modern Manuscripts, who helped me find Fodor's files on the Thornton Heath case. For advice on psychical research, thank you also to Melvyn Willin of the Society for Psychical Research, and to Leslie Price and Vivienne Roberts at the College of Psychic Studies. Thanks to Simon Ertz for researching material in the Hoover Institution at Stanford University on my behalf; and to AnnaLee Pauls at the Firestone Library, University of Princeton, for copies of correspondence between Fodor and Hereward Carrington. For information about the Fieldings' lives in Devon, thank you to Barbara Farquharson, John Torrance, Sue Dymond, Mark White, Jean Brinscombe and the late Sid Sweetland. My thanks to the Society for Psychical Research, the Syndics of Cambridge University Library and the Parapsychology Institute in New York for access to their papers. For advice on psychoanalytic ideas, thank you to Lorna Bradbury, David Hewison and their colleagues at Tavistock Relationships. For advice on the history of the paranormal, huge thanks to Christopher French, Malcolm Gaskill, Christopher Josiffe and Roger Luckhurst. Thank you to the staff at the British Library, the Cambridge University Library and Senate House Library, University of London.

Thanks so much to the friends and family who have discussed this story with me, especially those who have read parts or all of the draft. My thanks to everyone at Bloomsbury – among them Sara Helen Binney, Jonny Coward, Hannah Paget, Sarah Ruddick, my brilliant editors Alexandra Pringle and Allegra Le Fanu – and also to Kate Quarry and Gillian Stern. Thank you to the great team at Penguin Press, including Ann Godoff, Scott Moyers, Caroline Sydney and my superb editor Virginia Smith Younce. Thank you to my agent Melanie Jackson in New York and to the wonderful people at Rogers, Coleridge & White literary agency in London, including Laurence Laluyaux, Stephen Edwards, Honor Spreckley and – especially – Georgia Garrett. This book is dedicated to the memory of my friend and literary agent David Miller.

INDEX

A NOTE ON THE AUTHOR

Kate Summerscale is the author of the number one bestseller *The Suspicions of Mr Whicher*, winner of the Samuel Johnson Prize for Non-Fiction, the Galaxy British Book of the Year Award, a Richard & Judy Book Club pick and adapted into a major ITV drama. Her first book, the bestselling *The Queen of Whale Cay*, won a Somerset Maugham award and was shortlisted for the Whitbread Biography Award. Her third book, *Mrs Robinson's Disgrace*, was a *Sunday Times* bestseller, and her fourth, *The Wicked Boy*, won the Mystery Writers of America Edgar Award for Best Fact Crime. Kate Summerscale was elected a Fellow of the Royal Society of Literature in 2010. She lives in London.

katesummerscale.com

NOTE ON THE TYPE

The text of this book is set in Fournier. Fournier is derived from the romain du roi, which was created towards the end of the seventeenth century from designs made by a committee of the Académie of Sciences for the exclusive use of the Imprimerie Royale. The original Fournier types were cut by the famous Paris founder Pierre Simon Fournier in about 1742. These types were some of the most influential designs of the eight and are counted among the earliest examples of the 'transitional' style of typeface. This Monotype version dates from 1924. Fournier is a light, clear face whose distinctive features are capital letters that are quite tall and bold in relation to the lower-case letters, and *decorative italics, which show the influence of the calligraphy of Fournier's time.*